"C. S. Lewis wrote that friendship is bo[illegible] You too? I thought that no one but mysel[illegible] a new friend in this remarkable book. What makes this book both approachable and powerful is its honesty—that rare treasure we pastors are sometimes afraid to make our own. Zack Eswine gives us a front-row seat to his heart. In seeing him, we see ourselves. But far better, we also see Jesus in his all-sufficiency for us. To everyone who wants to serve the Lord with a heart set free from pretense, I commend *Sensing Jesus*."

Ray Ortlund, Lead Pastor, Immanuel Church, Nashville, Tennessee

"This is one of the finest books on being a pastor written in this generation. I plan to use *Sensing Jesus* as required reading for our pastoral theology students here at Covenant Seminary. The book is heart-wrenchingly honest about Zack's own hopes and dreams and about the challenges of dealing with the praise that is heaped on a gifted young communicator of God's Word. It is this rare honesty that makes the book a must-read for anyone called to a life of ministry. Along with this painful and necessary openness, Zack has written not only with a practical helpfulness but also with a kindness of spirit about the follies, sins, and troubles that anyone engaged in serving others is constantly encountering. His careful exposition of Scripture is interwoven with unforgettable stories that bind the points he makes to the hearts of his readers. This will be an outstanding addition to the library of every pastor and teacher, indeed of anyone committed to ministry."

Jerram Barrs, Resident Scholar of the Francis A. Schaeffer Institute at Covenant Theological Seminary; author, *Freedom and Discipleship* and *The Heart of Prayer*

"This book is simultaneously deeply distressing and profoundly comforting. The rhythmic interchange between these two seemingly opposite impacts surprisingly convinced me that this is one of the most helpful books on pastoring that I have read since my ordination in 1978. Ruthless self-address and unvarnished vulnerability are here wed to searching exegesis and an obvious purposed submission to the text of Holy Scripture. The reader of this work will likely find remaining neutral and numb to their own mediocrity a difficult task!"

Joe Novenson, Senior Teaching Pastor, Lookout Mountain Presbyterian Church, Lookout Mountain, Tennessee

"After marinating in *Sensing Jesus*, I have two responses—one of lament and one of joy. Where was this book when I was stuck in the unrelenting grind of performance-based pastoring; the spiritual schizophrenia of preaching the gospel of grace with a frozen heart; the lonely pedestal of a pulpit surrounded by thousands of people? But joy fills my heart as I realize what a great book I now have with which to mentor young pastors and preachers. Zack, thank you for stewarding your pain and God's gospel."

Scotty Smith, Founding Pastor, Christ Community Church, Franklin, Tennessee; author, *The Reign of Grace*; *Restoring Broken Things*; and *Everyday Prayers: 365 Days to a Gospel-Centered Faith*

"In prose that is warmly authentic and deeply rooted in the wisdom of Scripture and a life well examined, Zack Eswine invites those who minister to pause and reflect. Eswine unfolds a lovely biblical vision of ministry that embraces the localities, limits, physicality, and margins of our finiteness that God deems good. Devotional, rich in insight, gentle in teaching, *Sensing Jesus* is also profoundly convicting in challenging us to embody what we profess to believe. This is not abstract pastoral theology; it is an understanding of ministry for all ministers, lay or professional, who find, perhaps to their surprise or disappointment, that they are human beings, body and soul. If you do ministry, please believe me: *Sensing Jesus* is must reading."

Denis Haack, Director, Ransom Fellowship; Visiting Instructor in Practical Theology, Covenant Seminary

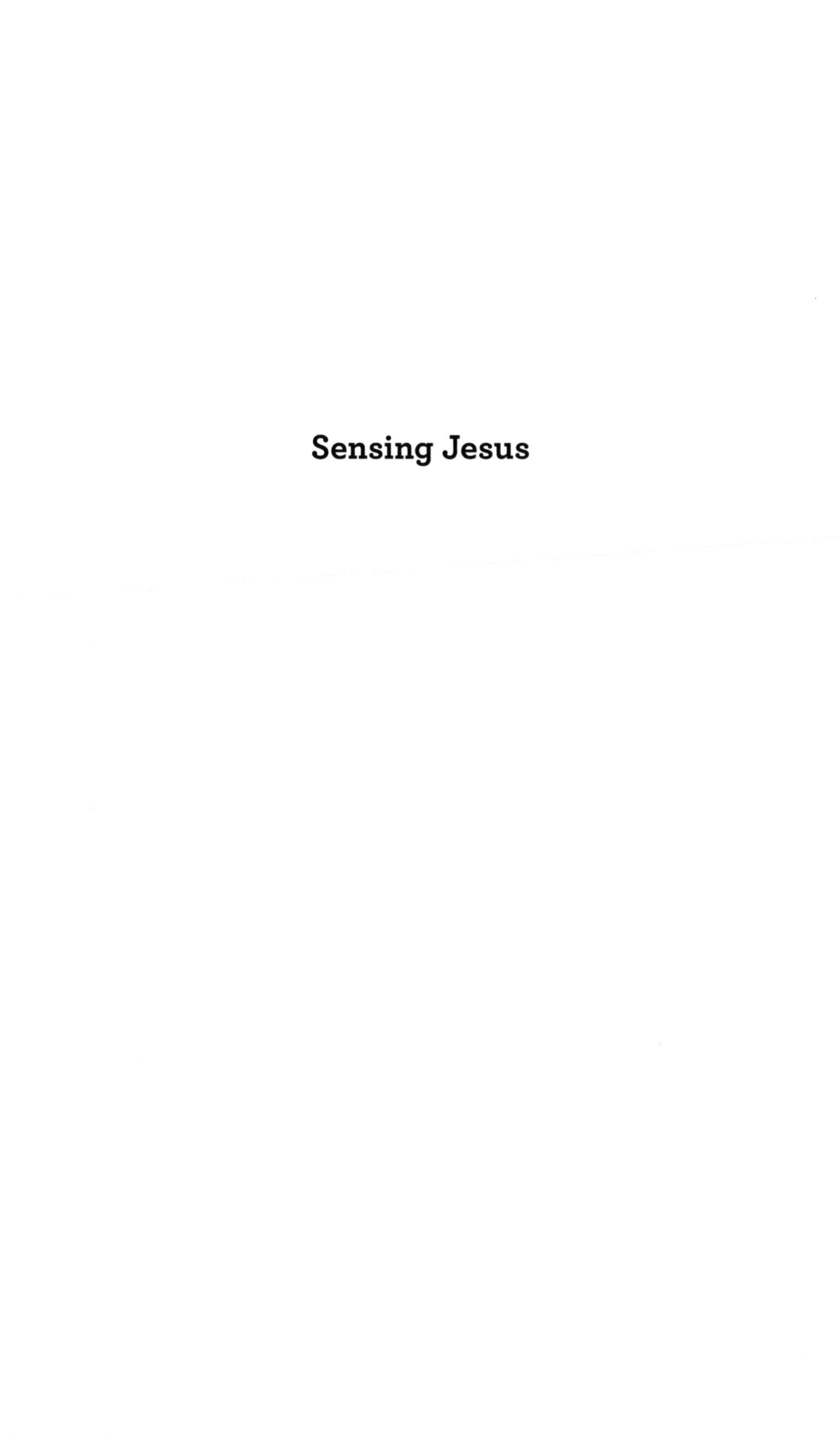

Sensing Jesus

Sensing Jesus

Life and Ministry as a Human Being

Zack Eswine

WHEATON, ILLINOIS

Sensing Jesus: Life and Ministry as a Human Being

Copyright © 2013 by Zachary W. Eswine

Published by Crossway
1300 Crescent Street
Wheaton, Illinois 60187

Cover and image design: Jeremy Holmes

First printing 2013

Printed in the United States of America

All emphases in Scripture quotations have been added by the author.

Trade paperback ISBN: 978-1-58134-969-6
PDF ISBN: 978-1-4335-1253-7
Mobipocket ISBN: 978-1-4335-1254-4
ePub ISBN: 978-1-4335-2099-0

Library of Congress Cataloging-in-Publication Data

Eswine, Zack, 1969-
Sensing Jesus : life and ministry as a human being / Zack Eswine.
p. cm.
Includes bibliographical references and index.
ISBN 978-1-58134-969-6
1. Clergy—Religious life. 2. Pastoral theology. I. Title.
BV4011.6.E89 2013
253'.2—dc23 2012019842

Crossway is a publishing ministry of Good News Publishers.

VP 22 21 20 19 18 17 16 15
15 14 13 12 11 10 9 8 7 6 5 4 3

For Mamaw, Papaw, and Jessica
I look forward to introducing you

Contents

Acknowledgments

Allan Fisher and Crossway have been gracious to me amid the various life challenges that have coincided with this writing project. Al's patience and counsel have blessed me. Thanks also to Lydia Brownback.

I want to thank Jim Roach for his early content editing and Mary Schawacker for her typing those edits for my original draft.

I also want to thank my staff team in ministry at Riverside Church: Matt Blazer, Lianne Johnson, and Simon Kim, as well as friends Seth Anderson, Ryan Anderson, Jerram and Vickie Barrs, Peter Boyd, Bruce Clark, Glenn Hoburgh, Zach Nielsen, and Dane Ortlund for reading drafts at various stages along the way and providing invaluable feedback.

I am grateful for my elders and colaborers Joe Farell, Brian Janous, Ty Schwieterman, and Greg Stokke for their support of my life, ministry, and family as well as for this project.

I am particularly grateful for Bob Smart for his counsel, suggestions, prayer, and abiding friendship in this and every endeavor of providence in my life.

I am blessed by Nathan, Abigail, and Caleb.

The partnership, listening ear, companionship, late-night readings, suggested edits, insightful questions, and prayers from my wife, Jessica, on this project and each day have been to me a gift of profound grace, strength, and joy.

Remembering Our Purpose

The place He gives us to inhabit.
The few things He gives us to do in that place.
The persons He invites us to know there.
These our days,
our lingering.

It is enough then,
this old work of hands
His and ours
to love here,
to learn His song here,

like crickets that scratch
and croon,
from nooks unseen,

carrying on with
what they were made for,
the night craft of
unnoticed faces,
with our wings unobserved,

until He walks again
in the cool of the day,
to call our names once more.

And we then,
with our stitched white flags,
will from behind His evergreens,
finally unhide ourselves,
unblushed with Him to stroll
once more.

CHAPTER ONE

Preaching Barefoot

Doing Something Great for God

> Chances are, the preacher reasons,
> You'll be more willing to listen
> Now that your city has fallen from what it was.[1]

I remember sitting out on the carport at a picnic table at my grandparents' house in Henryville, Indiana. I was in the third year of my first pastorate. The sky was blue. The wind drew near. It brushed occasional touches on my arms and hair as if to remind me that I was not alone.

I had taken a brief study leave to write my first article for a ministry journal. Mamaw, glad for my extended visit, made the spice cake she always made when I came to town. As I took up my pen and looked down Blue Lake Road, I felt what any man surely feels when he gets to do something that he knows he was made to do—that noble pleasure of feeling that somehow we are enough for the day, that the day cannot contain us because we will outshine it. In my case, I felt a growing desire to write something of significance for pastors. I wanted it to be exceptional. (And this, dear reader, is important to remember.)

That sabbatical week I devoured the subject that thrilled me the most at the time—early Princeton Seminary and preaching. This probably sounds annoying or incredibly boring to some. But to me the subject was like Mamaw's spice cake. The first principal of Princeton, Archibald Alexander, and his son seemed to have so much to say about preaching that fed my soul. It offered delightful food for the wounded pastor that I was becoming. I was in the beginning of my first pastorate at Grace Church. Looking back it sobers me to realize how new I was in ministry and yet how deeply tired I was already.

But somehow, the feeling that we are doing something significant can enable us to tell ourselves that things are not as bad as they seem. A good memory can likewise join this feeling. Together they can fuel a respite of hope. Dr. Calhoun had regularly shared his living room and some tea with me. Over the months he had passed his love of old Princeton on to me (and to others). With such a memory joining an opportunity to write and Mamaw's spice cake right in front of me, I felt energized. I had always hoped to change the world.

Looking back, I thought such change would come from an epic or grand moment. (Exceptional persons are not bound to a life of unexceptional moments, right?) Such epic moments when realized would leave nothing the same. Heaven itself will have touched us. This idea of a grand swoop flirted with my desires. The epic aspiration began to hold hands with my attempts to preach.

I was not alone in this. My colleagues with whom I graduated from seminary shared these dreams. Nor was this unreasonable in my mind. After all, my professors and my fellow students publicly recognized my preaching and affirmed these gifts. I had also read of how God attended preachers with his Spirit in the past, and I believed he might do so with us in the present. But two years into my first church, and all my preaching seemed to do at the time was give some people cause for checking out other churches.

So I began to desire as a pastor the epic moment outside the pulpit. But the level of strife that existed among my elders confounded me. I was hitting that stretch of highway in the desert that most new pastors must drive through in the first two to three years at a new call. But I didn't realize that then. Nor did I realize the large brokenness a little church can muster.

What was happening? I thought I was supposed to make an exceptional difference. I was a senior pastor at twenty-six years old and right out of seminary. I had a wife and a baby. We moved to a place we had never lived before among a people we did not know. In that sense we were missionaries, starting over in a new place far from our roots. But "I must be made for something special," I thought (and was told). "I want to do great things for God!" The church had eighteen acres of land and a new building. Its elders and deacons were made up of several high-powered businessmen. A young family right out of seminary, in a new place, untested in ministry and serving with a board of powerful men, all looking for a grand future. What could go wrong? Plenty.

So, I felt I needed a new hope. "Maybe this article is just the beginning," I thought. So, that week I drank Pepsi, ate spice cake, and gained a pound or two as Mamaw offered me seconds at every meal. If I couldn't preach or pastor exceptionally, maybe I could write what just might change the world for Jesus.

What Happens?

That was almost fifteen years ago now. My article was published, and I still had to brush my teeth and take out the garbage the next day. My mamaw has since died (Papaw too). I've eaten spice cake since, but it doesn't seem to taste as good as Mamaw made it. I've long since been called on from Grace Church. Grace has had its third pastor in the few years since I moved. It too has been trying to find its way, trying to find what it means to keep its namesake.

After six years at Grace, I went to teach preaching at a seminary. I dreamt there too, but those dreams were not to be. In fact, I am not what I thought I would have been by now. I do not mean this morbidly. I hope you will soon see that I am writing to you as one who feels profoundly rescued from himself by the abounding grace of Jesus. But the stale waters of celebrity, consumerism, and immediate gratification had infiltrated my drinking water, and I did not realize it. I fear a lot of us don't.

What I also did not know then was that my wife of fifteen years would suddenly walk away from Jesus and from me. So, when I dreamt of preaching with unusual unction, writing a great article in Henryville, and becoming exceptional for Jesus, I would never have imagined that my future would require me to learn to be a single dad with primary care of my kids amid a community of "scandal" and taking a long hard look in the mirror. Being declared "innocent in the matter" wouldn't remove the whispers or the slanders both in the community and in my own head. Neither did these remove what it meant for each of my three children and me to daily learn together to see the sun again and smile.

Too Much!

In this light, as we begin to talk about the purpose of this book it is strange what I remember. At the moment, I remember failing a seminary exam. At the time, I was trying to get licensed with the presbytery, find an apartment several states away in a place I had never lived, finish the preparations for taking that new call, packing to move my family, ending my part-time jobs, and taking four other exams. On my Old Testament Prophets exam, Dr. Vasholz wrote the words "What happened?" in red ink. "Too much happened," I had said. "It was all too much, and something just had to give."

If our lives are a story, his words and my answer in those early scenes would act as foreshadowing, because, in the years since, I've seen people come to saving faith in Jesus, marriages healed, addictions overcome. I've traveled, preached, gotten a PhD, taught, and written books. Jesus has revealed himself so kindly, truly, presently, and powerfully.

But of those laying hands on me at my ordination that November day, one pastor has since taken his own life, another died naturally, and another is no longer in the ministry due to moral misconduct. One elder and one deacon who were present have since been disciplined by the church, one for raging mistreatment and the other for a devastating affair. Another very dear friendship would fracture amid the politics of my eventual "scandal." And almost twelve years to the day after that ordination, my wife (who had stood with me at the time) walked away from Jesus and from me. So if there is anything exceptional about me and about this ministerial crowd of mine, it is that we are exceptionally broken. This wasn't what I dreamt when I first began to preach Jesus in my generation.

So now here I sit, years later, typing these words as pastor of a little church in Missouri. I had lost my pen and have only recently begun to slowly find it again. I'm asking, What happened? But not just for me. It seems that all around me lie the littered ministry remains and the suffered contusions of once ambitious Christian men and women. It wasn't just all around me though. It was all around, everywhere.

An irony whispers back to my thoughts. I am hoping that what I write to you now will prove significant. I shake my head and almost laugh—that short exhale of a laugh that comes through the nose. Funny how I once thought that significance lay somewhere beyond Henryville and Mamaw's spice cake—a local place and an ordinary love—as if an article in a journal would do more to glorify God and save others than either of these other created things. The irony has saddled up with me like the wind once did those years ago on the carport.

I was one of those guys to whom people would say these words, "You are among the finest preachers I have heard, and you are so young. I can't wait to hear you in ten years." Well, ten years have long since passed, and I have not become what was once projected.

Yet one thing has refreshingly changed by the grace of Jesus. I more fully understand some words that I first read on that carport those years ago. They felt like death to me at the time. Jesus nudged me with them but I quickly passed over them. They have come back to me, and I want to share them with you. They are hinting at life to me now. I hope you will soon see that there is life here for you as well.

Relinquishing

In the preface of his *Practical Sermons*, old age had humbled Archibald Alexander to admit his need for others in the gospel work and to acknowledge his limits in what he himself would be able to do. He wrote:

> If the author were not so far advanced in years, as to render the undertaking [of] new works presumptuous, he might make an attempt to supply the want, which exists. But he feels that he must shortly relinquish, not only his pen, but all earthly labours; and, therefore, he leaves this work to be performed by some other person.[2]

To relinquish; to admit that some dreams are presumptuous; to acknowledge that some needs outlast me; to recognize my inability to fully supply what is lacking; to admit that I am limited; to say no to competition with brothers and sisters, and to give to others what I strongly desired for myself; and in it all to still take up the pen or give voice to preach Jesus—these indicate a surrender to noble limits.

Alexander did his substantial part in his generation, even though many of us reading right now may never have heard of him (a fact that in itself highlights a humbling message for us).

God is the remembered one. But this does not mean we are forgotten—not by him. Not by a long shot. In fact, being remembered by him means we no longer fear being forgotten by the world. Living humanly within his remembrance is enough.

And this thought, dear reader, brings me to the purpose of this book. *I believe that Christian life and ministry are an apprenticeship with Jesus toward recovering our humanity and, through his Spirit, helping our neighbors do the same.* All of this is for, through, by, with, and in him for the glory of God.

I also believe that the general absence of this recovery of our humanity within Christian life and ministry for God's glory is spiritually killing us. I want something to be done about it. I realize that placing our humanity in Christ front and center for the Christian life and the pastoral task will make some of us uneasy, and rightly so. It could seem that I intend to droll out only more of the self-centered spirituality that our generation and our own hearts (including mine) harmfully want.

To allay such concerns, I simply offer this introductory thought. It was John the Baptist who said it. "I am not the Christ," he declared. It seems to me that while it is true that we can dangerously make too little of God by drawing improper attention to ourselves, it is equally true that we cannot fully magnify God without confessing that we are not him. "*A man*," John said, "can receive only what is given him from heaven" (John 3:27–28 NIV). Each of us is not God and is only human (I am not the Christ). The absence of such a confession is making us a ragged bunch.

Preaching Barefoot

Maybe this attempt to glorify God by owning my humanity is why, for my first Sunday as a new lead pastor, I preached barefoot. It is true: the lore had been that the previous pastor, a friend of mine, had likewise on occasion slipped off his flip-flops. On that junior-high auditorium hardwood, he occasionally stood on undressed arches and bald toes. He opened the Book and proclaimed the gospel.

I'd like to think that my own footwear removal flowed out of an attempt to reference holy ground, that it was designed to make a statement to the effect that when we preach, gather in worship, and hear the voice of God in Jesus, we lay our shoes next to those of Moses and bow down before the one who is "I AM."

I think some of the earlier shoeless gestures more than likely revealed the edgy, unplugged, and authentic kind of vibe the church was trying to demonstrate in its gospel pursuit of St. Louis twenty-somethings.

It had been a long time since I'd been twenty-something, and though I wish I had thought of it, I just wasn't pious enough to make the connection at the time to the biblical story of the burning bush. I confess it. My shoeless sermon arose from neither theological nor missional reasons.

But to stand there, holding the Bible on an ordinary and unhidden foundation with my hobbit hairs dangling across my knuckly toes, was an act of personal testimony, a silly but tangible reminder that I am not God.

You would think that as a preacher of the gospel, I already fully understood that I am not God. "Prone to wander, Lord I feel it. Prone to leave the God I love," describes not just my heart but each of ours. Jesus said as much when he taught us about the Bible teacher gone wrong (Luke 18:1). As a Bible teacher myself, Jesus has my attention, and I hope he has yours. Sometimes we trip over our own feet. Forgetting who we are as human beings in relation to God is often the cause.

Bible Teachers and Monks Tripped Up

Whatever he once was—earnest, or zealous, or genuine—Jesus teaches us that a breach within the being of this teacher has grown. But what's scary is that the teacher does not know this. He believes that what he sees in the mirror accurately reflects his true and not his false self. "A kind of empty image of righteousness in place of righteousness itself" has begun to "abundantly satisfy" him.[3] He has gotten "a distorted idea of [his and our] own nature."[4] On that account, he approaches God confidently, ignorant of how arrogant he has become.

So he says the awful thing with conviction and, of all places, in prayer: "God, I thank you that I am not like other men" (Luke 18:11). And there it is: the deadly air; the poisoned belief that in comparison to other men we can become exceptional in God's eyes. This Pharisee doesn't have to surrender to the same human reality that others do. So somewhere along the line this man of God began to say to himself statements such as, "For God's sake, I will not be ordinary." "Mine will be no usual life and no routine ministry." "I will do what no others can for God." "God will treat me more favorably than he does others." "I will preach, pray, and serve in a way that sets me apart from my neighbors and colleagues." "I do not sin like other men do."

My last twenty years in ministry have shown me that this Bible teacher and I have more in common than I ever dared to admit. That is why a monk, Thomas Merton, was on my mind. He wrote:

Am I not allowed to be hollow,
Or fall in the hole
Or break my bones (within me)
In the trap set by my own lie to myself? O my friend,
I too must sin and sin.

I too must hurt other people and
(since I am no exception)
I must be hated by them.[5]

I have heard myself say, "Lord, I feel as if there is nowhere I can turn to find grace." Those who have served long enough in ministry, and who feel their need of grace, will know what I mean. Our style of sermon, length of prayer, inadequate blog, tone of voice, or personal mannerism is cause enough for someone to criticize and leave us and our community for another church and another pastor over and again. Then there are those moments when someone encounters us at our worst, either due to our human limitations, our actual sins, or our ugly recovery from being sinned against. They see our true faults, and our fan base fades.

The monk beseeches his friend to "allow" him to be as other men. The holy man tries to express that he too is one who sins and is sinned against, and who therefore can feel sad or disgusted or hurt. He needs a savior too. It is this absence of permission to be "no exception" that leads many of us into the dark, doing in secret what the light of a gracious com-

munity would have freed us to confess and grow through. Trying to be an exception to the human race encourages arrogance among most of us and burnout among many of us—the two invasive fruits of having to prove that we are not flawed, that we do not need rescue from Jesus the way other neighbors do.

Thankfully, in defiance of this forbidden humanity, the decree the monk sets down to his "friend" is this: "I am no exception." Jesus's words to the Bible teacher come to mind. "Everyone who exalts himself will be humbled, but the one who humbles himself will be exalted" (Luke 18:14).

So I exposed my feet and preached Jesus. But it is not my feet that I need to uncover; it is my heart, my life in him. "I am not the Christ. I am a man," John said.

I hear myself saying, "I wish, Lord, that I could start again." I have a long track record of underestimating ordinary people and moments; I seek entitled praise because of my service to God. I struggle with believing that I am above others because of the superiority of my religious service.

And I am not alone. I have served people in churches for years who share the Bible teacher's ambition to become unlike other men in this trying-to-be-god kind of way. I have begun to harbor the pessimistic suspicion that I'll likely die before I've learned how to truly do life as an ordinary Christian. The saddest aspect of that reality is that I could be so unskilled for an ordinary Christian life, even though I went to school for twenty-three years, including "mastering" divinity and completing a PhD.

Starting Again with the Image of God

So, I want to start again with what it means to be human when I hold my Bible and speak of Jesus. I do not mean that I want to expunge the powerful theology that I learned. But by grace I want to apply it better. I learned many of those truths for a narrow reason—mainly to prove to others examining me that I am called to the ministry. I do not disparage this noble and necessary testing. I uphold its place. I cherish this knowledge. But I think I learned such truths in order to pass a test with good answers; I knew the arguments regarding a doctrine, but I had not thought through enough the implications for my own life and ministry. I could pick apart a blog post and learn that I too would be picked apart unless I get the words exactly as we were tested. But living the words and communicating for ordinary people in life was another matter.

Let's remind ourselves of an example. By doing so, let's wade into the waters of a theological pond just for a moment. We step in ankle deep and remind ourselves about why our being human matters for our testimony to Jesus.

Let's start with the doctrine of the image of God in persons. This doctrine is fundamental to our being human and God being God. I was well equipped to discuss and discern the difference between the communicable and incommunicable attributes of God and what these attributes of God reveal to me about who I am (and who I am not) as a human being, in relation to who God is and who God is not as the divine being. But what I underestimated is how my cultural and sinful tendencies toward disdain for what's common, my demand of entitlement, and a commitment to be exceptional among persons remained covert in how I applied this doctrine. These hidden agendas imported subtle and misguided meaning into the definitions. It is like the basketball nearly dead in a yard, worn out too soon by an eight-year-old who used it as a soccer ball. The basketball wasn't made to sustain constant kicking. Likewise, we sometimes do not use doctrines in the way they are meant. Our doctrines of God's image in us wear out, for example, when we kick them with our own and not his definitions of greatness, effectiveness, success.

After all, God's communicable attributes expose us to how we as human persons resemble God. He is personal, creative, loving, rational, truth-telling, willing. So are we, as beings made in his image (Gen. 1:28). Like my young son who places his boots into the fresh boot marks I forged in the snow as he walks behind me, so too I am meant to imitate and resemble the one who created and redeemed me in these ways (Eph. 5:1). Recovering this resemblance to God in my humanity describes what Jesus is restoring in his people by his grace (Col. 3:9–10). The goal of life and ministry is for his grace to recover us to our intended humanity in him. Recovering our proper place and extolling his glorifies him.

This is why we also need a dose of God's incommunicable attributes. These show how little of a resemblance to God we have. We are not infinite, everywhere at once, all-powerful, or all-knowing. We are not meant to try to be or to expect this of others. And this is my concern. Forgetting our place as only human, we grasp for incommunicable attributes and try to make them our own as we live and minister with others. Our worldly and church cultures often applaud this and urge us on. You can be like God! This makes us prone, especially in ministry, to try to do what only God is meant to. The paradox is this: only by surrender to our proper human place can we glorify and enjoy God the way we say we want to and the way he requires.

So, when I say I want to "start again" with my theology, this means that I admit that my resistance to being an unexceptional man and ordinary human being is ultimately rooted in the Serpent's lie to the man and the woman. "You will be like God," he said (Gen. 3:5).

When the Serpent tempted Eve and Adam to "be like God," the Serpent meant that we can rival God in what we resemble. The Serpent meant that we can also break the bonds of creaturely limits in order to infinitely know and do as our Creator knows and does. We can circumvent what legitimately limits us. The lie continues by whispering to us that in comparison to God, we are somehow extraordinary, entitled, and exceptional. We must therefore behave this way among the neighbors and creatures with which we do life. These whispers, and our attention to them, atrophy ministers from the inside out. I'm trying to say that Jesus intends to pound our chests and breathe our lungs full again.

How to Read This Book

I should simply and humanly admit at the start that I am cognizant of a few things that might challenge you a bit. First, I have begun this book on life and ministry with a bit of poetry. This book is filled with it. Though poetry inhabits the Bible's pages, some of us have no taste for such language. But I suggest that "even those Christians who cannot enjoy it will respect it; for Our Lord, soaked in the poetic tradition of His country, delighted to use it."[6]

I am also aware of the poets and the persons whom I quote. I do not know some of them to be Christian, and the monk in this chapter, for example, is a Christian mystic (and certainly not a Protestant). On both counts, some may feel that since I've gotten off on the wrong foot so early by quoting these ideas from suspect people, the rest of the book must be assuredly wobbly in a theological sense (especially if it goes unnoticed that I will quote John Calvin more than once—which in its own right, will still concern others). But I hope the apostle's refusal to censor a true statement even when found upon odd lips can calm such a concern (Acts 17:28).

Meanwhile, I've taken a very personal approach in my attempt to point us to Jesus. The danger of this approach, as with any of us who seek to testify about God in our own and others' lives, is to leave the reader with more of a sense of us than of Jesus.[7] On the other hand, the danger of eschewing a more personal approach is to try to point us to Jesus as if he has nothing to do with the real sights, sounds, and providences of his creation under the sun. Likewise, one cannot credibly learn to be a physician of the body without becoming acquainted with the lab and years of residencies with actual people. So, it seems to me, those studying to physician the soul are left disadvantaged without some kind of truth regarding what is actually out there and within our own hearts.

To get us closer to the lab and the residency, therefore, is my aim. To that end, I am taking my writing style cues from the Wisdom Literature of the Bible. The Psalms, Job, and Ecclesiastes often take the posture of a first-person voice that speaks transparently regarding God, the providences of the world, and the realities of the heart. We hear Job's personal thoughts and those of his "friends." "I thought in my heart," the preacher tells us. "I devoted myself, I have seen, I have heard." Ecclesiastes uses this posture to communicate God and our existence as his creatures under the sun. At one point, he even says, "I hated life" (Eccles. 2:17).

The Proverbs partner in this way to give us the sights and the sounds and quotes of everyone from scoundrels to saints in order to give case studies to the next generation of God's people. The young were meant to hear the sights and sounds of creation and providence and learn what they mean before they actually encountered them in real time; this was so they would know how to wisely navigate what is actually there and be not surprised or left ill-equipped or naive.

With that in mind, I recall a criticism often leveled at Charles Spurgeon: the complaint that he spoke with too many personal references and with too much of the world in his speech.[8] To the degree that we were left thinking more of him than of Jesus, the complaint is warranted. But rarely is this the case with him.

I am no Spurgeon; nonetheless, such a complaint may likewise come my way, and as it relates to my blind spots, such criticism will be warranted. But I do hope my efforts to apply our theology will more often than not leave us thinking about and worshiping at the feet of Jesus. I likewise hope that those of us more accustomed to a didactic and Pauline approach will remember how often Paul referred to himself and his stories in his letters as well as the fact that we know his personal story and not just his teachings, and this by God's design.

The book, therefore, has a slow-building, simmering-pot kind of embodiment to it. It is not a quick read, and this too is by design. Apprenticeship needs meditation and time.

I admit, therefore, that this book needs others. But my assumption is that we have no lack of those more didactic, linear, and quick helps for our young men and women. I hope this volume contributes alongside of these other fine helps to create together a full picture of the glory of Jesus in our humanity for life and ministry.

So on all these counts, I suppose you and I could be getting off to a rough start! And yet any of us who have tried to build a life, pastor a church, or begin a ministry know that the start (after the honeymoon period, of course) is often rough. In fact, most often it is the end rather than the beginning of a ministry or a marriage or a life that more readily reveals the true character of it all.

I think of Mamaw's porch in Henryville. I think of my shoeless sermon and the dark days in between. My message to you is simply this: all of us, whether loafered, high-heeled, laced, or tennis-shoed, preach nonetheless as those who are bare soled before the living God. With the recovery of this in Jesus, hope rises.

CHAPTER TWO

Recovering Eden

Giving Ourselves to the Word, the Supper, and the Place

> Our former minister had so much energy that simply pastoring wasn't enough.[1]

I had recently learned that a longtime pastor, mentor, and friend had committed suicide. I took a sabbatical from the seminary where I served as a professor and spent six months as interim pastor with my departed friend's family and congregation.

I had pastored a church before. I had served as an interim before. But not like this. We would forage together for scraps of grace and truth amid the wreckage. The living Christ would inhabit the heaps with us. We would learn from him in the trash. He would sup with us in the shadow's valley.

But presently I was standing with other professors and seasoned students in our jeans and tennis shoes. I was asked to give a word to future pastors and ministry leaders. Mostly young faces chewed hot dogs. Hands took napkins to wipe remnants of ketchup or mustard from their cheeks. Mountain Dew and root beer spoke to our thirst. Prayers were said. The evening had given this eager-to-succeed crowd the grace to laugh and relax. It was time to say something for a new minister to count on. It was time to find some words that could act as a compass. What could I say to help a rookie in ministry prepare to navigate the strange and lovely terrain of ministry leadership?

The atmosphere was light, but my heart was heavy. I was thinking about how my pastor friend could have stepped down from the ministry and still have mattered to all of us. But for him, stepping down in the midst of his inner haunting indicated not his humanity but his failure. He could not see himself useful if he no longer held the position of pastor with the care for others the position enabled. I missed him. I was, for the first time in my life, asking myself the same question. Did I know that I could serve Christ humanly and significantly (whether or not I was a pastor or ministry leader)? I did not know it at that time, but I would soon have to answer such a question in a painful and public way. For the moment, however, among those ministry students, with grief in my heart, and soberly confronting my assumptions about what it meant to lead in ministry, it was now my turn to speak. I breathed a quick prayer and stood. That's when I said it. "Jonathan Edwards, the great American theologian and preacher, farted."

Some laughed. Some smirked at my irreverence. Maybe I was irreverent. I wasn't trying to be funny. I probably could have found better language to describe what I was wrestling with. But a few sat back and reflected. Those few probably knew for some time what I was only just beginning to learn. Greatness, even in ministry, cannot escape humanity. How did I ever begin to assume that it was supposed to? Being human does not mar greatness; it informs it and sets its noble boundaries. Why had I come to think otherwise?

Forgetting How to Feel the Air

When I formally trained for the ministry, I was taught the doctrine of creation. I studied the facts of Genesis 1 and 2. I memorized the following catechism questions and answers for my ordination exams:

> *What is the work of creation?*
>
> The work of creation is, God's making all things of nothing, by the word of his power in the space of six days, and all very good.
>
> *How did God create man?*
>
> God created man male and female, after his own image, in knowledge, righteousness, and holiness, with dominion over the creatures.

I was asked to wrestle with the questions that in our generation flow from these truths. Mainly, I had to decide what I thought "in the space of six days" meant along with the questions posed by Darwin's legacy. I had to discern my views of gender roles and what it means to be male and female. I would be examined on these points.

I am grateful for this training and these purposes. This kind of training has benefited and blessed me. I believe that many of us need such training to help us.

However, after twenty years in vocational ministry, I now realize that I gave little thought to *how* such truths about God creating the world should shape the way I approach my daily life as a man and the ministry of the gospel as a pastor. Professor Jerram Barrs tried to help us.[2] He sought to teach us to view our lives with God and the lives of those we serve as human beings. But I did not yet have the ears of experience to hear. I derived my view of calling from places other than Eden. In his living room with tea, I once asked Jerram why he hadn't written more books over the years. He had taught us, traveled the world, and continued to give so much of himself for others. I told him how so many of us long to hear more from him and want to learn more. Pausing and shrugging his shoulders, he smiled broadly and set his teacup on his plate. What he said in response put ministry ambition and the doctrine of creation into perspective. "I'd like to write more," he said, "but I really enjoy my garden."

The Preacher and the Wind

The preacher in Ecclesiastes seems to proclaim something of Jerram's sentiment. He too speaks from a local calling (king over Israel) in a local place (in Jerusalem) (Eccles. 1:12). He too exposes the limits of good books. "Of making many books there is no end," says the preacher. "Much study is a weariness of the flesh" (Eccles. 12:12). And as he sifts through everything illusory that we chase in this world, he continues to call us back to Eden from the "under the sun" vanity that evicted it and changed the locks on the doors. We stand outside on the porch, wondering where then to go. The preacher, again and again, brings his refrain home to our hearts.

> There is *nothing better for a person than that he should eat and drink and find enjoyment in his toil. This also, I saw, is from the hand of God*, for apart from him who can eat or who can have enjoyment? (Eccles. 2:24–25)

> I perceived that there is nothing better for them than to be joyful and to do good as long as they live; also that *everyone should eat and drink and take pleasure in all his toil—this is God's gift to man.* (Eccles. 3:12–13)

Sensing Jesus

> Behold, *what I have seen to be good and fitting is to eat and drink and find enjoyment in all the toil* with which one toils under the sun the few days of his life that *God has given him*, for this is his lot. Everyone also to whom God has given wealth and possessions and power to enjoy them, and *to accept his lot and rejoice in his toil—this is the gift of God*. For he will not much remember the days of his life because God keeps him occupied with joy in his heart. (Eccles. 5:18–20)

> There is an evil that I have seen under the sun, and it lies heavy on mankind: a man to whom God gives wealth, possessions, and honor, so that he lacks nothing of all that he desires, yet God does not give him power to enjoy them, but a stranger enjoys them. This is vanity; it is a grievous evil. If a man fathers a hundred children and lives many years, so that the days of his years are many, *but his soul is not satisfied with life's good things* . . . (Eccles. 6:1–3)

> And I commend joy, *for man has nothing better under the sun but to eat and drink and be joyful*, for this will go with him *in his toil* through the days of his life that *God has given him* under the sun. (Eccles. 8:15)

> *Go, eat your bread with joy, and drink your wine with a merry heart, for God has already approved what you do*. Let your garments be always white. Let not oil be lacking on your head. *Enjoy life with the wife whom you love*, all the days of your vain life that he has given you under the sun, because *that is your portion in life and in your toil* at which you toil under the sun. (Eccles. 9:7–9)

As he exposes our illusions of gain, and compares them with the reality of gain that ordinary love for God and neighbor in a place is meant to have, the preacher declares, "Better is a handful of quietness than two hands full of toil and a striving after wind" (Eccles. 4:6). I think of Jerram's response to me about writing and the garden. I think of my ambitions. I hear the preacher's voice. I ask myself, why would his statement about quietness and striving after the wind be exempt to us who are pastors? I hear Jesus's words in my memory, "What will it profit a man if he gains the whole world and forfeits his soul?" (Matt. 16:26). Is there a kind of "world to gain" even in the ministry that in the end can damage my soul?

A poet has reminded us that in the shadows of what alarms us and calls us to action, there lies a (seemingly fragile yet) stronger and deeper call. "It's a flower in the parking lot of the Pentagon," the poet writes. "It says, 'Look around. Listen. Feel the air.'"[3] Ironically I had "learned" the doctrine of creation, and yet I possessed little ability to feel the air God has made. Perhaps this is why I am confounded by a notion that glorifying God leaves little time for writing more books because of the beckoning pleasure of plants and soil. And what about the Great Commission? How does planting and enjoying a garden bring about our call to go into all the world and make disciples of Jesus? (Matt. 28:18–20). My deep assumption is now exposed. Somehow I've come to believe that fulfilling the Great Commission has more to do with writing books than with planting gardens. Why is this? After all, when God determined to glorify himself and reveal himself in his pursuit of a people for himself, what did he do first? He planted a garden and invited Adam and Eve to it.

Going Away Sad

My pastor/mentor took his life amid a platform of ministry success. A two-fold building expansion was underway. The church was adding a gym for its school and a beautiful and towering sanctuary. The number of people attending the church was rapidly growing. He was invited to speak at other places. He had a staff. His counseling load was large. A church plant was in the works. There were the normal and painful divisions and debates about vision and the application of doctrine. He was a husband. He was a father of two. He preached with power. And internal to all these successes that surrounded him, he was a man whose thoughts were troubled. It's as if he could see the Pentagon and we could see his medals and need his briefings, but neither of us could feel the air anymore or see the flower in the church parking lot. He was a success, reaching the dreams that most young pastors aspire to and hope for. But as a man—as a human being—he must have begun to feel keenly what we say we all believe and what we tell our secular counterparts.

"No amount of money or growth in buildings or constituency will satisfy you," we say to the businessmen in our congregations. "Your hearts were made for a different kind of treasure, and it won't satisfy you until you let go of this fool's gold and take hold of what God created you for."

Sensing Jesus

While we applauded this pastor who was doing great things for God, none of those things that we thought were great had the power to satisfy and mend his soul.

The problem deepens, because when doing something great for God is measured by such outward successes, to let them go must mean that one is choosing failure. This is the logical conclusion when gospel "success" equals more money, larger numbers, and more expansion. Those who forfeit these "successes" appear unblessed by God. It is little wonder that when Jesus asked the rich man to give away his money, become poor, and follow Jesus, the rich man went away sad, and the disciples who looked on were perplexed (Mark 10:17–31).

My friend must have felt the weight of this truth deep in his being. If the success story in ministry was actually damaging his soul, could he let it go and still be useful to Jesus and significant for Jesus's kingdom? Perhaps he knew that he could but wondered if those around him could see it that way? Or would we have thought it a waste to be so gifted and yet let go of such "great" things? I do not know. I only know this for sure. Church success can damage our souls when definitions of success are removed from what God teaches us in Eden—when ordinary persons and places made in God's image and given by him are not extraordinary or exceptional enough for us.

Returning to Eden's Ground

In Eden the young couple had ministry to do. And they were in love. A match made truly in heaven—a partnership for God. What task had God given them? What great things for him did he want them to accomplish? They ate food. They cared for animals. They planted seeds. They prayed. It was a pornless world with naked rest. Pleasing God meant nothing more than listening to his words, following him in Eden, and gratefully swimming in the safe waters of each other's company. They needn't be anything other than who they were, nowhere other than where they were, and possessing nothing more than what they had for God to be glorified by their lives. God was enough, and so were they. There was no striving for ministry advancement, no glad-handing and networking to get to the next strategic level. Nothing more was needed. More money was not their hope for ministry success, nor did they strategize how to enlarge the garden for God (as if what they had was too small to bring him glory). Holding hands, mowing the lawn, resisting foul temptations, and learning to love the one who created them was enough for a significant life. God was glorified by what we might call "the love of inconsiderable things."[4]

"Inconsiderable things" are those exceptional and extraordinary beauties that we no longer value. As themselves they are "considerable"; they are weighty, solid, yet they no longer capture our attention or maintain our interest. This is partly what happened to the Prodigal Son in Jesus's parable (Luke 15:11–32). The good life with his family on the farm had become a bore that stifled him. He could no longer see its "considerableness" because of the alluring sirens that sang to him in the world. For the purposes of this chapter, I draw your attention to three such inconsiderable things that God gave all of humanity in Eden.

1) We were to regard him (and nothing else) as God and love him and surrender to him as such. In other words, we were to love God.

2) We were to love each other (hold fast to his wife), relate appropriately to our extended family (leave father and mother), and cultivate a family and ultimately a community of neighbors for neighbor love (be fruitful and multiply). In other words, we were meant to love our neighbors.

3) We were to recognize the goodness and sacredness of the place, the creatures, and the things that God had created and to watch over these good things. We were to contribute to cultivating the creation (to work it and keep it) and a culture that reflected the goodness of God in the things he had made in a place he called us to.

Human life was given for the love of God and the love of our neighbors in a local place for God's glory and the common good. Therefore, God intends to glorify himself and give you enjoyment in him by giving you three core truths by which to arrange your life and ministry.

1) God has given you himself to surrender to and love. This means that to daily orient your life toward a moment-by-moment relation-

ship with God is a great thing that brings glory to him. You needn't be anywhere else than where you are, because Jesus is there too.

2) God has given you a handful of persons that you are meant to love. This means you are meant for relationships with people. To enter this way of love for neighbor is to do a great thing that glorifies God. You needn't become somebody else or overlook those people who are right in front of you. The Lord is at work here doing great things.

3) God will give you a place to inhabit, which means that you get to become attentive to what is there where you are. This means that to dwell knowledgeably and hospitably in and toward the place God gives you is to glorify him. God will give you a few things that he intends for you to do in your inhabited place and with those people. To do what God gives you to do is to strengthen the common good and to glorify him.

As pastors we will personally struggle with this. "I constantly feel that I am out of my depth," my pastor friend said. "Me too," I said. We both stared quietly into the distance for a moment. Then a few questions occurred to us. Why do we lament the fact that we do not know everything? Why do we speak of our being out of our depth with sadness and heavy sighing, as if we are failing something we were supposed to attain? "It is as if we feel we are supposed to repent for having limits with our knowledge," I said. "Who has taught us this?" he wondered. "Where does  this expectation to know it all come from?" he asked. We paused and then laughed with shared embarrassment. We concluded that if we were to say to God, "Father, I constantly feel out of my depth," God would gently ask, "And why is that a problem?"

Or consider another struggle pastors have. When Richard was fresh out of graduate school and contemplating his first pastorate, the rural farming community of Cana, Illinois, was one of his ministry options. Richard felt hesitant.

"I'm looking for a significant ministry," he said to his dad. "Cana is very nice, but is it significant?"

"Significant?" his father replied. "You've been preparing for this—for more than ten years. You've piled up more schooling after high school than most people accumulate in a lifetime. These people are saying, 'Come, we've been waiting for you. You can be our pastor,' which is what you said you wanted all along. And now it has to be *significant*? Isn't the ministry significant? I thought it was. All of it. Everywhere."

"Yes. Right. Yeah," Richard replied. "I guess I want to have an impact on people's lives."

"There are people in Cana, in case you hadn't noticed," his dad retorted.

Richard shot back, "You don't understand what I want. I am weighing this offer, but it has to be right for me."

"It's not an offer," his dad interrupted. "It's a call."[5]

Ambition and Significance

The problem isn't that Richard might be called to Las Vegas or Manhattan or London instead of Cana, Illinois—as if going into rural ministry reveals more maturity or has greater weight than an urban one. The problem is that Richard misread the dignity of both. He could not see the greatness of an ordinary life in Cana, and he was illusory and arrogant in his implied feeling that somehow being somewhere other than Cana would prove more significant. More importantly, Richard didn't seem to understand that no matter where he was called, his purpose would be the same either way—to seek an apprenticeship with Jesus for recovering people's humanity—to recover again in Christ the daily and edenic purpose of loving God and neighbor in a place until he comes.

In other words, our goal of greatness isn't the problem. How we define the word *great* is. The trees in the garden were desirable, good, and pleasant (Gen. 2:9). But when Eve saw the one tree, she desired it in a way that was bent. She sought to consume it apart from God and in spite of his stated purpose for that tree (Gen. 3:6). She exerted desire for a truly desirable thing in all the wrong ways.

Like Eve and Adam, we too are tempted to prize the Serpent's cunning.

1) We are tempted to something like omnipresence—the ability to be at all places at all times. The Serpent says, "You shall not die," and we try to act like this is true, as if we have no limits of space or time, as if we can be everywhere for everyone with no limits, no rest, and no need to adjust due to our aging bodies.

2) We are tempted to something like omnipotence—the possession

of unlimited power. "When [Eve] saw that the tree was good . . . she took of its fruit" (Gen. 3:6). She acted as if apart from God she could wield the power she needed to get what she wanted. Ever since, we too try to act as if we have the personal or social resources to fix, control, and overcome whatever faces us. We take what we can as fast as we can to fix persons and things and to make them work the way we want them to. This is why we feel we have the right to never wait in line for our agenda. We should expect to get what we want immediately. So we consume creatures and things as a means to advance ourselves, as if everything was made to serve our personal agenda for ministry or for life.

3) We are tempted to something like omniscience. We want to know everything as God does. ("You will be like God, knowing good and evil," v. 5). This is why we sometimes feel that we deserve celebrity status. We feel that we warrant fame, praise, and deference and to be counted exceptional among persons. We are meant to be the unique one and everyone else to pale in comparison to our lives or our ministries.

No matter what size our church or where we serve, these temptations enable us to generate a buzz, gain respect, sometimes produce large followings, and often give us quantifiable measurements to report and feel that God is greatly using us in our generation. We rally and program, and machine-like we produce for God.

But these temptations also make it difficult to ever hear someone say to us: "I want to tell you, every time I have been here, I feel like a human being."[6]

What does this teach us about ambition and greatness? Some of us will be called to a well-known ministry (Prov. 22:29). Such a calling, moment, or place is not the problem we have. The problem we have rises when we suggest that obscurity and greatness are opposites, that fame in our culture and greatness as God sees it are synonyms. This is why I say the goal of greatness isn't our problem. How we have come to infuse our definitions of greatness with this devilish sentiment is.

Jesus seeks to save us from ourselves and from this devilish lie about greatness. In Jesus, we do not do away with possessing an ambition for great things. Rather, we learn in him to make sure that the greatness we strive for is the kind that he values. In this regard, Jesus sees our fights for greatness, pushes through the crowds to get to us, separates us from each other, and commands, "Not so with you."

> A dispute also arose among them, as to which of them was to be regarded as the greatest. And he said to them, "The kings of the Gentiles exercise lordship over them, and those in authority over them are called benefactors. But not so with you. Rather, let the greatest among you become as the youngest, and the leader as one who serves. For who is the greater, one who reclines at table or one who serves? Is it not the one who reclines at table? But I am among you as the one who serves. (Luke 22:24–27)

Jesus commends a greatness of a different kind—one that foregoes using power and position to achieve it. Whether one has position has very little to do with whether one is a great man or woman. Yet, in the world of congregations and ministries and businesses and neighborhoods, we are tempted to live as if greatness is tied to being the one who owns the table and not to the one who has no table and must work as a server for a living. This view partially explains why conference speakers are generally those whose churches are larger or whose books are more widely read. In theory we know that an unknown pastor in a long and faithful ministry who doesn't write books would have a great deal to share with us for our growth. But in practice we find this very difficult to act on. Because of this, faithful persons in large ministries often get used like a commodity, while faithful persons in small settings often get overlooked.

But Jesus turns these and other worldly and churchly definitions of greatness on their heads. "I am among you as the one who serves," he says. That "leader" who is great in Jesus's eyes is the one who lives as a servant or who, as an aged one, uses his or her position as if younger, like one who is overlooked and relates to others as if lacking advantages or special honor at the table.

By this metaphor, Jesus isn't calling upon those with position to act childishly or irresponsibly, as if their position is worthy of disrespect. Instead, Jesus is saying that we carry those positions of responsibility as those who believe that greatness has little relation to the position one has  and more to do with the quality of life in Christ that one humbly offers. Every moment of obscure service makes the hall of fame in heaven. This means that everybody, no matter what color, what economic reality, what gender, or what position they have or will never have in this life can do something great for God.

The fact that I preach or write or attend larger or smaller congregations actually has very little to do with being great in God's eyes. Having a large national pulpit does not mean that I am favored or blessed, just as having no national pulpit has little to do with being overlooked or unfavored. Because my business is large does not make me blessed, as if having a smaller business means that I am less blessed. If this line of reasoning were true, then the way to get more favor from God has to do with size, money, and notoriety, and the way to lose favor with God has to do with lessening size, money, and notoriety. But Jesus directly opposes this view of greatness. In the eyes of some congregation members, constituencies, and colleagues and in the deep places of many of our hearts, greatness has everything to do with gaining and not losing size, position, money, or degree of notoriety. But not so with Jesus. Jesus calls us to a greatness of a different kind.

Therefore, those of you searching for something larger, faster, and more significant, who feel that if you could just be somewhere else doing something else as somebody else, then your life would really matter—Jesus has come to confound you. I'm not referring to those who need to flee to somewhere else for safety's sake. I am referring to the discontented who have not yet learned what it means that Jesus is our portion and that he is enough for us. You have wandered far from home. You cannot glorify God by trying to become him. You cannot honor him by overlooking his creatures and the places he has given them in which to enjoy him. This Shepherd is searching for you. His shoulders are ready for you. He may just decide to pick you up and carry you to somewhere sexy in order to undo you! He may call you to courageously prize what is overlooked and mundane among those whose cravings for the next and the now might cause them to soon overlook you for another more hip pastor. Or he may call you to nowhere sexy so that you can learn that you can make a difference in Jesus even if you are somewhere forgotten by the world.

A business model might try to make lemonade out of this perceived lemon of a situation. But for a church, when greatness is defined as "big, efficient, and now," ruin follows, even if the shell of the ministry boasts of strength. When the ordinary, the common, and the unexceptional are yawned at, we no longer see the value of the ordinary people and places and creation in front of us. We believe nothing in front of us is valuable enough, and something more must be made of it. We become pastors who no longer see people and are not content to sit with them in their ordinary places among their mundane toil.

In other words, we flirt with the very definition of greatness that ruined Eden. Bible college and seminary students feel this.

When a woman marries a man, for example, she imagines him to be her best friend, a soul companion, a partner in laughter, a friend in tears. When a man marries a woman, he imagines these same ideals. We do so because we were created to esteem such inconsiderable things as treasures.

But when a Bible student graduates, and when a couple enters ministry, the young love of ordinary life is pressed out of them if they are not careful. She has often just given birth to a child. Or maybe they are newly married. But mostly they are already exhausted from the Bible training pace of quantity and haste that has mentored them. All of this for the sake of the call. They are starting the work of ministry as those who already need a break to rest for a while. But the start of a work for God offers little time for residual fatigue. So the spouse goes with her ministry leader without roots to a new place with a new child and a newer job. The church expects him to hit the ground running. He wants to show that he was worth their hire. He overworks all hours for the sake of Jesus while his new bride and newer baby try to learn to trust Jesus amid the dishwater and Sesame Street with no local friends and no knowledge of street names.

The single person graduating Bible training likewise fills all waking hours for God, exhausts herself, and tells herself that if she ever gets married, then she will slow down (not realizing that the habit of the present pace will be very difficult to interrupt).

Why do we pressure our young ones in ministry to produce ministry results in this way? Why do they feel they must become something other than a normal human being who is single or someone other than a young couple in sacred love having their first baby and learning their first call in the world?

Recovering Eden's Goals

Perhaps we biblically conclude that when Adam and Eve fell into sin, God changed his mind about what he would derive glory from among human beings. After the fall, perhaps we imply that the garden and its goals became too small for God or no longer valued.

But I commend to you that God has been about nothing but seeking to restore and recover what was lost in Eden. Throughout the Old Testament narratives, God gives his people a place to dwell and cultivate—a land in which to raise their families and go to be with their fathers. In that place, they were meant to regard him above all else and to love their neighbors and give themselves to daily labor. This way of life would, in God's hands, become a blessing to the nations. Captivity was so terrible because it removed this way of life. It snatched God's people to another place that distorted and devalued God, love for neighbor, and love of place.

The sum of the law is love for God and neighbor in the place where people dwell for the sake of their families and the nations. The prophets call out to a people who remove love for God from the heart, who damage neighbors and violate neighbor love, who misuse animals, and who keep looking beyond the place God gave them to larger, more prestigious places (such as Egypt).

In the Wisdom Literature, the story is the same. Ecclesiastes is a chronicle of fallen Eden. For what does "life under the sun" describe? It describes the Eden that once was and the vanity that now is. The refrain harkens back to Eden. There is nothing better for a man than to eat, love his wife, and work, for this is God's gift and this is man's joy and lot. In the Psalms, God's provision is pictured as his preparing a table for us to sit together with him and eat, even in the presence of our enemies. Green pastures and still waters for rest are where he leads us.

Had Adam and Eve resisted the Serpent, this would be what they know. They would have supped with God and each other in the cool of the day, in the venomless presence of their defanged foe.

Likewise, our Lord Jesus does not introduce essentially new things. He fulfills and recovers existing old ones.

> Jesus prayed to the Father that his disciples would not be taken out of the world but kept in the world from the evil one (Jn. 17:15). In line with this, Christians did not have to go out of the world (1 Cor. 5:10), but to remain in their occupations (1 Cor. 7:17–23); to obey the powers God had ordained (Rom. 13:1); to regard all things their own (1 Cor. 3:21–23); to

> enjoy every gift of God with thanksgiving (1 Tim. 4:3–5); and to consider godliness as of value in every way, as it holds promise for the present life and also for the life to come (1 Tim. 4:8). . . . Nature commends grace; grace commends nature.[7]

Jesus demonstrates greatness within the creation as one of the least and as a servant of all. His ministry is revealed at tables with food, with ordinary and diverse people in the marketplace, and the intimacy of daily friendship. He eats fish and bread. He blesses and reveres God. He loves even his enemies. The cross of Jesus does not free us from loving God and neighbor in a particular place; it recovers us to value this idea of greatness again. "Grace, accordingly, serves not to avoid, to suppress, or to kill the natural, but precisely to free it from its sinful corruption and to make it truly natural again."[8]

This is why Paul teaches us that great preaching, knowledge of mysteries, great acts of faith, and sacrificial martyrdom for Jesus mean nothing in themselves and are no measure of health in a church or a soul. What gives meaning to the world and glory to God is our love for him and for our neighbor in the place in which we have been called (1 Cor. 13:1–8). Only from and for such tangible daily love do preaching, doctrine, faith, and sacrificial service have their meaning.

Therefore, Paul teaches us to pray for our leaders, not so that we can escape this life but so that we can lead a quiet and peaceful life (1 Tim. 2:1–8). He calls upon us to aspire to live quietly, to mind our own affairs and to work with our hands (1 Thess. 4:11). This is the outworking of the Great Commission. Paul would give his life and teaching to others, whether he was in cosmopolitan Corinth or dingy Crete, so that they too would live differently and Christianly in their ordinary places with their neighbors until Christ comes. This is why the letters from Paul, Peter, and John (for example) each discuss how the gospel is meant to transform ways of relating as spouses, parents, and neighbors, and to governments and different races, ages, and genders.

And what then is heaven but our existing with love for God and each other in a place of his choosing for the rest of our lives? And that with neighbors from every tribe, tongue, and nation and all for his glory!

Imagine how at odds this edenic purpose and measure of success are to a church planter. He has a time clock of three years. What must he do in that time in order to retain viability as a pastor in the eyes of his financial supporters? Biblically, success has relational and character-oriented measures in Jesus, irrespective of numeric interest, for the good of a locality. But quantitative results often shadow these more relational measures of success. In fact, a board member in America will be tempted to expect the word *more* or *larger* to attend the organizational, programmatic, and economic matters of the new church plant or ministry institution year by year as a measure of whether the organization is moving forward in the gospel. But nowhere does Jesus teach us that forward gospel movement is measured in dollars and cents. Navigating the institutional side of Jesus ministry is not easy. But when we are not at our best, there is something in our hearts that resists "the love of inconsiderable things." These inconsiderable things fade in our view and rarely inform what it means to actually move forward as Jesus, not the world, would see it.

Confusion

I now see that this inattention to inconsiderable things was in my heart as I first began to pastor a church. I now see how I did not understand that my gospel purpose was to enable persons to recover what was lost about their humanity and to live from there in Jesus. I also saw this absence in some (not all) of the leaders of the church.

As for my heart, I was twenty-six. Amid the boxes and the moving truck, Richard Baxter's words were on my mind. "I preached as a dying man to dying men," he said.[9] I took Baxter's words seriously. I vowed that I would not compromise with the shortness of this life, but every chance I got would expose it and its attempt to burgle God's true treasures from us.

Getting my feet on the ground and making my first attempts at preaching week after week, I longed for that "sense of God's presence" that Martyn Lloyd-Jones had spoken of and had recovered from the forgotten history of spiritual revivals in the West. I hoped that my ministry too would consist of "theology coming through a man who is on fire." I hoped that God's Spirit would set the truth of his Word aflame in our souls.[10]

I prayed, therefore, for a visitation from God. As I began to make my first pastoral visits in a new community, I remembered Daniel Rowland praying for the godless place he was called to as a pastor. In his lifetime, he saw those prayers answered more bountifully than he could have imagined.[11] I also recalled what Benjamin Franklin wrote in his autobiography. Though he himself did not believe in Jesus, this father of America observed the arrival and preaching of George Whitefield and marveled at how "the whole town had gone religious." Franklin recounted how he "could not walk through the town at night without hearing psalms being sung by each household." That made me think, "What if God were to come with such power at my church in Hudson, Ohio?"

My first sermon series outlined the primary aspects of our core vision as a church. In each sermon, I said what I meant with all my heart. "May God so work in us in these days," I beckoned, "that years from now long after we here are gone, those who come after us will look back and say, 'Surely God was in this place.'"

I do not disparage these longings and prayers for God to work powerfully and truly in my life and for my generation. Many of us excuse our lack of seeking God in this way from hearts of unbelief and cynicism or cowardliness.

What I'm trying to say is not that I should not have had such longings, but that there was something obvious within them that I was tragically overlooking about myself. I was overlooking that, as I preached with all my heart for God, I ate Froot Loops and Raisin Bran for breakfast; that I prayed with all my soul as a man who used cream for the acne on his face and tried to figure out the two cowlicks in his hair each morning. As I visited and dispensed pastoral counsel, I did so as a young father who had been frustrated at 3:00 that morning with my inability to stop my infant from crying.

My point is that God does great works! But God's great works may have nothing to do with enlarging my ministry or saving me from having to experience what every other human being has to go through in this life. I didn't see that a great work from God would profoundly anchor me into a more authentic love for him and my neighbors where I lived, and that, no matter what God did, large or small, I would still need to use Q-Tips or a washcloth for my ears every now and then.

My church leaders struggled too. We had eighteen acres of land. With our number of ministries, our money, our acreage, and our theology, we dreamt of being movers and shakers for God. So when I proposed that we cut half of our ministry programs so that our people could rest more with their families and be at home in their neighborhoods with the gospel, some judged me as taking the church backwards (even though we had some thirty programs in a church of eighty-five people).

And while we as a leadership could argue tirelessly about our vision statements and eloquently debate tedious questions (such as whether John Calvin would have removed the wooden cross hanging on the wall in our sanctuary, or whether as Protestants we should rebaptize someone previously baptized in the Catholic Church, or whether we should have the name "Presbyterian" in our church logo), we as human men often had little ability to show one another the love, grace, or humility of Jesus in our daily relationships. Our dreams and plans for doing something great for God energized us. Our dealings with one another, however, only wounded and fatigued us. As leaders, we damaged others too. We did not know that it is easy to do a great thing for God so long as greatness does not require interior humility, practical love for the people right in front of us, or submission to the presence of Jesus in the place we already are.

When one raging man in Christ becomes gentle, there is more power here than in thirty raging men who came to our event and went home unchanged. The problem for my heart and for many of those with whom I have served is that thirty in attendance sounds greater than one. And even if, our Lord willing, thirty came and thirty were changed, for all of our rejoicing we'd still have to use the bathroom at some point.

I Am Not the Christ

Great things from God do not remove us from our humanity. Great things from God establish for us that no one but God is God. Human we remain. And because God created us and our places, we already possess in Jesus the extraordinary calling we long for.

To this end, Jay, a dear teacher friend of mine, has been known to have each of his ministerial students stand up in the classroom. There, each student must individually turn and face the rest of the class. Then he or she must confess out loud to the rest, "I am not the Christ." Why? Because to say, "I am not the Christ" is simultaneously to expose for all to see that we pastors, leaders, and caregivers are merely human and only local.

I use the words *merely* human and *only* local in order to differentiate us from Jesus. Jesus is human, but not *merely.* Jesus is local, but not *only.* We clarify this distinction between Jesus and us as an act of worship and commitment. As ministry leaders we endeavor to give of our lives in such a way that every neighbor we minister to will know that we are not God. The Serpent's invitation to celebrity, immediate gratification, and using people to advance ourselves as if we are God poisons the air. Jesus recovers our lungs! To exalt Jesus as Lord is to free us to the derivative glory of belonging humanly to him.

I had overlooked my being human in my aspirations to greatness. Maybe this is partially what happened to my pastor friend who killed himself. He was a "success." I was becoming one. That's why I said it that day, "Jonathan Edwards farted."

Our Work

Two texts are helping me as I seek to grow in loving God and neighbor in my local place for a global good in Jesus. The first is Ruth. The second is Titus. May I briefly remind you of both?

Consider the biblical story of Ruth. I know that the call of prophet and king sounds more noble than widow and farmer. Therefore, we aspire to such grand positions and heroic moments for our generation. I do not disparage this. We long for a generation in which God would grant us such leaders. We take up Elijah on Mount Carmel, for example, and long that we too could stand against the false prophets and teachings of our age with such courage. We long for God to work in such a miraculous and powerful way. And no wonder! For consider that in the days of the judges, when "everyone did what was right in his own eyes" (Judg. 21:25), God raised up men and women for mighty deeds and champion events (Judg. 2:16). Oh, to rise like Deborah or Gideon or Samson! We look at our times. We see everyone doing what is right in their own eyes. We, too, rightly long for such reformation and revival. Those of us prone to resignation need Jesus to reawaken such longings for our generation.

But those among us prone to romanticism need at least four remembrances.

Sensing Jesus

First, there are heroes that never receive the limelight of their generation. While the judges publicly participated in substantial cultural change, a farmer named Boaz quietly walked the muddy fields, planted grain, fairly treated his workers, and sought the common good of his community with ordinary, daily, prayerful, and hard work. This farmer loved a Gentile woman and her family. They made an ordinary life of real love together. They loved God. Those who know the story will argue that this ordinary love and life proved equal to if not greater than the mighty deeds of the judges in that generation.

Second, heroic moments are heavenly but not heaven. What relief, what celebration, what gratitude and happiness arise when a people is delivered from oppression, corruption, and foul treatment; when souls are awakened; when dignity and integrity and decency form again not just the slogans but the actions of a land! And yet the effects of heroic moments fade. This was true in the times of the judges. The human heart was not intrinsically changed in a universal way by mighty deeds. In a matter of time, another generation would need another judge. And even these powerful deliverances could not bring back Naomi's family or Ruth's husband. The revivals came but the gravestones still remained in Moab.

Third, sometimes visitations from God are discovered when ordinary bread is placed on the table of an ordinary family (Ruth 1:6). Sometimes the aid of God is found in the provision of a mundane grain or an ordinary friend.

Fourth, what is the heroic moment meant to do but recover the ordinary greatness that God originally intended? Deborah and Gideon are raised up by God so that everyone can return to ordinary love and life and food with freedom and without harm in their locality with God. We get rid of evil so that people can live their ordinary lives without harassment. The great triumph of a fictional Superman is to free the citizens of Metropolis from evil so that they can work, marry, live, eat, and find meaning. The great triumph of the Greatest Generation was to free the world for a time from tyranny so that people could go back to the blessing and joy of daily life. The true act of heroism in Jesus on the cross and emptying the tomb is to return us to the grace of doing life with God in a place with love for our neighbors and finding the enjoyment in that which God created for us. Heroic moments have as their aim the recovery of the ordinary.

Romantic Realism

Without these remembrances, some of us will burn ourselves out with romanticism. We cannot find God in the ordinary. We restlessly move ourselves from one grand moment to the next. We regularly push others into the same whirlwind. We have little room in our ministry for a Naomi who does not get her husband back or a locality in which the visitation from God is that the supper tables have food again. We have trouble seeing how it is glorifying to God to eat food, learn to love, go to bed, and get up the next day for work. The thought of living and ministering in one or two unknown and ordinary places for fifty years and then going home to be with the Lord feels like death. Of what account to God is an ordinary life in the grain fields?

Others of us inwardly decay through resignation. We too cannot find God in the ordinary, but we have long given up on anything extraordinary being given by God or accomplished through us. "Call me Mara," we say with Naomi (Ruth 1:20). No love will ever find Ruth again. No bread will come to our table. No judge will save us. All is bitter and with little point in trying. I think my pastor friend who took his life must have landed here. Of what account to God is an ordinary life in the grain fields?

The result is an "all or nothing" kind of thinking. Either everything is grand or nothing is—and either way a grain field isn't grand enough (i.e., Adam and Eve with Eden). Romanticism and resignation both have this motto in common.

In contrast to both, Jesus calls us to a romantic realism. He purchased this for us on the cross. We long for heroic moments but recognize that they aren't heaven and that someone else among a rare few will most likely have that momentary role. We are realistic about the fact that heroic moments are not the normal way that God daily visits his people. And yet we still believe that God is doing something larger than we can presently see. Out of his love for us, he is recovering in Jesus what was lost. We are realistically romantic. We see bread on a table and give thanks to God! Bread isn't just bread anymore. Bread is a gift—God has remembered us. Ordinary love the way it is meant to be, along with a long life of ordinary faithfulness to God, accomplishes more than we know. A farmer, a widow, and a Gentile in an unknown place all of their lives may actually reveal in the end the true greatness of God. A romantic realist talks like this:

Sensing Jesus

> If you were to rank the most important people in the generation of the judges, who would they be? Gideon? Deborah? Samson? What mighty deeds! What help God brought through them. But Jesus purchased new eyes to see more than the heroic. Matthew, in the first Gospel of the New Testament, tells us of two others who likewise lived during the times of those awesome judges. He records for us "the book of the genealogy of Jesus Christ, the son of David, the son of Abraham" (1:1). In verses 5 and 6, Matthew says this: "Boaz the father of Obed by Ruth, and Obed the father of Jesse, and Jesse the father of David the king."

While everyone did what was right in his own eyes and reformers sought powerfully to turn the spiritual tide, the promise of Genesis 3:15 was being pursued by God on a mundane farm amid the shattered and recovered dreams of ordinary love and life.

The romanticized and the resigned—neither would have seen Ruth, the royal lady in the line of the King. While the romanticized stood in line to get the autograph of someone like Gideon, and while the resigned stayed home and complained about the hype, neither would have noticed the tremendous movement of God in their midst.

Congregation and Story

And this is what makes me think about Titus. He was a stand-out in his class. The apostle Paul would serve as Titus's first reference on his résumé. Titus had traveled and ministered with Paul and had become a true son and intimate friend of the apostle. What kind of life and ministry should such a powerhouse of gifts, experience, ability, and résumé have? What kind of position would you counsel such a one to ignore, and what kinds of jobs would you counsel him to go after instead?

The call Titus is left with is Crete. It was a start-up church in need of real help and difficult labor. It was out of the way, without prestige and without reputation, except that it was notoriously corrupt. To make a global difference means that every local place—whether it is Brooklyn, Vegas, Henryville, or Webster Groves—needs attention. Locality is the way a global difference is made. Local people in a local place—this is where Titus works each day.

There is a story brewing in Crete. Jesus has something to say there.

Titus goes, a particular man to a particular place for a particular people. His goal? To teach people how to do ordinary life soundly in Jesus with love for God and each other where they live. This congregation becomes Titus's workshop, or farm, or office. How is Titus to go about this God-glorifying goal? What does a great man with superior gifts do for Jesus? Paul teaches him.

- *He will pay attention to local and ordinary persons for leadership* (Titus 1:5, "appoint elders"). He knows the names and stories of local people.
- *He will do so for the sake of local and ordinary towns* (v. 5, "in every town"). He knows the towns.
- *He will do so in light of local and ordinary expressions of gospel hindrance* (vv. 10–11, "There are many who . . . must be silenced"). He knows the local teachings and personalities that challenge the gospel in those towns among those persons.
- *He will do so for the sake of local and ordinary families* (v. 11, "They are upsetting whole families"). He seeks to equip families to deal with these local gospel challenges.
- *He will need to gain local knowledge* (v. 12, "One of the Cretans, a prophet [poet] of their own, said . . .). He reads the news and local spokespersons.
- *He will invest in the local and ordinary relational lives of those particular people* (vv. 1–6, older men, younger men, older women, younger women). He cares about strengthening the relational soundness of the ordinary persons in his community according to the gospel and in contrast to local norms.

What does this mean but that Jesus has recovered the greatness of the ordinary? Jesus returns us to an Eden-like posture in a place before God. He delivers us from trying to become something only he was meant to be. Right in front of us is everything we've longed for. Jesus intends to content us with this vigor of a courageous joy in the mundane.

Ruth, Boaz, Paul, and Titus each learned of grace to live out the kind of life that Eden would have meant for them and the new kingdom will provide. No matter how great or gifted we are, God invites us to himself for the sake of local people in a local place with the long learning of local knowledge in Jesus until he comes. This means that if you are wearing yourselves out trying to be and do more than this, Jesus is calling you to stop all of this tramping about and come finally home. The great work to be done is right in front of you with the persons and places that his providence has granted you. For me, this means reading the *Webster-Kirkwood Times* or the *St. Louis Post Dispatch,* when it sounds much more sexy and feels much more important to read the *New York Times* or *USA Today.* I can read the former without the latter but not the other way around, because here is where he has called me. Here is where he is working. Here is my post, my place, my life, his glory.

Word and Sacrament

Romantic realism explains why we give ourselves to the reading and preaching of God's Word along with the regular embrace of the bread and the cup.

Some romantically incant this biblical text as if magic lay buried in the page and ink. Others resign themselves to nothing more but the recitation of old words on a dead surface. But Paul the apostle confounds both views and speaks of a time instead in which preaching comes to the local place and its people, "not only in word, but also in power and in the Holy Spirit and with full conviction" (1 Thess. 1:5).

Some romantically exaggerate the voice as if holiness has a loud pitch, as if God speaks with a foghorn articulation that is laden with tremor or in contrast as only a timorous voice whispering shouts of glory. Others x-ray these vocal antics and are cynical of the song. "Voice," they say "is nothing more." Voice is vocal-chord limited, empty. Voice is as cold as religion.

But Paul tells us otherwise. There are times in which the human voice speaks in all of its grandeur and frailty, but what the congregation hears is God himself speaking to them by and with this inked text and human voice. "When you received the word of God, which you heard from us, you accepted it not as the word of men but as what it really is, the word of God" (1 Thess. 2:13).

The Spirit takes up this Word, read and preached. The ordinary alphabet, the mundane voice, these giving life by the Spirit's breath, and ordinary people respond as if God is present. His Spirit in Jesus was speaking to them, and with their flaws and limits, they actually "turned to God from idols to serve the living and true God, and to wait for his Son from heaven" (1 Thess. 1:9–10).

Likewise, the bread and cup "proclaim the Lord's death" (1 Cor. 11:26). Loaf and juice, wafer or wine, are nothing more than that. We bought them on sale around the corner. And yet he draws near here; uniquely we taste and see, not only the dough and crushed grapes but the very goodness of the living Christ. Remembering him becomes greeting him. He meets us with real presence, while in faith we chew and swallow and pray. Death lurks here among the pieces. Life rises as we gather together. The body of the Lord is discerned here. Sacred we eat (1 Cor. 11:27–29).

What I am learning is that the romantic realist finds his or her way toward a long rhythm in a local place. Because by faith there is more to this ink and text, these varied human-preacher voices, these local people with their daily stories, this store-bought or stove-baked bread, and these cups of juice or cheap wine—there is more here, I am saying, than meets our eyes. God is here. The same old, same old has wings.

PART 1

EXPOSING OUR TEMPTATIONS

In this section, we are asking Jesus to expose the primary temptations that hinder the recovery of our humanity and our seeing his glory. In so doing, Jesus will begin to show us three noble limits that are ours for surrender.

First, we can only be at one place at one time, which means that Jesus will teach most of us to live a local life. We will resist and want to act like we are omnipresent. But he will patiently teach us that as human beings we cannot be, and this admission will glorify God. Others will likewise resist Jesus and want you to be omnipresent. They will use his name to praise or critique you accordingly, but they too will have to learn that only Jesus can be with them wherever they are at all times. This fact is actually good news for them and for us.

We will explore how in taking one day at a time by recognizing the four portions of each day, Jesus graciously recovers our local attention.

Second, we cannot do everything that needs to be done, which means that Jesus will teach us to live with the things that we can neither control nor fix. We will want to resist Jesus and act as if we are omnipotent, but we will harm others and ourselves when we try. Others will also resist Jesus. Using his name, they will praise or critique us according to their desire that we fix everything for them and that we do it immediately. But they will have to learn too that only Jesus can fix everything and that there are some things Jesus leaves unfixed for his glory.

We will explore how psalm-making is a means that Jesus gives us to pour out our hearts to him and by which we wait upon his means for fixing what needs it. We will also examine how calling for the elders to pray forms part of entrusting ourselves to a power of a more gospel kind.

Third, we are unable to know everyone or everything, which means that Jesus will teach us to live with ignorance, our own and others'. In other words, we are not omniscient. Jesus will require us to stop pretending that we are. Others will resist Jesus and in his name praise us or critique us on the basis of their estimation of what we should know. They will have to learn that only Jesus knows everything they need; his invitation to faith and to trust in his knowing is a good one.

In this light, we will explore how trying to act as a know-it-all damages our capacity for making wise decisions and dealing with one another in our sin. We will look at how entrusting ourselves to what Jesus knows frees us to engage decisions and discipline as the gospel would.

Ask yourself this question: Which are you more tempted to pretend that you are: an everywhere-for-all, a fix-it-all, or a know-it-all? What do you feel you will lose if you stop pretending in these ways and entrust yourself to Jesus?

Now think about those you serve in family and ministry. Perhaps think about those who put the most pressure upon you by their praise or their criticism. Which temptation are these people desirous to add to your job description? Do they criticize you for not being an everywhere-at-all, a fix-it-all, or a know-it-all? Or for which of these do they praise you? What would it mean for them to have to enter the awkward uncontrol and wait upon Jesus for what they are mistakenly requiring of you?

Jesus invites everywhere-for-alls, fix-it-alls, and know-it-alls to the cross, the empty tomb, and the throne of his grace for their time of need.

CHAPTER THREE

Everywhere-for-All

Cultivating the Four Portions of Each Day

> There is a day when the road neither comes nor goes, and the way is not a way, but a place.[1]

"Zack, your life is like a five-alarm fire. You are coming and going in so many directions. I worry about you." Bill's words shook me as a young man.

One of my bosses echoed the same sentiment ten years later. "You are doing so many different things," she said. "We are afraid you are going to burn out. We want you around here for a long time, so pace yourself, okay?"

Her voice was soon joined by others'. Two colleagues invited me to lunch. Another called on the phone. "We are worried about you," they said.

Then I received a letter. It was the old-fashioned kind of letter with a stamp on the envelope. The words were written by hand with a pen. I opened it and heard my mom's voice as I read. She too must have heard the alarm. "Son," she wrote, "a tree has to have roots to provide shade."

God is a shade giver. "The Lord is your keeper" the psalmist sings. "The Lord is your shade on your right hand" (Ps. 121:5). The Lord is a "shelter from the storm" for the poor. He is for the distressed like "shade from the heat" (Isa. 25:4). It makes sense then that God's kingdom gives shade. When the kingdom is full grown, Jesus says, it "becomes larger than all the garden plants and puts out large branches, so that the birds of the air can make nests in its shade" (Mark 4:32).

To give shade is to pity. Pity gives shelter. Shade is a refuge. Nests are built there. Eggs are hatched. Baby birds are cared for and taught to fly. Shade is sturdy.

Calling and Ambition

So what does it mean that giving shade requires deep roots? Those called into pastoral ministry are ambitious to give shade. This ambition is necessary for a pastoral call to the ministry. "If anyone aspires to the office of overseer," Paul says, "he desires a noble task" (1 Tim. 3:1).

But aspirations, even noble ones, can go awry. Human nature is restless. "Its ambition," Calvin said, "longs to embrace various things at once."[2] Discontent with one thing at a time locally exposes the longing for grander things that can tempt even a shepherd. *Shepherd* is one of the primary images used in the Bible to describe a shade giver. The ambition of a shepherd can err. God rebukes erring shepherds. The error includes the lack of locality in their ambition:

> The weak you have not strengthened, the sick you have not healed, the injured you have not bound up, the strayed you have not brought back, the lost you have not sought, and with force and harshness you have ruled them. . . . My sheep were scattered over all the face of the earth, with none to search or seek for them. (Ezek. 34:4–6)

Shepherds are meant to give shelter and refuge to an ordinary people in a particular place. So, when I think about giving shade locally, I feel Calvin's point. Each of us longs to embrace various things at once. Locality can mess with one's contentment. That is why leaders sometimes strive to be everywhere at once. But to be everywhere generally is to reside nowhere particularly. To strive for various things at once is to announce one's secession from place. The driven have no places in what they imagine; only positions and postures.

An image from Walt Whitman comes to mind. He spoke of blacksmiths who as a team brought down their hammers in tandem. "They do not hasten," he observed. "Each man hits in his place."[3]

My personal struggle to hit in place and not hasten has an irony within it. I once had the ability to make a day's work out of tying my shoes and getting my book bag for school. This talent daily exposed my potential for tardiness and pushed my mom to keep time. "Slow as molasses," my mom would say. But that was then. Somewhere along the line, I had since taken up the hammer and lost my place.

Shade is hard to give when roots remain shallow.

Learning the Names of Trees

I grew up in the Ohio River Valley, in the lower southeast region of Indiana near Louisville, Kentucky. Many of those towns are named after men—

Charlestown, Georgetown, Scottsburg. In Clarksville I learned confidence with football and shyness with girls. In Floyd's Knobs I learned to drive. As a teenager I could drive Buck Creek Road with my eyes closed.

But Henryville is designated as the glue for my life. My name is scribbled in chalk there in a closet underneath the stairs in the house that my papaw built. The Henryville United Methodist Church has had a long, beautiful, and sometimes tumultuous relationship with my family. Mount Zion Cemetery gives rest to many of my people—those I have known, loved, and miss—and those I've only heard stories about. In fact, my mom and my pop, the Guernseys and the Eswines, both have their roots in this small town. My papaw had a mug down at Tanners reserved just for him. He and his longtime friends had named themselves "the liars' club." They sat most mornings to enjoy each other's company before the work of the day began. There are people who live in Henryville that once changed my diaper. I meet them at funerals. Just by looking at me, they tell me that I must be Vern's son.

What I am trying to say is that I have a hometown—a physical space of people, birds, roads, weather, happenings, and things in which I have come to know and recognize something of what the world is like. Reasons to mourn and reasons for laughter were framed for me there. Who I am in St. Louis, Missouri (where I now live), has been shaped for better and for worse by what was and is in southern Indiana. There is no escaping this fact. Some of my best and worst memories have taken place there. They inform my place here.

Place exposes limits. Limits repulse the driven. The driven therefore struggle with the sense of place that Jesus had. Amid the aromas of freshly cut woods, the bone and blood in Jesus's hands would form an alliance. With this, he would shape and sand long trunks and planks of wood into tables and chairs. Jesus knew the names of trees. He built from them what his mind imagined and what his skill learned over time could call forth. He crafted bark during what theologians refer to as his "years of obscurity." I think of this when I remember my papaw and mamaw visiting my home in St. Louis. They told me in a few minutes what I had not learned in two years—the names of the trees and bushes on my rented property. We walked slowly. I needed to listen, but listening required resting. I struggled with both as papaw and mamaw named my place for me.

Exposing Our Temptations

It seems that both Henryville and Jesus expose my restlessness. I puzzle over what Jesus is doing among the wood chips. What is the meaning of this sawdust caught in Jesus's beard and dangling from his smile—and all of this for thirty years? Thirty years! Jesus had a world to save, injustice to confront, lepers to touch—*shade to give*. Isn't greatness squandered by years of obscurity? What business does a savior have learning the names of trees?

When "here" seems to be where his future will unfold, and when moving on must stop, a pastor begins to ask such questions. This time will come for every pastor, the moment when he realizes, "This is where I'll be, and this is not what I had imagined for my legacy."

Jesus of Nazareth

The demons first drew my attention to Jesus's sense of place (I refer, of course, to those demons that the Bible mentions). I'm not accustomed to learning from demons. A man who has little time for the trees on his property will have even less time for unseen spooks. But Mark's Gospel records a conversation between Jesus and demons. "What have you to do with us, Jesus of Nazareth?" they hissed. "Have you come to destroy us? I know who you are—the Holy One of God" (Mark 1:24).

The demons intertwined two laces. First, they identified Jesus with Nazareth; and second, they knew this Jesus as the Holy One from God. I pondered the connection. I rolled it over in my mind. Jesus *of Nazareth* is *the Holy One of God*. The Holy One of God is Jesus *of Nazareth*. Suddenly the nightlight was turned on. I saw in the room what had before eluded me. If the Holy One of God is Jesus *of Nazareth*, then the Holy One of God has a hometown. The shade giver has roots.

Though Jesus would later identify Capernaum as his "own city" (Matt. 9:1), Nazareth followed Jesus. When Jesus entered Jerusalem on the Palm Sunday donkey, people said, "This is the prophet Jesus, *from Nazareth* of Galilee" (Matt. 21:11). When Jesus was crucified, Pontius Pilate had the description posted on the cross: "Jesus *of Nazareth*," it read; "the King of the Jews" (John 19:19). Even the resurrected Jesus, when confronting Saul of Tarsus on the road to Damascus, identified himself by saying, "I am Jesus *of Nazareth*, whom you are persecuting" (Acts 22:8).

Why Nazareth?

Certainly, Nazareth is a place of ancient promise. To identify Jesus with such a place is to attach prophetic significance to him (Matt. 2:23; 4:12–13). But practicality is also involved. "Jesus" was a common name. In my son's fifth-grade class, for example, there were three boys named Alex. In order to know which Alex is which, they for a long time identified themselves as "Alex M.," "Alex O.," and "Alex C." However, one of the boys has since changed his name altogether in order to make it easier for everybody. He simply calls himself "Steve"! In the same way, the phrase "of Nazareth" identifies which Jesus people are discussing.

As a theological student, I already knew that Jesus had roots. The apostle John had made that clear. Jesus was God and "was in the beginning with God" (John 1:2). But I had little thought about how God rooted himself in a physical place for a time and walked among us. This action made me wonder. When a customer picked up her newly built table or freshly crafted chair from Jesus's woodshop, if that customer had asked sixteen-year-old Jesus where he was from, how would Jesus have answered: "I am from the eternal residence of God," or "I am from Nazareth"?

What I do know is that when Jesus took up his hammer, he did not hasten out of place. The Bible says plainly that Jesus had a hometown.[4] He grew up not in every place, but in one place. He had a home church. He had a family and a trade that was known and sometimes challenged by his community (Luke 4:16–30). If the Ohio River looms ever-present in my upbringing, for Jesus it was the River Jordan. I fished and boated in Patoka and Deam Lakes. The lake known as the Sea of Galilee offered shores, waters, and fish for Jesus. He knew the shortcuts and paths in the Galilee region as I knew those particular to the Ohio Valley. The Holy One of God became a man—and this incarnation included limiting himself and inhabiting a locality on the earth. I think this is something of what my Mom meant by "roots." This divine condescension to locality challenges my ambition that is restless to embrace various things at once.

Climbing Mountains

What is the cause of such hurry? Brooks Williams denotes phases of life as one possible answer.

Young men watch the sky and they wish that they could fly
Old men watch the sky and they marvel at its light
I am neither young nor old and I wonder if I watch at all.[5]

But phases aren't the only answer. Agendas often drive the formation of corporate-world relationships. We plan in order to meet, and we meet in order to plan. "Somewhere else doing something else" is the unspoken motto of our advancement. It is likely that the longing to be everywhere is a cultural habit. Better means bigger. Such sentiments drive one into a discontented mood. There is little doubt that my five-alarm fire was partially ignited by these cultural sparks.

After all, Henryville does not offer a corporate advancement. Advancing forward is of a different sort. Meaning is found where you are and in what you do. One expects that he will do tomorrow what he does today. People live where they are. They do not plan to get somewhere else.

I've noticed that when one is not concerned with being somewhere else, she tends to notice where she is. In such an environment, daily moments naturally become the topic of evening conversation. What one lived that day becomes what one talks about that night. For example, the granddaughter's smile down at the A&P becomes a fifteen-minute story that draws everyone into belly laughter. The smile was important enough to notice and the story valuable enough to tell. The laughter, the story, and the smile each form a sufficient agenda for conversation. Nothing more is required to share time together. In my younger years, I found this attention to the mundane lacking. I wanted "real" conversation about "real" life. I wanted us to talk about things that mattered, things that make a difference. Now I'm beginning to reflect more on those feelings. When did it happen that to talk about what one lives is not enough for real conversation? When did it happen that a granddaughter's smile is not substantial enough to speak of?

But I am afraid that my restlessness has more than a seasonal and cultural cause. Calvin discerned restless ambition in the nature of human beings. I am no exception. When George Mallory was once asked why he wanted to climb Mount Everest, he famously answered, "Because it is there." But on another occasion George expanded his answer:

> If you cannot understand that there is something in man which responds to the challenge of this mountain and goes out to meet it, that the strug-

> gle is the struggle of life itself upward and forever upward, then you won't see why we go. What we get from this adventure is just sheer joy. And joy is, after all, the end of life.[6]

A personal letter to George's wife, Ruth, reveals even more about what drove him to climb the mountain. "Dearest," he wrote, ". . . you must know that the spur to do my best is you and you again. . . . I want more than anything to prove worthy of you."

The fact of the mountain's existence, the quest for joy that drives humanity to struggle upward, and the desire to prove worthy of his family were among the motives that drove George's famous expeditions. He left a meaningful legacy that proved worthy of history's remembrance. But George's son John wrote something that has challenged me. Proud of his father but sad too, John wrote, "I would so much rather have known my father than to have grown up in the shadow of a legend, a hero, as some people perceive him to be."[7]

The answers George gave concerning his motives have confronted my own. The mountain "was there," but so was John, George's son. The mountain brought a sense of joy and gave a sense of the human struggle upward for life itself. But George's knowing his son would have brought him joy and a sense of striving for the purpose of life too. Climbing the mountain enabled George to prove worthy of his family. But so would have loving and providing for his family in the ordinary routines of a long life, day upon day. So why did George choose to engage the challenges of the mountain but not the living room?

At this point, I am leery, sensing that I have established a false dichotomy between one's work or dreams and one's family and routine. After all, there is nothing morally wrong with climbing Mount Everest. George Mallory was a schoolmaster with three children. Though he and Ruth were geographically apart as much as they were together, there is indication that this was not easy on George. So I must refocus the question. Why did George Mallory choose the mountain when he understood that it might take his life?[8] Why was Mallory's pursuit of joy, the meaning of life, the worthiness of family, and the loyalty to complete a task connected more with climbing a mountain than with the daily routines of love and life, work and play at home? I do not have that answer. But I do recognize something of myself and my restless tendency to hasten out of place with my hammer.

Perhaps my nagging desire to be somewhere else doing something else is forged in what Charles Cummings once referred to as the numbing effect of the ordinary. "We get nothing out of the ordinary, and so conclude that nothing of value is there," Cummings observed. "Instead we seek extraordinary experiences and the special techniques that might induce such states."[9]

It seems foreign to suggest that playing blocks in the living room or folding clothes by the washer can provide either joy or meaning. After all, what meaning has a life with no mountains to climb? Yet I hear the voices of Bill and my colleagues. I think of Nazareth and of my mom's concern about roots. I feel the absence of laughter at a toddler's smile. So, what if the ordinary is the larger mountain?

Advancing by Limitation

I remember walking the fields late at night at Ball State University in Northern Indiana. Regularly I'd cry to God, saying, "O Lord, I'll go anywhere you want; send me!" I never anticipated that he might say in response, "I am sending you to nowhere else but where you are." Like the tomb dweller whom Jesus healed and who then begged to travel along, God may say, "Go home to your friends and tell them how much the Lord has done for you" (Mark 5:19). Going home may not require you to return to childhood neighborhoods. It may simply require you to stop trying to get somewhere other than where you already are.

I am beginning to see the folly in how I imagined what a missionary life must be. And what is a pastoral life if it is not also missional? So many of us move to places we have never been to love people far from home. I used to think of such ministry as a glory without a place. But the missionary must do her laundry, cook her food, and love people too. Any place she goes will require her to either avoid there or live there.

But the fact of being there is something none of us can escape. In other words, "to take up one's cross" is to let a particular tree press upon our

actual shoulders, on a local road within a specific community. This seems like death and it is—a death to one's self. Without realizing it, I had always imagined self-sacrifice in ways limitless and placeless. I do not think that

I am alone. Many who are ambitious to oversee others rarely envision the mundane of the place in which their greatness will land. So when sacrifice requires limits and locality, great mountains somewhere else seem to offer fewer challenges and more glories. But Chesterton's words challenge and offer help at this point:

> Every act of will is an act of self-limitation. To desire action is to desire limitation. In that sense, every act is an act of self-sacrifice. When you choose anything, you reject everything else. . . . Every act is an irrevocable selection and exclusion. Just as when you marry one woman you give up all the others, so when you take one course of action, you give up all the other courses. If you become King of England, you give up the post of Beadle in Brompton. If you go to Rome, you sacrifice a rich suggestive life in Wimbledon.[10]

If we want to give shade, we are required to take a step. But in whatever direction we place our foot, we necessarily leave every other direction empty for the footsteps of another. To choose, therefore, is to limit. Yet limitation is the only way forward.

Something in me hates this confession. I do not think that I am alone in this. Twitter, Facebook, virtual conferencing—these allow us the illusion of being somewhere other than where we are. Positively we have a voice in places otherwise absent to us. But we type on our keyboards while sitting in a chair where we are—the local knowledge and work of the day in our place awaiting our presence. The danger here is that it allows us to give our gifts without giving ourselves.

I remember giving an interview on the radio. The subject matter concerned Christ-centered preaching for various cultural settings. Those who heard the interview were greatly helped and let me know it. But I gave that interview in my pajamas from a retreat house in the woods of Missouri while trying to recover from a terrible season in my life. I would never have spoken in person that way, and if I had tried, I would have had to do a great deal of pretending. My point is that no matter how far technology allows our gifts to travel, we ourselves, the persons that we actually are, remain rooted to one place at one time. Coming clean with our locality makes pretending a lot harder and forces our hearers to resist celebritizing us. After all, Jesus, whom we represent, never disembodies his gifts from his person. With him, to access one is to access both.

I'm trying to suggest that our surrender to the limits of Eden that God gave challenges us. The alarm my friends sounded forth in my own life indicated their response to my resisting this surrender. Only God is omnipresent. To embrace everything at once is at heart to covet God's position. Only God is worthy of fame, and that same God humbled himself and became flesh and walked among us.

Exulting in Monotony

A placeless ambition can likewise rob us of the kind of happiness that God intends. J. W. Alexander once noted this in his *Thoughts on Preaching*. A pastor without care for locality becomes what Alexander called a "ceremonious visitor" of the people he serves. His body is present but his mind is always looking elsewhere for meaning and success. But "the minister of the gospel," is meant to find the "source of happiness in his parochial work and social communion" that God gave to him. Alexander continues:

> The genuine bond is as strong and tender as any on earth, and as productive of happiness. Think of this when you are tempted to discontent. What is it that really constitutes the happiness of a residence? Is it a fine house, furniture, equipage . . . large salary, wealthy pew holders? Nay, it is LOVE. It is the affectionate and mutual attachment. It is the daily flow of emotion, and commingling of interest in common sorrows and common joys; in the sick-room, and the house of bereavement, at the deathbed and the grave, at baptisms and communions. . . . The declaration of what one believes, and the praise of what one loves, always give delight: and what but this is the minister's work?[11]

Happiness with the people and place we are in confounds many of us. But what if this is what Paul meant when he said that he loved people, that they were his joy and his crown (Phil. 4:1; 1 Thess. 2:19)?

With this thought, a sinking feeling infuriates the pounding within my chest. To dignify the ordinary with glory will require a radical shift

in my habitual approach to life. In Chesterton's words, like other pastors I will have to relearn how to "exult in monotony."

> A child kicks his legs rhythmically through excess, not absence of life. Because children have abounding vitality, because they are in spirit fierce and free, therefore they want things repeated and unchanged. They always say, "Do it again"; and the grown-up person does it again until he is nearly dead. For grown-up people are not strong enough to exult in monotony. But perhaps God is strong enough to exult in monotony. It is possible that God says every morning, "Do it again" to the sun; and every evening, "Do it again" to the moon. It may not be automatic necessity that makes all daisies alike; it may be that God makes every daisy separately, but has never got tired of making them.[12]

And now it dawns on me. Restless discontent is a kind of fatigue. When a finite creature covets omnipresence he loses sight of sight itself. Imagination becomes placeless. Detail loses relevance. Routine becomes boring; arrogance and impatience bid a person to never look twice or long before moving onto somewhere or to something else. To exult in monotony is to deepen roots. To deepen roots is to look twice and long at the smiles that happen at the A&P. Such awareness of life extends the shade we can give. And I remember Jesus *of Nazareth*—born in Bethlehem, a refugee in Egypt, growing up in his particular place. The Holy One of God with a local breath. My bloomless battle to give shade without roots, it seems, must be fought at this point. No longer can I imagine great work apart from local places. A global work is a local thing. A local work has global implications. This will mean that I must inhabit wherever I am, differently. Milosz demonstrates one aspect of this "strange occupation":

> There was time when I dreamed of an international role for myself. . . . How glad I am now that I clung to my native language (for the simple reason that I was a Polish poet and could not have been otherwise) . . . . One would like to astound the world, to save the world but one can do neither. We are summoned to deeds that are of moment only to our village.[13]

Milosz was exiled from Communist Poland. Yet he gave himself to the "strange occupation of writing poems in Polish while living in France or America."[14] He stated his reasons. "If I am to nourish the hope of writing with a free hand," he said, "with gaiety and not under pressure, then I must proceed by keeping only a few Polish readers in mind."[15] This "strange occupation" through his local place in time produced a global implication. An old man scribbling Polish words on scraps of paper while teaching in English in Berkeley, California, must have looked obscure and inefficient to the rootless shade providers who raced around him.

Milosz was awarded the Nobel Prize in Literature in 1980.

International implications are not placeless or void of personality. Global implications are found, rather, in a carpenter living in Capernaum and hailing from Nazareth. To follow Jesus is a physical thing. As he did, I must come from a place, inhabit it, work in it, love in it, carry a cross in it, die in it, and rise from it.

I am not speaking here of settling with evil or returning to an abusive home to be bruised. I am speaking here of a glorious nonescape from the ordinary of life. Difference making takes place in a garden. The God who created a garden in the vast expanse of the universe returned to Nazareth. I must learn, like him, to return to the same old, same old and dwell there for its redemption. I must not resign my longing to give shade. I must, rather, learn how shade is properly given. Shade giving will require that I learn about roots. Root growing will require me to touch my desk.

Coming Full Circle

"There is a day," says Wendell Berry, "when the road neither comes nor goes, and the way is not a way but a place."[16] Forward requires a present and a past. "There" is not always preferable to "here," because the requirements of love are the same in both places. Furthermore, "here" is the only genuine way one can travel "there," at least if one intends to give shade when inhabiting either place. Consequently, I must not imagine where I will be without standing where I am. Likewise, I must not imagine where I will be as though my future moments will require no connection to a place and a people. Place is advance. Imagination disconnected from place leaks fruitless urgency into our habits.

For example, I am a preacher by vocation. If I had ever asked God to enable me to be like my heroes, he might have said, in this regard, "Which one?" If I would choose Spurgeon, I would have to live in Dickens's London and inhabit that community and care for that people. To be like Alexander, I would have made Princeton, New Jersey, my boundary and labor for its good. But I cannot do both, and neither could they.

I spoke about this to my mamaw before she died. We sat in old chairs, in Henryville.

"For a long time I've been trying to get away from here," I said. "Now it seems I'm sad for the distance and the absence."

"Well," she said, looking through the walls like they were windows, "sounds like you've come full circle."

That is what roots require of a man who is nowhere in particular. He must first come full circle and there find the grace to say "Do it again" to the mundane beauties around him. He must learn to tell old stories in familiar places among a people he thoroughly knows. He must believe that this is enough to give life meaning. How can we find such grace but in him who knew the names of trees? He who called you to where you are declares that you needn't repent of being in one place at one time. You needn't repent of doing only a long, small work in an extraordinary but unknown place. Standing long in one place allows the roots to deepen. The shade grows and a life gives. It is Jesus *of Nazareth* who walks with you.

Stability and the Four Portions of Each Day

When, by grace, we begin to stop trying to be everywhere but where we are, things feel worse for us for a while. Jesus takes us through a kind of withdrawal or detox not unlike those "crawling out of your skin" experiences that one can feel during the initial hours and weeks of alcohol-, drug-, or cigarette-free living. The caffeine addict has to endure a season of headaches if she wants to rid herself of her coffee or soda necessity. The food habit tortures us with fierce hunger pangs when simplicity and health first begin to inform and reorient our menu choices.

So it is with we who have been addicted to self-promoting celebrity, to consuming and using, and to the long-practice of immediate gratification. Busyness, constant planning, a driven pace, quick spending, and spontaneous time fillers have been our drugs of choice to deal with the swirling restlessness within us. Remove one or more of these drugs and our interior storm rages on with nothing in our schedule to unquiet it and no numbing activity or one more Bible study to distract us from its tornado warnings.

Exposing Our Temptations

Just look at how often people leave a church not because of doctrinal concern but because they don't like the music, or the Bible study, or the nursery, or the boredom that loving an ordinary neighbor in a place requires. Or they feel offended by a relationship and speak of forgiveness but do not act on it in order to move forward to the other side with each other.

One dear couple pulled their children out of our children's program until we "got right" the process for teaching kids that they expected. When I suggested that we could learn from them, they could learn from us, and we could walk through it together and come out on the other side with a stronger ministry to our children, the idea was a foreign category. They soon left our church. Staying put was not an option if preferences weren't met and if they were expected to contribute to the remedy.

Our spiritual inability to remain with a people in a place as a family through thick and thin when not everything is how we prefer it or want it becomes apparent. We do not believe we need to stay in a place in which our feelings and needs are incompletely met. After we've left church after church, or job after job, or relationship after relationship, we still haven't yet learned to ask if some spiritual skill might be lacking in us, that maybe all of these churches, jobs, and people acting imperfectly aren't alone in their need of help. We too might need some.

Benedict called this spiritual skill "stability," the spiritual skill for "staying put to get somewhere."[17] Whatever one thinks about all things "monkish," one cannot easily deny the reality that few of us know what it is to steadily love one another through the ups and downs of our ordinary moods, circumstances, and changes. Jesus recovers us.

Moment by Moment

To recover this kind of stamina for an enjoyment of the local, to rest watchful again or for the first time among the sacred margins, and to remain intact when others beg us or berate us not to attempt the glad obscurity of a long perseverance, we need Jesus to graciously and patiently teach us how to find God's portion in each ordinary day. Jesus calls us to a "one-day-at-a-time" assumption:

> Therefore do not be anxious about tomorrow, for tomorrow will be anxious for itself. Sufficient for the day is its own trouble. (Matt. 6:34)

We are often humbled into such an outlook when we are sick, experiencing trauma, seeking to change a long addiction or habit, or even aging into our elderly years.

When my papaw, for example, labored through fluid-filled lungs in the last season of his life, I would call him on the phone. I was in St. Louis. Papaw was in Henryville.

Inevitably he would answer, "What do you know, young man?" I could hear the wheeze of depleted breath in his voice.

"Oh, I'm just thinking about you, Papaw," I would say. "You are on my mind. How is it going for you today?"

"Oh, I'm all right. It is what it is," he'd say. "Ain't no use in complaining, huh?" Then he would add the piece of advice that had become familiar ground for him. He seemed determined to pass that advice on. "Just taking one day at a time," he'd say. "You know that's all we can do anyway, huh? All we can do anyway is take one day at a time. Ain't that right, young man?"

I would pause in my own confounded attempts to practice in my being what he was saying. "Well, yes, I think so, Papaw. I have a lot to learn about that," I'd muster. I'd hear a smile in his voice, his lungs muscling through each bit of air.

Then I'd say, "I love you, Papaw."

"I love you too, Zack," he'd say (words rarely uttered by him when he was a younger man but wonderfully and freely spoken now). Then he added what had become his regular request: "Don't forget to say a prayer for this old man."

"I won't, Papaw. I pray for you all the time," I'd assure him.

Such times in our lives force us to face what is actually true every day: "The Christian life is moment by moment."[18] But without a moment-by-moment approach to a day, we tend to use our days as if they are highways. They enable us to speed from one place to another without having to notice the people, the yards, the farms, the streets, the hospitals, the funeral processions, the balloons, the squirrels, or the trash in between. Each day becomes a blur on our way to getting somewhere.

When Jesus says that we are wise to limit ourselves to a this-present-day focus, he teaches us not that we must never think about tomorrow, but that this day in front of us contains enough within it to sustain our attention and purpose. The person who wants to be everywhere-for-all struggles to believe this (Matt. 6:34).

Some of our literary best have sought to help us. For example, the opening paragraph of Solzhenitsyn's famous story tells us that it's "5 o'clock as always . . . time to get up." That same story ends in this way:

> The end of an unclouded day. Almost a happy one. Just one of the 3,653 days of his sentence, from bell to bell.[19]

Like Wendell Berry's *The Memory of Old Jack* or James Joyce's *Ulysses*, Solzhenitsyn's whole story takes place in one day—in this case, *One Day in the Life of Ivan Denisovich*, a prisoner in a Soviet labor camp. So much of life is already in front of us if we but learn the grace eyes to see it and to entrust it to the Lord. To linger long enough to look requires that we entrust an intruding tomorrow to its proper place. We will get to tomorrow, tomorrow. Today we will handle today.

In the Bible we get a glimpse of what I think of as the four seasons or portions of each day. The psalmist, for example, breaks down his day and expresses it poetically in this way:

> Evening and morning and at noon
> I utter my complaint and moan,
> and he [God] hears my voice. (Ps. 55:17)

Sometimes, the psalmist gets more specific about what "evening" can encompass and, like other places in the Bible (e.g., Lam. 2:19), he refers to the night watches: "I remember you upon my bed, and meditate on you in the watches of the night" (Ps. 63:6).

One way to learn a stamina for doing one day at a time in our local and ordinary places is to find a similar kind of rhythm to our day—to think of our day as containing four seasons or portions. A *season* is a poetic term that describes a period of time that has a beginning and an end. In between its beginning and end it offers conditions and experiences that distinguish it from other seasons. Likewise, a portion describes a provision that has been given to us. God is our portion, which means that at any given moment of our day he is enough for us. He is our shepherd. We shall not want. Each day has different seasons in which God demonstrates to you that he is your portion.

- Morning: sunrise or 6:00 AM to noon
- Noon: noon to 6:00 PM
- Evening: sunset or 6:00 PM to 10:00 PM (sometimes known as the "first night watch")
- The night watches: 10:00 PM to 6:00 AM[20]

Jesus's earthly life and ministry is often identified with these different seasons and portions of a day. Let's take a moment to see how the Psalms poetically describe these daily seasons and how our Lord historically inhabited these daily portions.

The Grace of the Morning

> For years, early morning was a time I dreaded. In the process of waking up, my mind would run with panic. All the worries of the previous day would still be with me, spinning around with old regrets as well as fears for the future.[21]

What Kathleen Norris describes there resonates with many of us. For some persons, morning is all sunshine and light. Smiling they awake. The day awaits, and they are eager to meet it.

But not so for me. Most mornings for me are a melancholy sadness. All that troubles me buzzes about like a crowd around the bed of my mind waiting with anticipation for me to stir. As soon as I do, they all in tandem begin to shout their moody concerns at me. The morning is a "call in sick on life" time.

A change took place in Norris. She finds that more often than not when she emerges from the night, she does so now with more hope than fear. I have yet to find this morning transformation. But what we are talking about now gives me hope.

The New Testament tells us things about Jesus in the morning: he prayed (Mark 1:35). He was hungry. He walked (Matt. 21:18). He taught (John 8:2).

For the psalmist, the morning in God's hands testifies to us that tears end, relief is signified, and "joy comes" (Ps. 30:5). In the morning songs of praise and thanksgiving can rise because God's strength has gotten us through the night (Ps. 59:16). The night didn't win. We awake and see once again that God's love hasn't quit on us, and we ask that he will go with us and guide us into what awaits us (Ps. 143:8). The morning stirs us to pray, therefore, and to watch how God will answer those prayers through the day (Ps. 5:3).

The new dawn also calls out to us that the help of God has come (Ps. 46:5). Morning is meant as a poem or sermon to console the downcast. Their soul cry is given new invitation to ask again and to have hope that the dawn of God will soon come to answer. The morning enables us to think again of God's goodness and to ask him why he waits to reveal that goodness to us (Ps. 88:13–14). The ending of night also rouses us to a renewed conviction to use the day as a means of opposing what is wretched in the world and protecting what is good and beautiful and right (Ps. 101:8).

Because God gives this meaning to the morning, he poetically pictures the sun as a bridegroom love-struck and happily longing to see his bride. The sun is no melancholy like me, tired of shining again unnoticed, traveling the same old path every day and bored with it all. No! The sun is like that runner in the story *Chariots of Fire*, who, when he ran, lifted his head as one who joyfully feels the pleasure of God (Ps. 19:5). The sun shines love-stubborn above the thunderclouds. No stormy sky can quench it!

One of our mistaken uses of the morning, therefore, is to look at the circumstances and appointments awaiting us on our calendar without attending them with an awareness of their service or surrender to God and what God may wish to reveal to us with them or in spite of them. The Bible teachers of Jesus's day particularly struggled in this way (Matt. 16:3). They could name things and describe the conditions of a day but they had no discernment regarding God's presence or purposes.

This is why I am coming personally to think of the morning as the time of grace. Of course, the whole day and night is dependent upon grace. I just mean that grace seems to rise to the forefront in the morning portion because we feel we are not enough to meet what awaits us, or because we wonder if the sun will shine in our circumstances the way it shines in the morning.

The sun shines to remind that God has not quit. There is joy still residing in the world. The outstretched hand and the cry of the soul have a hearing.

The sinner can start again and take up with forgiveness. God is bounding forth like a man smitten in love with his bride to gather her into his arms.

This must surely describe something of what Jesus sought out in those early mornings of prayer in desolate places. Was he like the psalmist watching at dawn for the steadfast love, the joy that comes, the hope of answered prayer? Was he refreshing the conviction to oppose evil, gaining anew the illumination of the Father's redemptive intention?

Historically, it was the morning when Jesus's enemies bound his hands and determined to kill him (Mark 15:1). But poetically was there some hope the sunrise gave to our Lord as men possessed by the terrors of the night threw him out into the street? It was the morning. He knew it, didn't he? So many mornings he had known the intimacy of his Father. There had been many mornings before these ensnared men were born. Mornings would go on after they died. In fact, there would come a morning on the third day while it was still dark when death would die, these foul men would be confounded, and Jesus would rise again! The morning proclaims that resurrection and life have outlasted the night. Did that proclamation whisper to him? Was this part of the "joy . . . set before him" (Heb. 12:2)? Did the sun somehow wink at Jesus as they bound his hands and sought to take his breath away?

Morning is the time of grace and hope for the chained and mistreated, for the lost and compass needing, for the forgiveness dependent. We rise; God's love is here! We pray; God's guidance is with us! We hope again and cry out anew; God is overcoming the darkness! We eat the daily bit we have; God has provided! We get to the work before us; God has something to show us! The dawn has come; the tomb is empty! The season of morning begins and ends. Noon comes.

Noonday Wisdom

Jesus's wisdom is needed always. Certainly we must not think it wise to be foolish in the mornings or in the night watches, but it seems to me that it is in the noon portion of each day that this provision of wisdom from God is often and peculiarly felt. In the Psalms, "the noonday" symbolizes for God's people the light within which justice and virtue shine (Ps. 37:6). It is here that we act with wise choices regarding the work, the circumstances, and the persons at hand.

For this reason, afternoon is fatiguing. The business of the day gets its second wind and picks up speed. Work must get done. Decisions must be made. Calls logged, tasks completed, e-mails written, meetings and agendas kept, fields plowed, bolts tightened, three more diapers to change, dinner to prepare, sickness to endure. On one occasion Jesus poetically pictures the noon season as that time of day in which we labor under "the burden of the day and the scorching heat." It is the time of day when work fusses us to its conclusion, paychecks are handed out, and the bones pop within our aching muscles (Matt. 20:2, 12).

Often, two hours after lunch the weariness sets in. For some of us, we experience the "noon-day demon," a dark cloud of a mood that wriggles our legs, squirms us in our seats, and twiddles our thumbs. Such moods instill in us "a hatred for the place," a hatred for the life we've been given, and "a hatred for manual labor."[22] It is little wonder that cocktails and happy hours tempt men and women of business in the afternoon. Distraction calls out to us. Procrastination keeps calling. Flirtations and imagined rendezvous for the night are given consideration.

This combination of enduring hard work, feeling fatigue, wanting relief, and looking for distraction explains why the noon hour through 6:00 PM often puts to the test the virtuous path that grace has purchased for us. It illumines the degree to which we will surrender to the paths of grace in Jesus or will resist him and stumble instead through the brush. If the morning is the time for taking our tears, plans, work, and questions of the day to his throne of grace and there finding hope, the afternoon seems to be the time of illumination in which our intention to lean on that grace is sifted and the true objects of our hope take off their masks.

Historically, it was at noon that Jesus was weary and thirsty. He sat down to take a break. There he met a woman whose barren heart needed living water. Her sins were exposed. The afternoon brought her face to face with her folly and his wisdom. He had water for her thirst there at noon. Because of him, her place and its people became a kind of sanctuary and a congregation into which she testified, "Come, see," and then told them all about "a man" who revealed her heart and changed her life (John 4:6–30).

It was noon when Pontius Pilate tried to escape virtue and placate the heart-ensnared brutality of a murderous brood. Politics, agendas, self-interest, and alliances rattled the sunlit moment. At noon the sun is at its highest and gives its strongest light by which to see, its strongest heat by which to be humbled. We are meant to resemble it. But he faltered. And so did God's people.

"Behold your King!" he offered them.

"Crucify him! We have no king but Caesar!" they responded.

It was in the noon portion that Pilate chose political advantage and ordered the innocent to be mistreated, the Son of God to die (John 19:14–15).

It was also at noon when Jesus breathed his last and the sun's light inexplicably failed (Luke 23:44). The dark and the sunlit noon traded places. They turned the day upside down as if to resemble the evil that was being called good, and the good that was being accused of evil.

Noon is the time when we make the choices we had prayed about or ignored in the morning. If the morning beckons us to sing, the afternoon humbles us into a remembrance that we need his salvation. The morning teaches us to praise. The afternoon teaches us patience and perseverance. The noonday has a beginning and an end. The evening comes.

Evening Hospitality

> Now when it was evening, the disciples came to him and said, "This is a desolate place, and the day is now over; send the crowds away to go into the villages and buy food for themselves." But Jesus said, "They need not go away; you give them something to eat." They said to him, "We have only five loaves here and two fish." (Matt. 14:15–17)

"The day is now over." The teacher and teaching come to a close. It is time for food and a bit of rest in the company of others who also are at rest and could likewise use a bite to eat. The limits of our food do not prevent but only remind us that our true portion is Jesus and that he will prove sufficient to rest us and nourish us amid the company of the evening. We needn't take our work with us. Workless in the evening matters. In order to learn how to rest in life, we need the spiritual grace to set down our work and to rest when an ordinary evening arrives. An inability to do this where we are in our ordinary place on a given and routine evening will render it nearly impossible to cultivate a life of stability "out there" amid the chatter and the frenzy.

By "hospitality," I have in mind extending the kindness and protection of a peaceable presence to our neighbors. It is kind because it takes our neighbor's bodily and soul needs into account and provides them a room-giving acceptance and practical sustenance. Hospitality is also protective because remaining hospitable toward another means that we do not transgress, misuse, or consume them. We allow them to take up company in our presence in such a way that they know that we will not use them to satisfy our lust, mandate that they act as if they are not tired or in need of nourishment, or require them to take the heat for the afternoon moods that we are carrying with us and misplacing on them.

Grace and wisdom are, of course, necessary evening friends. But hospitality seems to take a front seat in the evening. Blessing, rest, good food, friendship, acceptance, honesty, freedom from misuse, reclining at rest at the table prepared for us—the welcomed reward from a long day of solid work. The prayers of thanksgiving rise from our lips, and we raise our hands in gratitude to God for his faithfulness through the day (Ps. 141:2). The morning teaches us to sing. The afternoon teaches us to persevere. The evening teaches us to enjoy the blessing of ordinary goodnesses and to give thanks to God for the sacred boredom of mundane blessings that we can count.

But the poetry of the Psalms also pictures the evening as a shadow time (Ps. 102:11; 104:23). Light of day is fading; the morning and afternoon are withering into their end (Ps. 90:6). Those whose afternoons were entertained by folly's seduction threaten hospitality. Happy hour imaginations come to fruition in the evening (Prov. 7:7–9). Those who took no time to pause and take their foul moods to God prior to the evening's inauguration likewise rabble-rouse us. Irritable many of us come to our dinner tables. We litter the evening living room with the trash of our untended frustrations and anxieties. Those in our crowd pay for it without warrant—often and especially those who are closest to us, those whom we would say we love the most. In such cases, the dark of the evening emboldens the illicit misuse of one another. The dark gives rise to those who disregard God.

> Each evening they come back,
>   howling like dogs
>   and prowling about the city.
> There they are, bellowing with their mouths
>   with swords in their lips—
> for "Who," they think, "will hear us?" (Ps. 59:6–7)

For this reason, our evenings need Jesus. Some evenings he went away to pray (Matt. 14:23). He acted as if he might go on. So we say to him with those on the road to Emmaus, "Stay with us, for it is toward evening and the day is now far spent." Like them, our hearts burn as he stays with us and breaks bread with us and speaks of himself in the Scriptures for us (Luke 24:29–31).

In the evening, the troubled found their way to Jesus. He welcomed and was hospitable to the sick and the demon possessed (Mark 1:32). Twice it was amid evening storms that Jesus showed his followers that he was with them amid what frightened them in the night (Mark 4:35; 6:37). Locked behind closed doors for fear of what the crucifying community would do to them, it was in the evening when Jesus pursued them and spoke to them, "Peace be with you," and made their hearts glad (John 20:19). Gladness for his goodness redeems the evening, and this is very kind of God, because the night watches are coming. How kind to direct our meditation to ordinary joys amid neighbor love before the "night thieves" come to bogeyman us.

Solitude and the Night Watches

> My soul will be satisfied as with fat and rich food,
> and my mouth will praise you with joyful lips,
> when I remember you upon my bed,
> and meditate on you in the watches of the night. (Ps. 63:5–6)

I have always assumed solitude as a morning feature. But the poetry of the Psalms pictures the night watches as a place of solitude. Historically, when Jesus was up alone in the night in the desolate places of prayer, surely this testimony from Psalm 63:5–6 was the kind of portion that Jesus experienced with the Father (Luke 6:12).

The night watches picture for us a military soldier posted as a lookout. The watchman stays awake and peers into the potential movements of the night in order to protect his community from an enemy so that they can sleep. He also watches for a messenger or reinforcements who come bringing clarity or rescue by stealth. Bed for rest, watchfulness for clarity and rescue; sleep and sleeplessness—these are the two movements of the night. Jesus accounts for these night watches in his parable:

> Therefore stay awake—for you do not know when the master of the house will come, in the evening, or at midnight, or when the rooster crows [3:00 AM], or in the morning. (Mark 13:35)

In the night watches, between 10:00 PM and 6:00 AM, solitude therefore emerges among our ongoing need for grace, wisdom, and hospitality. Solitude regards our aloneness before God—who we are as he knows us to be. This is no "quiet time" in general, parsing out abstract truths. Solitude takes up with God the very real leftover emotions and questions from the day.

> Be angry, and do not sin;
> ponder in your own hearts on your beds, and be silent. (Ps. 4:4)

One purpose for our bed in the night is to ponder in our hearts what troubles us and to speak such things to God. We entrust to him now what we pray the morning will relieve with fresh hope. Sleep results. Sleep is a Sabbath-like act. We rest from it all and leave it all for God's keeping while we lie motionless in the world for a while. If we hope to enact such trust out there on the horizon of another place, the practice this very night affords to us is our best hope.

> In peace I will both lie down and sleep;
> for you alone, O Lord, make me dwell in safety. (Ps. 4:8)

Sleep is a gift, a discipline, and sometimes a luxury. As a gift it provides for our limits. As a discipline it humbles us to admit to everyone that we are finite and must stop for a while. Soldiers, crisis-care workers, and the chronically ill know well that sometimes sleep is a luxury. Sleep is meant for our refreshment and strength. Its patterns change as we age. By it we are freed to be human.

But there are terrors in the night, too (Ps. 91:5). Nightmares. Sleepless weeping can linger (Ps. 30:5). Trouble can hold our "eyelids open" (Ps. 77:4). Once there was a "song in the night" (v. 6). Praise in the barren dark on our bed, it sounded forth from our whispered voice taking strength from the happy praise of God.

But now the desolate silence allows our heart questions to search in frenzied unrest. No melody. No song. Anxiety fills the night watches:

Will the Lord spurn forever,
   and never again be favorable?
Has his steadfast love forever ceased?
   Are his promises at an end for all time?
Has God forgotten to be gracious?
   Has he in anger shut up his compassion? (vv. 7–9)

Our agitated questions with no answers lead us to a remembrance in the night. We, the unrelieved and sleepless, become rememberers of God's faithfulness with no one to applaud us (vv. 10–11).

But it is also true that our unchecked afternoon folly can lead us into an inhospitable evening and fill our night watches with stumbling. "Come let us take our fill of love until morning," the affair choosers say (Prov. 7:18). The predawn dark often haunts us with guilt and shame. We hail a cab half drunk, with our dignity left for misuse from a stranger's bed, wondering what we were thinking. Or we pulled an all-nighter due to procrastination or work. We have no sleep or solitude to strengthen us into the morning. The deep night then becomes a confessional, a school for God's counsel to find us and instruct us (Ps. 16:7).

I rise before dawn and cry for help;
   I hope in your words.
My eyes are awake before the watches of the night,
   that I may meditate on your promise. (Ps. 119:147–48)

Historically, night upon night Jesus enjoyed sweet solitude with God as well as blessed sleep. But solitude of an ugly kind formed the one night of our Savior's Gethsemane. It was not time for sleep, though sleep was all his three friends could muster. Sometimes sleep more than anything else, along with a bit of food, is what we need for a while in order to recover from a trauma in our past (1 Kings 19:1–8). But sleep rarely gives the power to face what comes tomorrow. Only the exhausted prayer of the watchman in the night can give that kind of strength (Luke 22:44–46). Jesus is that watchman. His strength in the night enables us both to sleep and to awake according to the times God has for us. He leads us to our aloneness with the Father and steadies us for what lurks to harm or what waits to bless.

Some of us dream in the night of our sleeping. Dreams can trouble or bless us. May I say just a word about them? Dreams come from one of three places, just as our thoughts do when we are awake. They originate with us, they are set upon us by our enemy the Devil, or they are whispered to us by God. Either way, dreams are providential; that is, they too are one of the circumstances in our lives that God governs and through which he holds us for his glory and our true good (Job 33:15–18).

Because of this, in general, it is normally helpful for us to focus more upon the impressions, thoughts, and emotions with which we awake than on trying to figure out the symbolic meaning of every detail. When we transition from one portion of the day to the next, we pause for a few minutes to take note of what has gone before and to take such things to God in prayer. So I suggest we do here with dreams.

Whatever foul or marvelous thoughts or feelings that linger with us, we take them as they are to God, just as we do when we are awake. Generally, dreams of strange images of ordinary things in our lives arise from us. Dark, murderous, treacherous, adulterous, slanderous, brutal terrors arise from our enemy who either solely suggests them to us or seizes our own experiences and makes an exaggerated haunting or scandal out of them. Dreams from God are rare and treasured. Often they are remarkable because of the lasting impression of his love and our forgiveness and identity in him as his own dear children in Jesus. Endeavors by grace after new obedience to Jesus follow from such dreams. "But if any are led by dreams to pursue a course repugnant to the dictates of common sense or the precepts of Scripture, such dreams may rightly be considered diabolical."[23] Such is not from us or from God but from our enemy. This thought alone can comfort the distraught believer who dreamt of doing horrible sins. The imagination of such heartbreaking scenes does not mean that they came from us or that they represent our true hearts or desires.

In any case, we needn't get agitated if we cannot presently discern which origin of a dream is before us. Whatever our dream, we take its contents and resulting thoughts and emotions to God. With him we can rest their poetic business and our frame of heart in Jesus. If there are persons in our dreams that stand out to us, we can intercede for them, just as we often do when persons come to our minds during our waking hours. We likewise entrust such fearful or celebratory impressions to him believing that he will as he always does, inform us and change us and lead us according to his love and grace and perfect timing in Jesus.

After the night and the dreaming the dawn comes. The morning returns. The promise again of light, joy, promise, a fresh start. Night is ending. Our hearts are poured out, clarity comes, sleep blesses. The Lord who keeps you does not slumber but attends you (Ps. 121:4). The sun begins to break forth for his bride.

Getting Seasonal with Our Daily Calendars

Some days seem too small to us. They do not have enough, we believe, to sustain our attention. Other days are too big for us. We feel that we cannot handle what looms before us. Either way, learning to notice and inhabit the seasons of each day can help us. If we learn to slow down and notice all that fills an ordinary day, we find ample provisions of creation and providence to keep our attention. If we learn to slow down into each daily season, we learn to manage what troubles us and seems too large.

Since I have no skills with this kind of biblical rhythm of Jesus's grace for a day, I have needed help. One of the places I have turned might seem strange to some of us. I am not a monk. I've moved a lot in my life. But unlike me and many that I've done church life with, these quirky followers of Jesus attempt to go a long distance in one community together. This fact has meant that they have tried to learn what it means to take one day at a time. It seems to me that they operate on the premise that a long life of stability begins by learning the grace to spiritually manage an ordinary day, which is arranged around times of prayer and Word they have called "divine hours" or "divine offices."

In contrast, my days in my community couldn't be more different. My Franklin Covey daily planner begins with blank early-morning time slots. Then it formalizes each morning at 8:00 AM and assumes a continuous stream of planning activities for twelve uninterrupted hours (through 8:00 PM). More blank time slots for more scheduling await use at the bottom of the page. A North American congregant or neighbor like me is likely to blur each day into the next by practicing a continuous unbroken stream of daily activity in order to make the best use of the shortest amount of time, all the time, every day.

Helpful books about our need to find margin or boundaries in our lives address this frenetic pace. Some cultures such as Britain or New Zealand break for tea in the morning and afternoon. Some ministry organizations such as L'Abri divide the day into morning study and afternoon work, knit together by tea and meals.

But our problem goes beyond our need to say no to activities and the need, however pleasant and helpful, to find more time for tea in our day, for we can learn to say no and can positively lighten our schedules without addressing our desire to be like God and to be everywhere-for-all. In other words, we can remain self-centered, blurry-eyed, and God-numb with boundaries and a cup of tea in our hands just as much as we can without them.

We are meant to replace what we've emptied, not with just anything but with the provision and grace of Jesus. Otherwise, the emptier schedule will drive us nuts because we do not know what to do with the quiet. Likewise, without him the things we do schedule will drive us off the mark because we still do not know how to schedule or do our local tasks as if in God's presence and with his grace to hear his voice intrude into our day and content our souls with him.

How do we everywhere-for-alls learn to stay put in the workaday world when we are out and about? This is something I have been attempting slowly with a great deal of imperfection, a lot of false starts, and gratitude for Jesus. Here is how I have started. Maybe it can offer some help to you too.

1) Think of morning, noon, evening, and night as portions large enough for your attention and small enough to manage each day. No longer seek to blur them together or rush past them.

2) Learn over time, by grace, to begin each portion with an intrusion of God's Word to you. One way to do this is to begin each season of the day with a reading from the Psalms or the Gospels.

3) Then enter that portion of the day hopeful for his leading.

4) As that portion of the day draws to a close, pause and look back before you start the new portion and rush forward. Give thanks to God for the tokens of his grace that you experienced. Or cry at the pains and lament. Or recognize your agitated moods and petition

> him for what originates them. Ask him to show you your errors, sins, and faults from that portion that he can lead you to confess and gratefully turn from. Or intercede for any situation or purpose that stuck out to you during that time. Then, out of this pause, praise him and ask him to lead you by the hand into the next portion of the day.[24]

In this regard, let's say it's 11:47 AM. The morning is about to rest. We take a few moments to observe the graces given and the moods fouling us up. Wisdom will be required for the noonday. But for now it is his presence and grace we linger with for a few more minutes. With his grace we await noon's arrival.

Or the evening is coming. It's 5:30 PM or so (or 6:30 because we are behind). Food is simmering on the stove. Traffic awaits our commute home. We pause and reflect. We conclude the afternoon with Jesus. We ask forgiveness; we seek his courage to make things right where we need to as much as it is possible with us; we give thanks for the strength he gave and for the morning prayers he answered; and we celebrate the virtue of his Spirit that, by his grace, lasted. We notice our aching muscles or tired brain. We seek his rest. What this afternoon's work left unfinished we wrestle to believe it will be there tomorrow waiting for us. The morning will give us time to take it to the Lord before it comes back around. It will all get done. For now, there are kids to play with, spouses to come alongside of, and neighbors to encourage. Leave the noon for now. Take its moods to Jesus so as not to unduly take them with us and hoist them upon others at the dinner table.

Or maybe, it's 9:45 PM or somewhere thereabout. Our table is cleared. The TV is turned off. Our kids are in bed (unless we have teenagers). Our friends are heading home. We pause to give thanks for the good food and good company with which he has blessed us. We seek forgiveness for the foul moods we spilled upon others. We take heart that the morning will give us a new moment to take such things to him and sing again and hopefully find praise again. We take our fears, our sickness, and our oppressions felt from the evening community to him. He stays with us and speaks peace. We brush our teeth. The time for bed approaches for some of us. For others, the time for quiet and prayer arrives. Third-shift jobs, hospital stays, seasonal parties, last-minute homework—each of these realities informs the night. But the second and third watches of the night are not normatively made for our TV watching, our leftover work from the day, or our after-party carousing, not as a norm anyway. The night is coming. The late night was made for our solitude with God.

Conclusion

Each of us who are tempted to try to be like God and be an everywhere-for-all can find God's provision in the seasons of a twenty-four-hour day. Our individual circumstances, jobs, and cultures take hold of our days differently. But whether we work the night shift or during the day, one-day-at-a-time Jesus leads us humanly into his grace, his wisdom, his hospitality, and his solitude. Sometimes we need to leave the place we inhabit for safety or sanity. But wherever we land, Jesus intends our stability there. He teaches us gently and slowly what it means to praise, to persevere, to give thanks, and to believe. Without having to be any other place but where we are, the morning, noon, the evening, and the night watches give us the "one day at a time" that frees us to slow down in the place we have been given. From that locality and smallness, we discover in him what is universal and grand. In Jesus, we needn't try to be omnipresent like God anymore. He and such meaningful portions were here all along. Chesterton was right. The quickest way to get home is to stay there.[25]

CHAPTER FOUR

Fix-It-All

The Inner Ring, Psalm Making, and Calling for the Elders

> I have seen a man on the bank of the river buried up to his knees in mud and some men came to give him a hand to help him out, but they pushed him further in up to his neck.[1]

Lori was in high school. She was beautiful but didn't feel it. Maybe it was because she was adopted and the mystery of unanswered abandonment still lay buried deep in her being. Maybe she knew the looks of boys only for misuse and rarely for love. I don't know. But looking back, we also didn't know that beneath her contagious smile, anorexia was beginning to consume her young life.

I remember the phone call from a pastor in another state. Lori was in jail for shoplifting. Somehow the pastor, while visiting the local jail, had come into contact with her. He called to tell me she was okay. Lori and I had met on several occasions for counsel. I had held several living-room sessions with her mom and dad.

The front porch is what I probably remember most. There she lay, curled up in a ball, barefoot and in pajamas, leaning fetal into the aluminum screen door. Her mom was there but would not open the door for her. She had been ordered by her husband to keep Lori out. The dad, a former military man, had begun to resort to "tough love" with Lori. He had called the police on her a few weeks before. Exasperated, the dad was trying force to fix the situation. The mom was pleading with tears. As for me, two other elders and I had been walking the streets of her neighborhood searching for Lori. "She had run away again" is all we knew. Our search ended on the front porch. There Lori lay, locked out in her tears, and there we stood in ours.

Dealing with Our Surprise

In his book *Strong at the Broken Places*, Richard Cohen observes, "We the injured are everywhere."[2] This fact should not have surprised me. After all, Jesus had clearly revealed our injured world in the Gospels. He regularly walked his disciples down roads filled with the sights, sounds, and smells of persons broken by bodily or soulish sicknesses and hardships. But I have been surprised, surprised by the nature of the injury.

Somehow the injury of once-Eden set before me in Christian theology was memorized but not understood. "Into what estate did the fall bring mankind?" the Westminster Larger Catechism asks. The estate of "sin and misery," it answers. Then it tells us the kind of sin and misery that live in our neighborhoods: "blindness of mind, a reprobate sense, strong delusions, hardness of heart, horror of conscience, vile affections" including all the "evils that befall us in our bodies, names, estates, relations and employments, together with death itself."[3]

I shouldn't have been surprised. I had experienced firsthand in my own life that my family, my friends, my church, my generation, and I were among the injured who are everywhere.

Yet, for all of my knowing, I was not prepared for this condition's implications for how an ordinary day can feel in the world and therefore in ministry. I did not recognize how deeply cracked the crevices of persons and families can be or the molten lava that volcanic choices and feeling can erupt, the once fruitful Pompeii now ashen and gone. Sins and miseries describe how the front porch of a normally welcoming home can become an island of exile, a banishment that is decreed and felt on either side of a wall-like door, an uncivil war waged among those who love each other while men with Bibles stand there with their verses.

Somehow I had not imagined that ministry in Jesus's name would mean that my life would be lived among such porches. I'm not sure why. "In the world, you will have tribulation," my Lord Jesus has told me. Therefore, Peter and John both say to me, "Do not be surprised," as if to say that "fiery trials" and "hatreds" in the world are something I am meant to assume (1 Pet. 4:12; 1 John 3:13). The apostle Paul likewise lists the sinful expressions that are like a swamp through which all of us must trudge in this world. Things like enmity and strife, fits of rage and jealousy, rivalry and sexual damage toilet paper our trees (Gal. 5:19–21). He describes the miseries too. They include distress, persecution, famine, nakedness, and sword (Rom. 8:35). To seek Jesus's ministry to others is to follow him into this condition. This means that an ordinary Tuesday can feel kind of rough, and this before I've gotten out of bed.

But the implications of this pervasive condition and the impact of these conditions on an ordinary day are not the only surprises. There is another surprise, an assumption really, that I have needed Jesus to remove from me. It is this: Jesus doesn't see victory in this world the way I wish he would.

To introduce what I mean about our limited power and confounding purpose, let's start by considering the problems of heart, mind, and choice that brought us all to that porch on that morning. They are all of them beyond my ability to mend. I can search, find, and become present on that porch with Lori lying there and her mom weeping behind the locked door, her dad angry (or afraid?) on the phone. But none of us has the power necessary to heal the incision that seeps there. For all of our Bible quoting, planning, counseling, reasonableness, force, pleadings, laws, and graces, something only Jesus can do humbles us into waiting for him to do it.

So, behind that door and in the weeping the mom needs Jesus to meet her. On the phone and in the bellowing the dad needs Jesus to meet him. On the porch rubbled like leftovers, Lori needs Jesus to meet her. Standing in our work clothes and clutching our Bibles, we elders, each in our own way, need Jesus to meet us. This is what such porches expose. Jesus-less, our powers are exposed and fragile.

We would get Lori up off of that porch that day, go on into our normal routines of chores, food, prayer, Bible reading, music lessons for our kids, and sleeping. But the thing that brought Lori to the porch in the first place would remain unrepaired that night and for many, many nights to come. Each of us therefore would have to learn how to live each day with each other and none of it or us fixed. It is no wonder the Serpent's pledge glitters and shines into preference. "You will be like God," the Serpent promised (Gen. 3:5). "You will not surely die," the Serpent hissed (v. 4). I want this promise on the porch, and if I'm not careful, I will take of its cursed fruit. I can be god on the porch for them. I can fix them. "All is not this bad," I can tell them. "You will surely not die," I will say. "I will make this go away for you." Immediate remedy beckons. Eve saw it and took it. And so do I.

Exposing Our Temptations

Anything I can grab and eat or say or quote will do, anything to make me feel like I'm doing something constructive amid my helplessness. I scratch and claw to be omnipotent on the porch. This fact brings me back to the second surprise. Even if I could be god for people and fix-it-all, the fact remains. Jesus often does not have the kind of fixing in mind that I would want to bring.

Mounting an Offense

In her remarkable memoir regarding her ongoing battle with chronic rheumatoid arthritis, Mary Felstiner asks: "How can a soul rise to the occasion of illness?"[4] By "illness," Mary meant the diseased wrecking of one's body into disrepair. By inquiring how a soul rises to this occasion, she meant choosing and learning to live stubbornly, vibrantly, and lovingly onward within the carnage that once was her fingers or legs.

Her disease is a sadist with joints and bones. It pulverizes them with a grin. It wrenches them out and yanks at them. It twists them into a mangle while chuckling. So when I hear her call us to "rise to the occasion," I recognize that she intends to fight—not whenever these sins and miseries disappear, or so that they will disappear but, rather, fighting while knowing the disease will remain unevicted from her. She accepts its occupation of her territory, and she chooses to rise anyway.

The mentoring of an old movie comes to mind. The underdog fighter has no chance to win. But when his wife, who lies sick in a hospital bed, pulls him close, she says with all the courage she can muster, "Win. Win for me." At that exact moment, as these defiant words take their stand on her weakened lips, the music begins. One lone bell rings and then pauses. It sounds again then pauses. It shouts again and then pauses. And then the trumpets begin in force. The fighter, Rocky Balboa, revives. He must rise to the occasion. Something within him has changed. Whether he wins or loses is no longer the issue. The question is, will he step into the ring anyway? He will, and the crowd will cheer for him, "Rocky! Rocky! Rocky!" He will face the fighter in the ring.

But I think to myself, "Why fight if winning isn't possible?" What if every movie ended with Rocky losing the fight? Would I still cheer for him? Would I lose interest in watching movies if the hero fought but was knocked out every time? Would I tolerate all of that buildup of music, drama, relationships, and hope only to watch him lose at the end of every match? Felstiner's description of how the soul must rise to meet its nemesis startled me. "At least now I know what the job is," she says. "Mount an offense when no match is mine to win."[5]

Powerless to win, we nonetheless take up our cause? Is she suggesting that victory is more fundamentally tied to entering the ring and rising to the occasion than to becoming champion or being delivered completely from the disease? Is there a victory even when our foe dances over us with arms raised and gloves glistening, taunting us while we lie limp and seemingly down for the count?

Words from the Bible come to mind: "He saved others; let him save himself, if he is the Christ of God, his Chosen One!" they shouted (Luke 23:35).

Others taunted him as he lay heaving and pinned down to the wood. "If you are the King of the Jews save yourself!" they jeered (v. 37).

Then one who had made a perversion of neighbor love as a way of life railed against him. "Are you not the Christ? Save yourself and us!" (v. 39).

Their shouts make sense. Wouldn't this be the moment when the Chosen One, the King, the Christ, would "rise to the occasion?" As he lay sprawled on the mat with the referee counting closer and closer to ten, isn't this the instant in which the hero is supposed to grab the ropes and will himself into standing? And while the crowd's excitement reaches a fevered pitch will we see fear in the foe's eyes as our hero wills to win for us?

But this is no movie. This is not how the winning back of once-Eden came. "Father, forgive them," he said (v. 34).

"I thirst," he said (John 19:28).

"My God, my God, why have you forsaken me?" he begged (Matt. 27:46).

"Father, into your hands I commit my spirit!" he said. "And having said this, he breathed his last" (Luke 23:46).

Herod, Peter, and Our Winsome Harming

It's clear to me that King Herod would not have watched a series of movies if the fighter kept losing at the end. For Herod, winning happens only by a decision in his favor from those who judge the performance or by a knockout. Herod liked to fight. He raged and manipulated his hearers into submission. He never learned.

Peter on the other hand thought to fight as well. He raised his sword and cut off the servant's ear. It was not that Jesus was without warriors for his aid. Legions of angels would have swooped down in an instant had he called them. And this is the point. Jesus did not call upon them, and he told Peter to put away his sword. Peter would learn. Jesus would fix things by a different means. Jesus uses his power differently than others do.

It's also become clear to me over the years that many of us who are tempted to be a fix-it-all often unwittingly mimic Herod's or Peter's example when confronted by troubling porch situations. This is because a person who defines victory only as the eradication of what troubles him will make destruction from the trouble he finds on the porch. This assumption of what it means to "rise to the occasion" illuminates why, when King Herod was troubled, so was "all Jerusalem with him" (Matt. 2:3). When Herod wasn't happy, nobody was. He could not allow anyone else to have any other mood but his. He used the force of decree, words, will, power, or violence to fix what troubled him.

And it worked. The trouble was dealt with and fixed. But his actions healed nothing in once-Eden. In fact, how Herod chose to fix what troubled him tragically only violated love for God and neighbor all the more and advanced the result of humanity's sins and miseries. "A voice was heard in Ramah, weeping and loud lamentation, Rachel weeping for her children; she refused to be comforted, because they are no more" (Matt. 2:18).

In light of a Herodian approach to fixing what troubles us in the world, it is legitimate for Henri Nouwen to remind us that in Christ we are meant, in contrast to this Herodian approach, to serve as "wounded healers" among the broken porches of our ministries.[6] The reason is that the dominant tendency of persons and leaders, even those of us who, thankfully, know little of a Herodian extreme, is nonetheless to try to fix what troubles us as "winsome harmers." Like Peter, we are often kinder than Herod but no less deadly.

Consider the long line of ministry leaders whose sincere harm is documented in the Bible. Job's friends, lacking sincere empathy, thought they knew more than they did. In their hands, doctrine excused ignorance. Correctness validates a cruel word. Truth, we learn from them, can be used unfeelingly and foolishly. Truth can be used to hurt people.

The mandate to speak truth with love mutated into "I'll tell it like it is." Likewise, the shepherds of Ezekiel 33 used ministry to manipulate people in order to gain status, comfort, and reputation. They left the broken, the lost, and the harassed to the wolves. Similarly, the elder brother of the Prodigal Son represented the Pharisees (Luke 15:11–32). These Bible teachers justified ingratitude and bitterness in the name of standing for righteousness. They gracelessly pounded people with religious virtues. Or consider the religious leaders in the good Samaritan story (Luke 10:25–37). These ministry leaders had no concept of love for neighbor when they were "off duty." Even Judas stole from the money jar and took a bribe. The Gentiles who lorded their leadership over one another (Matt. 20:25) used their positions to slam rather than to serve people, and they abused the nature of ministry among the troubled porches. For any of us who consider the vocation of ministry, it is sobering to realize that the harshest things that Jesus ever said (like the prophets who foreshadowed Jesus) were for the ministry leaders of his day (Matt. 23:1–36).

The best of us are not immune to sometimes pushing others even farther into the mud in the name of helping people and fixing their trouble. Peruse the heroes of our faith. Notice that we receive their teaching in the context of their greatness but also with full disclosure about the mercy that they themselves required from God. We know about Noah's drunken debacle alongside of knowing of his courage and faith. We rightly honor Abraham's faith, while rightly remembering the fact that selfish fear could get the best of him. Moses murdered. He shrank back. His temper squandered his opportunity to physically step into the Promised Land. Yet, he also believed and courageously led. We sing the psalms of a man after God's own heart. But this man also did terrible deeds and at times made tragic choices far beneath his calling and the grace given him. Jonah raised his fists at grace. Paul teaches us. But God made sure that we receive Paul's teaching and integrity while knowing Saul of Tarsus's bitter story. Peter exalts Christ for us. But we are not gullible regarding the kind of cowardly sin that Peter exemplified when Jesus was arrested.

Somehow I thought the contours of my life and ministry would look distant from these biblical leaders and heroes. I thought that I would not make their mistakes or share their vulnerabilities. Though I would say that  they were each like broken jars through whom the power of God's grace was shown through their weakness, I failed to connect the dots to my own story. Standing on that porch (and at all other times), I am a broken pot and without any superhero cape. We're all broken, earthen vessels—the mom behind the door, the dad on the phone, the two elders with me, and the girl piled in the ruins.

So, when preaching about David's sin, my tendency was to say, "See what he did? Now don't you do that." But the problem is that David did sin. So now what? So what can you say there on the porch? You can say, "Don't be there!" The problem is that everyone already is. What if I am prone as Peter was to the same temptations to lie amid my fear of men? What if I have already shrunk back in self-centered fear as Abraham did? What if, like Jonah, I raise my fists at God's desire to forgive the kind of person who broke the knees of my world and left me crumpled on the ground in pain? Now what? What if God's reason for showing us these broken heroes is that we learn who not to be but also that we can come to our senses about who we already are?

The point is that Jesus is the anti-Herod in handling what troubles us. There need be no immediate decision in our favor or knockout punch on the porch that morning in order for healing and victory to be learned. Jesus exposes the hints of Herod within us. He invites us instead to the way of the clay jar. We are broken pots, fragile and chipped, within which the strength of Christ shines upon the valleys of our sins, miseries, and weaknesses (2 Cor. 4:7–8). His is the strength our broken porches need.

Paul admitted that he prayed three times for healing, that God did not relieve, that the thorn remained, and that therefore the grace of Jesus amid our weakness must become the path by which we handle what troubles us (2 Cor. 12:7–10). Herod would have turned the channel or walked out of that movie. But we who follow Jesus must learn the grace that keeps us in our seats, waiting. Otherwise true power is lost.

The Peace Jesus Gives

But what if waiting in our seats means we have to welcome feelings we do not want for a purpose that is not ours so that what we most need can come from the only one who can truly give it? Fix-it-alls need the grace to learn what Jesus says to us: "Peace I leave with you; my peace I give to you," Jesus says, but "*not as the world gives do I give to you*. Let not your hearts be troubled, neither let them be afraid" (John 14:27).

He does not untrouble us the way Herod tries or the world assumes—and this is a marvelous grace to all of us. By doing so Jesus resists our habit of adding insult to injury, of choosing gasoline as our means for dousing a fire. Yet, Jesus's peace, while not adding to the wreckage, is powerful enough to linger with the wreckage. In this way, he often does not give peace how we wish he would.

I remember walking into the hospital room. Steve was there. I first met Steve years earlier at my first Bible study at Grand Village Retirement Home. I had asked God for an opportunity to serve widows and widowers. The phone call came from this place that I had not heard of before. A person I had never met was asking me if I would come lead a Bible study.

The only one who came my first day was Steve. I was nervous and pushed to say a prayer and end the meeting right away. But this Purple Heart recipient had other ideas on his mind. "Father, I've not been to church in over fifty years," he said to me. I was not Catholic, but I was a "Father" to this ninety-year-old. "God could never forgive me for all the things I've done," he said, as he stared past me into a world that pained him. That day, grace gave me words to speak of Jesus and his forgiveness. Jesus drew Steve to himself.

Now, here Steve was in the hospital room. His hands were tied down because he kept tearing his tubes out of his arms. He was in a hallucinatory world now. He told me to watch out for the postman standing at the edge of his bed waiting to do me harm. I assured Steve that I was okay. I told Steve that I loved him. He gave no indication that he heard me. He was all fidgety groaning in the world he was imagining. I sat for a long while. I sang. I prayed. All the while Steve didn't recognize me. Then, as I was leaving, I leaned over and said, "I love you, Steve."

Steve shot me a look. The fidget, the moans, and the illusions collapsed from his eyes. For a moment he saw me clear. "I heard ya the first time," he declared. Then for an instant more, Steve and Zack looked at each other and Steve saw me. Then the moment left. The turmoil returned to Steve. And yet, love asserted itself there amid the hallucinations, the tied hands, and the fading mind. There is a kind of power that Jesus gives. It goes where other kinds of power will not. It does what other kinds of power cannot.

His power is found when singing "Amazing Grace" to a woman in hospice, wheezing in the dark for breath. Singing of his grace makes the lungs relax, and the breathing eases. Death will not stop. But grace has come. Something more powerful than death hums softly alongside of her and holds her hands. The grace will outlast the death.

The things moaning on that porch with Lori, behind the door with her mom, on the phone with her dad, require a power that does not cease when the knockout comes. Things such as love, joy, peace, patience, kindness, goodness, faithfulness, gentleness, and self-control begin to mount an offense at the porches of our troubles (Gal. 5:22). Such a power exists. To find it, we will have to come to terms with the presence of inconsolable things.

The Inconsolable Things

"Inconsolable things" are the sins and miseries that will not be eradicated until heaven comes home, the things that only Jesus, and no one of us, can overcome. We cannot expect to change what Jesus has left unfixed for the

moment. The presence of inconsolable things does not mean the absence of Jesus's power, however. Rather, it establishes the context for it. There in the midst of what is inconsolable to us, the true unique nature and quality of Jesus's power shows itself to be unlike any other power we have seen.

This is what I mean. Jesus teaches us that the faith of a mustard seed can move a mountain. "Nothing will be impossible for you" (Matt. 17:20). So we bring faith to what troubles us. And according to Jesus it would seem that there is nothing in the world that we can't fix if we just have the smallest seed of faith.

But this is not the conclusion Jesus draws for us. This challenges our Herodian ideas. Though nothing will be impossible for us with faith, "you always have the poor with you," Jesus says (Matt. 26:11). The paradox emerges. When it comes to poverty, there is no knockout punch or decision in your favor. You must step into the ring with faith, knowing that you will not win in the way you want to. Faith takes its stand amid an unremoved trouble.

The inconsolable things, therefore, are identified first by the "cannots" of Jesus's teaching. These things he identifies as impossible for any human being. For example, no matter who we are, "no one can serve two masters," no one (Matt. 6:24). Even if we are wise and knowledgeable by his grace, there are still things and seasons in our lives that we "cannot bear . . . now" (John 16:12). No matter how strong a will a person has, "the branch cannot bear fruit by itself" (John 15:4). No matter how many oaths we take or how much we spin words into boast, we "cannot make one hair black or white," Jesus says (Matt. 5:36).

These cannots from Jesus teach us that sickness, death, poverty, and the sin that bores into and infests the human being will not be removed on the basis of any human effort, no matter how strong, godly, or wise that effort is. The power to give this salvation is inconsolable as it relates to us. We cannot give people the new birth with God (John 3:3–5). We cannot justify someone, make her righteous, sanctify her, give her adoption, convict her of sin, or change her heart (Luke 19:27; 1 Cor. 12:3).

This presence of inconsolable things reminds us that healing is not the same as heaven. Miracles are real and powerful, but they do not remove the inconsolable things. Those whose leprosy Jesus healed coughed again or skinned their elbows. Those who were blind but now able to see could still get a speck of burning sand stuck in their eye. The formerly lame could still fall and break their leg. Lazarus was raised from the dead only to find his resumed life filled with death threats. Moreover, the raised friend of Jesus would die again someday, along with this company of the healed. Bodily healing in this world is not heaven. Sickness and death are inconsolable things. Their healing reveals Jesus but does not remove sickness or death from life under the sun. A soldier survives combat only to die in a car accident on the way home (or forty years later of cancer). Miracles never remove our need for Jesus.

In my first pastorate we began to make ourselves available as elders once a quarter on a Sunday evening. Our intention was to invite people to what James teaches us in his letter about coming to the elders when sick for prayer and anointing with oil (James 5:13–15). During those seasons of prayer and worship nearly everyone was nourished and encouraged in their faith. A handful of them were even healed. I remember a young girl whose eyes were fading into blindness. The doctors that week were astonished to learn that the cause of the trouble had disappeared. We all rejoiced in amazement and gave thanks to Jesus. I still do. The peace he gives is a sign, as we will see in a moment, that he is here.

Yet, Joni's healed eyes did not remove eye disease or blindness from the world. Healed eyes humbled us into tears of gratitude, but this did not mean that Joni's life was now heaven or that ours was. She was still a middle-school girl within a lovely but broken family, with all the realities of a fallen world and an untamed heart. So were we. It's like being a hero. The moment the hero rushed into the burning home to save a young boy resounds with sacred dignity. At the same time, we know that buildings still burn. The little boy still has a whole life ahead of him of grace and joy but also of ache and inconsolable things. The hero herself still lives on too for another forty years. But heroes aren't always so, as a long life of broken moments reminds each of us.

Inconsolable things reveal and refer to the ache that exists in every created thing and within even those who have the Spirit of God (Rom. 8:18–23). There is an ache within us that will remain even if what ails on the porch is blessedly mended. Jesus demonstrated there are some things he did not change but left as they were for a time, until he comes. We minister the peace of Jesus amid the troubling unremoved. He walks there with us and leads us through. Jesus empowers us to resist both adding to the damage and hastily trying to do what only Jesus can.

The Inner Ring

In life and in ministry, our Herodian tendencies are intensified by what C. S. Lewis called "the Inner Ring": "Of all the passions, the passion for the Inner Ring is most skillful at making a man who is not yet a very bad man do very bad things,"[7] Lewis observed. It tempts us to let go of "friends whom you really loved and who might have lasted a lifetime, in order to court the friendship of those who appear more important."[8]

What is an inner ring? "From outside, if you have despaired of getting into it, you call it, 'that gang' or 'they' or 'so-and-so and his set.'"[9] Deacons, elders, presbyters, boards, assemblies, donor bases, constituencies, committees, ministry teams, personalities, friendships, families—these function as inner rings.

At their best, these facilitate the Jesus-versus-Herodian way of bringing peace to what troubles us. At their worst, local inner rings, expose "our longing to enter them, our anguish when we are excluded, and the kind of pleasure we feel when we get in."[10]

The idol of the inner ring exposes why we are prone to excuse a person whom we love even though he or she is damaging others. We see his dignity so plainly, and we are blessed by his use of certain gifts. So when we experience pain or concern from darker sides of his character, we feel disoriented, find rationalizations, or get anxious about losing our relationship or our jobs or of upsetting others. The wisdom of being slow to judge one's weaknesses transitions into the folly of making a marathon of excuses.

In this regard, I remember a man nominated to be an elder in one of the churches I have served. There was a division among the other leaders as to whether this man was ready or gifted to serve as a shepherd to others. Those who were cautious and thought it best to wait were outvoted. Two painful things surfaced almost immediately.

First, only weeks later, at the end of a congregational meeting, a church member actually shouted out loud from a hallway, "Pastor! Pastor!" As the pastor came quickly to the situation, the parishioner was near tears, and the brand-new elder was intense in the face. The parishioner appealed to the pastor for help, saying he was hurt and confused as to why this new elder had cornered him and was talking to him in this harsh way. The new elder had been unsatisfied with an answer the member had given during the congregational meeting and had taken it upon himself to immediately corner and intensely correct the member.

Second, it came to light that no congregation members had actually nominated the man for leadership. Only his friends who were current elders had done so. Naively, these well-intentioned men, out of loyalty and love for a friend, usurped wise practice. They knew that no one in the congregation had yet recognized any gifts of shepherding in this person. But they excused that, because in their eyes the man was qualified, and they after all were the leaders. So they closed their eyes to the fact that he was untested with actual people and their care. The result is that the elder was defended (but not helped to grow) while the congregation was misused.

To slow down damage done by inner-ring leaders, Paul reminds Timothy, "Doing nothing from partiality. . . . Do not be hasty in the laying on of hands, nor take part in the sins of others. . . . The sins of some men are conspicuous . . . but the sins of others appear later" (1 Tim. 5:21–24).

On the other hand, a ministry leader can face the intimidation of a congregation with its various pockets of inner rings. Well-meaning friends can quickly pile on critiques of a leader. If one person in a close-knit small group begins to speak critically of a pastor, for example, the critique presses loyalties of the rest in the group. After recognizing a pattern of this kind of pastor critique, will they risk relationship with their pastor friend by suggesting that the group is not the forum for tearing down the pastor, or that the all-or-nothing way of speaking about the pastor probably isn't accurate to who Jesus is in the pastor's life? Because of each one's desire to remain accepted by the inner ring, each will be tempted either to remain consistently silent or to join in.

To slow down the damage that inner rings within congregations can cause, Paul counsels Timothy, "Let the elders who rule well be considered worthy of double honor. . . . Do not admit a charge against an elder except on the evidence of two or three witnesses" (1 Tim. 5:17, 19).

Imagine if we had used partiality as our chosen tool for trying to fix the brokenness that we discovered on the porch that morning. Fear could have driven us to preserve our sense of belonging with the dad on the phone, the mom at the door, or the daughter curled on the concrete. With imagined voices of disapproval in our heads, we could have lost the capacity to speak the fullness of what the gospel could say to each of them and to us according to our individual needs, strengths, and sins.

By grace, the once-partial apostle warns us about partiality in order to helpfully teach us. We are meant to admonish not the fainthearted or the weak but only those who are idle. We are meant to encourage not those who are idle but those who are fainthearted and weak. Patience is to orient our way of relating, no matter to whom we are ministering (1 Thess. 5:14). Partiality to preserve the inner ring creates an organizational culture that defends what should be abandoned and abandons what should be defended and leaves both the abandoned and the defended without the gospel. Jesus took on the shame, slander, and abandonment of inner rings who preserved themselves by rejecting and crucifying him.

Fear and Intimidation

When partiality takes the gospel's place as the thing we trust to preserve our group or institution, we begin to practice fear and intimidation as a leadership strategy.

> Nevertheless, many even of the authorities believed in him, but for fear of the Pharisees they did not confess it, so that they would not be put out of the synagogue. (John 12:42)

We struggle to believe that Jesus will preserve us even if we lose our title or our place. Deep within us a question nags. Can I still follow Jesus and have a fruitful life of service in him if this group disapproves of me? In such an environment, everyone involved learns, from the example made of those who have gone before, that their jobs or their futures are in the hands of those they must please. If we suggest, even out of love, with grace, and for the sake of true loyalty that someone in the group could grow or that we could better serve if changed, we know that those above us can make phone calls and with innuendo close the doors that would otherwise remain open to us.

The problem, of course, is that fear and intimidation work. They do keep the group or institution together. They do keep appearances up and perceptions high; but at what cost? Somewhere along the line, the gospel begins to erode and no longer forms the foundations of the building. Sooner or later what we uphold by fear will come crashing down. Happy perceptions built by fear cannot represent the realities that grace desires or create the conditions that grace warrants.

I remember talking with a dear man who shared an example of getting caught up in an inner ring. He took part with a ministry leader who was struggling with a personal crisis. The elder was charged with this ministry leader's care and formed an official delegation to meet with the ministry leader "to learn how they could pastorally care for him." Even though pastoral care formed the stated goal, the meeting collapsed into an interrogation, which ended with accusations and harsh words on everyone's part. The elder shared with me that he felt so sorry about that situation as he looked back on it. He said he had given in to the pressure of knowing that others involved were going to ask him very tough questions. So he had to make sure that nothing was left unturned in order to appease them. With their examination of him in his mind, he actually pointed at the man needing care and, with red-faced intensity, called him a hypocrite.

I know this temptation well. Most of us in ministry do. Seeking someone's approval rather than Jesus's gospel, we get tripped up. We take on a manner designed to appease the inner ring and let go of the manner that Jesus purchased for us. Implied or imagined threats rather than grace and truth become our way of relating. Often, we are long into the inner ring before we recognize this. Some of us never do.

The point is that fear, intimidation, and threat will not fix a girl with anorexia in a fetal position on the porch while her mother and father avalanche with anxiety. Actually, fear and intimidation won't fix much at all. When we've begun to trust fear and control to save our groups, Jesus will bring us to a porch so broken that neither fear nor control can fix it.

Multiplying Words

My oldest son was four. We were watching an animated Bible story about Stephen, who was killed by stoning for his faith (Acts 7:54–60). My son was getting anxious. As the G-rated cartoon showed Stephen dying amid the Herod-like fury, my son jumped up off of the couch and pled with me, "Daddy!" he cried. "I wish Batman were there!" My son was caught by the discomfort I too feel. If the story was of Batman, Batman would somehow have wriggled free. Then with sheer force and skill he would have pummeled every one of those stone throwers, vanquished his foes, and gone on to live another day. But in this story Jesus doesn't save Stephen from a cruel, unjust death. Instead, Jesus stands with Stephen in the midst of it. Together they do not escape the horror. Together they walk through it and outlast it.

When we use the substitute saviors of partiality, fear, and intimidation, we also begin to trust our ability with words and force in order to fix things. We call for Batman or try to be him ourselves. The problem is that our power with words and force is as fictional as his.

Job's friends struggled mightily here. They encounter Job on his broken porch. The presence of inconsolable things wears out their ability to wait very long in silence or empathy. Impatient for an answer and a remedy, they begin, first, to multiply their words. Job is not only faced with all that ails him; he must also deal with all of the daily texts, e-mails, letters, and phone calls of those trying to fix him in God's name.

Just as a case study can help a young minister to hear the difference between true and unsound doctrine in his Bible class, so the Proverbs likewise remind us to look out our windows and to listen to what the real world can sound like (Prov. 7:6–23). The sights and sounds can be tragic. As an example, imagine that a husband is leaving his wife. Imagine that the woman is a director of a ministry and a vibrant communicator.

"I'm not a Christian anymore!" he yells to her.

"You don't have to follow Jesus for us to remain married and find a good life," she responds. "I'm yours; I'm committed to you. We can get counseling. We can ask for help," she assures him.

"I'm not going to counseling together, and I'm not going to ask for help, especially from God," he declares. "I'm tired of the hypocrisy of churches. I hate this life," he retorts.

"I'll resign tomorrow," she pleads. "I don't have to be in ministry. Where do you want to go? We can go anywhere and start over," she begs. "I love you," she says.

"But I don't love you, and I never have," he retorts. "I don't want to be with you. I never have."

She is silent. Her words begin to falter. Maybe as you listen in, your words begin to fail you too.

"For me this marriage ended ten years ago," he reveals.

"You don't mean that," she mutters. "I can't believe that is true," she mumbles. You notice that she almost says the next words to herself rather than to him. "What about our kids, our memories, our life together over these years?"

"I need some air," he says and gets up from the couch. "I'm done with this."

At that moment, when her words fail, you watch her do something she has never done in fifteen years of marriage.

What does a baseball pitcher do when the other team hits his best pitch? Where does the "little engine that could" turn when she faces a mountain larger than all the others and too steep to overcome? What happens when the little engine can't? Having no answer, seeing him walk away, wordless to stop him, she stands up, grabs him, and tries physically to block his way. He moves one way and so does she. Words dissolve into the force of will.

"I'm not letting you go!" she shouts.

"Let me through!" he yells and begins to push.

Conscience calls to her. She lets him through but then gives in to multiplying words again. She follows him in a chase down the hall, through the living room to the front door.

"Leave me alone!" he yells and then slams the door behind him.

"I'm not leaving you!" she bellows through the door.

"That's just it!" he shouts as he walks to the car. "I'm leaving you!"

Throwing Bible Words About

In the days that follow, you watch as friends, family members, and church folks multiply words too. "He just needs to know what the Bible says and do it," one minister says to her. "You've let your looks go. You just need to get pretty and he will notice you more," another says to her.

It is not that we do not need God's Word in this. What else but his Word in the hands of his Spirit will light our path in Jesus? Appealing to his Word is paramount. The problem isn't God's Word. The problem is that we fall prey to what Job's friends did. We can be tempted to quote the Bible at people, to hurl verses almost as an incantation. We sometime act as though there is power in speaking the words themselves, like a witch reciting her spells. Get the words spoken correctly and the spell works. Misspeak the syllables and the spell won't work.

But the presence of things that we cannot control or immediately fix reminds us that though the Bible is God's revelation, it in itself is not his magic remedy. It lights our path by his Spirit, but it cannot always shield us from what he shows us there. Only the Christ that the Bible verses reveal can do this.

The husband walking out the door can quote Bible verses too. "I'm the unbeliever, and I want to leave," he quotes to his pastor. "The apostle Paul tells you that you have to let me go" (1 Cor. 7:15). He too has a power with words of his own.

One of the first signs that we are approaching the borders of attempting omnipotence is this: we believe that another is choosing a course of action because he or she simply isn't clear on what is right. Therefore, we believe that if we just work hard to explain what is right, then he or she will do the right thing. We think that all will be well if we simply make something plain to someone.

While our first step should always include making sure things have been made clear, most of us know from our own lives that often it is not a lack of clarity that troubles us. Often we already know the right thing to do, and we still choose otherwise. So why do leaders, parents, spouses, and friends often assume that if we just arrange the quotes the right way, or just say the verses enough times or loud enough, that such a change will immediately start to happen?

The Bible simply does not teach us that if we say the right words, right things will follow. Jesus taught us that the self-centered heart is tamed not by human will but by God's intervention. No one was more plain, reasonable, and clear than Jesus, and they crucified him. Somewhere along the way, those of us gifted with words will receive a painful reminder that it is Jesus and not our explanations that can change a heart. Words aren't strings. People aren't puppets. Eloquent speech isn't magic.

Imagine what the porch that morning would have become if we had believed that the best hope for that girl, her mom, and her dad amid the ruins was our formula of words, our multiplied pontifications choking out the space and the silence? There are hints of Herod in such an approach.

Jesus instead will often invite us to the more powerful way of quiet, prayer, and time. In this regard, Job's friends got it right when they sat silent with him in the ashes. The damage began when they spoke. Jesus will sit in the ashes on the broken porches of our lives and teach us how to trust him more than our multiplied words.

Raising Our Voices and Pointing Our Fingers

Then, when words and Scripture quoting fail, our temptation is to raise our voices and, in addition, to imply a more sinister or scandalous story. For those of us who have served a while in ministry, this temptation is very real because of the lies we have believed and the secrets that have burned us in the past. As words fail to solve someone's problem, those involved start to get louder and target character. Don't get me wrong—our character often warrants correction. But sometimes not in the ways we imagine. Job was not above needing correction and growth. But the character attacks made by Job's friends were misguided and cruel.

Fix-it-alls begin to think something like this: "This situation or person couldn't possibly be what it appears to be. We have quoted the Bible and made our arguments. Things should be fixed by now. There must be some hidden mischief here. We need to speak some more, but this time, louder and more accusatory."

So, we project onto our present situation the darkness that we imagine. We project something from one of our own similar past experiences. When that happens, we become like one who talks louder to a blind person or raises his voice at a foreigner who does not speak his language.

So now imagine again the situation of the director of ministry. Perhaps some men and women become red-faced finger pointers and call her a hypocrite. They maneuver to find some hidden debauchery in her life, tidbits and morsels for conversations and prayers. She warrants blame. She needs more growth and change than she knows.

But the growth and change she needs is more subtle and therefore not easily recognized apart from grace and nuanced mentoring. Her sins in this case, you see, are not of the talk-show variety. She has no gossip-magazine scandal hidden in her closets. Her sins and limits do not justify her husband's leaving. Yet a community of Jesus, behind closed doors, is tempted to whisper dark speculations in meetings opened with prayer. So sometimes the porch isn't enough. There must be dirt beneath it. We create foul scenarios and speak them.

"Did you have an affair?" someone asks her. "Are you a nag? Are you misusing the kids? What did you do to cause him to leave and to wreck your ministry?"

In my experience, when it is the woman who leaves the man in ministry, the accusations can sometimes become even more sinister and cruel.

Either way, it is easier for us to handle an illness when it has a clear name and a precise cause. Sitting in the doctor's office amid undiagnosed days of "I don't know" is much more difficult. We hate the feelings that come with unfixable and uncontrollable moments. We do not know how to do a day with unfixed feelings, so we flail about and knock the dishes off of their counters instead. At least we are exerting our power, we justify. We feel like we are doing something.

Similarly, a clearly named and precisely defined sin is easier to explain to an anxious constituency. The path for what to do seems plain, and our donor bases are made more secure. The stress more quickly abates.

So it is for our ministry plans and family hopes. Writing a nasty e-mail with words placed in ALL CAPS might feel empowering. But in the end this has as little power as reasoned words to fix what ails us. Imagine how we would have handled the porch that morning if we had believed that ALL CAPS dialogue would untrouble and control it? Imagine if we had projected onto the girl, the mom, and the dad worse things than were actually there, and filled the porch with pointing fingers?

Jesus will teach us the refusal to exaggerate another's sin or brokenness and will reveal his kindness and self-control on the porch. Time and patience become a means of finding the peace that Jesus gives and that everyone on that porch truly needs. Things needn't always be worse than they are. Sometimes they are bad enough already. The grace we need is to stop gossiping about it and instead wade into its waters so the peace of Jesus will find us there.

When adding accusations to our multiplied words, we can act as if we are in control of what others do. It is like what the mom says to the oldest son: "If you would just control your brother, then none of this would have happened." "If you would just change," one friend says to another, "then I would be okay." Translation: "My mood is your fault!" Job's friends sounded like this. When words and getting louder seem to fail, we blame with mean-spirited force. (We can even use money, positions, severances, and reputations as a threat to force another into action.)

In this case, there are areas in which the ministry director needs to grow and change. She knows that. But some believe that if she had just willed things correctly and clearly, then he would not have left her. They wonder how she could have allowed him to choose the prodigal life. They treat her as if her husband was only a child who warranted time-out if he disobeyed her. He left because she didn't control him.

So it is back on the porch. If the dad had just been loud enough and forceful on the phone and with the police, the daughter would naturally have complied. If the mom had just pleaded enough and cried enough, then the girl would naturally have willed the right thing.

But as human beings, men and women have their own wills. They have their own accountability to our Lord, quite apart from us. "Our will be done" is not the way the prayer goes. "Our will" is not the guide of another's conscience. We are accountable to God for how we relate to our neighbors, but we are not responsible or a lord for another's conscience and actions. Sometimes ministry leaders need help remembering this, especially on the porch.

Exposing Our Temptations

Defensiveness

When our place in the inner ring is threatened, we can add defensiveness to our faulty attempts to fix it all.

I remember this well regarding my own personal broken porches. As a single dad, with my children living with me and trying to care for them amid the loss of my ministry, amid a community of rumor and accusation, a man asked me directly, "Do you realize that you are a failure as a man?"

"Would you ask that if I was a woman and my husband had just left me?" I snapped back.

Another accused me of having a hidden secret that caused my wife to leave.

"It could seem likely that you are an abuser of your wife in secret. Are you? Are you an abuser?" I asked why the kids would be with me if that were true.

"Maybe you put her up to it," was the response.

I got up to walk out.

Rumors reached the ears of friends, colleagues, my kids. I try to set the records straight with multiplied words, long e-mails, and uncomforted emotions.

I leave five voice mail messages for a friend—within ten minutes.

A neighbor knocks to tell me my grass needs mowing. I close the front door.

An instructor for a kids' activity tells me that I've been late to the activities and need to do better. "Back off," I groan.

My pastor tells me that I'm like a man with both legs cut off and bleeding to death, while those around me are treating me like I broke my arm and did so on purpose. Yet when that same caring pastor asks me how I'm doing, I sometimes clam up or cynically snap back, "Why do you want to know?"

If my defensiveness has come in the form of emotional blasts, others defend by calm record keeping. Record keepers defend themselves in the way that I imagine the clergy in the good Samaritan story might have. Theirs was not a sin of commission—something they did. Theirs was the sin of omission—something they did not do. Leaving the broken man beaten by the side of the road, they could have easily defended themselves. They could have readily shown that they did all of their duty that day and never drawn attention to the beaten man. After all, his presence did not fall into their normal responsibilities. If someone did discover the broken man, the record keeper could have shown that they did nothing wrong to the man and justified why they respectively handled him the way they did.

Interestingly, the inner ring generally overlooks a cool record keeper much longer than it overlooks an emotional blaster. The first kind of defensiveness, emotional blasting, is easy to see and makes the inner ring squirm to retake control. The second kind, record keeping, functions to keep the inner ring more comfortable, more apparently in control with detailed defense, and so our ability to recognize this gospel substitute takes much longer.

Defensiveness only proves the point of our brokenness and exaggerates our faults in the eyes of others, particularly if those others already see what they want to be true about us rather than what actually is true about us. Although we are not the first to throw the punch when a bad call is made during a football game, our reactions are often what the referee sees. Or when we are the first to throw a punch and we get caught, we protest. Defensiveness has no power to heal. But the gospel does!

I sit for a while with a friend. "Anger does not bring about the kingdom of God," he gently says to me. We sit in the silence sipping tea. We sit in the ashes and wait together. We wait for Jesus. Gradually, he gives the stamina to be quiet when slandered, silent when gossiped about, entrusting our reputations more and more to him and less and less to our words, emotions, or record keeping.

The inner-ring politician, the word multiplier, the character assassin, the gossip, the intimidator, the record keeper, the trite Bible quoter, and the emotional blaster can each find forgiveness in Jesus, along with a kind of power that not only fixes but also heals. In Jesus, a power of a different kind triumphs.

Psalm Making

What does all this mean for us then, there on the cracked porch, when we're tempted to take up a Herodian strategy? By his grace Jesus intends to teach us psalm making as a way of life.

Exposing Our Temptations

> In the days of his flesh, Jesus offered up prayers and supplications, with loud cries and tears, to him who was able to save him from death, and he was heard because of his reverence. (Heb. 5:7)

The disciples had heard the Jesus way of praying. They had seen the rhythms of prayer by which Jesus ordered his days. They had asked him to teach them to pray (Luke 11:1). And three of them were meant to join him when resisting the Herodian way would test them most severely, but the sleep of sorrow and exhaustion kept them from it (Luke 22:45). In time, grace would teach them. They too would enjoy prayer as a way of life. In fact, they would in time tell pastors that prayer is the thing they are meant to busy themselves with (Acts 6:4).

For years, by Jesus's grace, my mentor Bob has prayed in the quiet, away from others and in the midst of it all too. Sitting in a lawn chair in his suburban garage while he peeked out onto his neighborhood street, he took up a pen in the early morning to pour out his cares upon the Lord, like water pouring over and drenching the pages of his journal. Lying prostrate, writhing, pained into the floor of his bedroom in the middle of the night, he appealed for vindication amid terrible slanders while he refused to defend himself. God was his shield and refuge. Herodian ways for securing relief pounded on Bob's door but found no audience.

I, on the other hand, have been slow to learn. I remember the glen in Colorado. Bob took a bunch of us college students there for a conference with the Navigators. It was 2:00 in the morning. "Zachary," he said. "Zachary."

My ears began to tune in the frequency from my sound sleep. "What?" I countered with irritation.

"Let's go pray."

"What?!" I replied in disbelief.

"Let's go pray," Bob repeated.

What Bob pursued that night and I entered with strong grousing became among the most memorable times of prayer I have known. Bob was gently, by example, trying to teach me something that Jesus had been teaching him. I did not take advantage of such a rare example, not until the dark events of my life left no one holding a candle, and my own floor gathered the writhing tears of my loud cries to God.

By "psalm making," I do not intend that we possess King David's place or a prophetic role of inspiration. The psalms we make are not authoritative for the instruction of the people of God. But David's psalm making is instructive for us. His psalms divinely reveal to us what it sounds like and looks like for a human being to choose God through prayer rather than choose the flesh when the going gets tough and unfixable. Through psalm making, God enables us to sit with the anointed praying man and to learn what it means to cast our cares upon the Lord because he cares for us (1 Pet. 5:7). "The Psalms, in other words, are the school for people learning to pray."[11] Many of us, acquainted with praying, have yet to learn what it means to resist Herodian schemes, edicts, or tantrums on the porch and to instead choose prayer as our way for handling what frightens us there.

On several occasions we are shown how David responded with psalms when in danger, or slandered, or facing a situation that he as king could not fix. Resisting taking his own revenge, for example, Psalm 59 was written "when Saul sent men to watch [David's] house in order to kill him" (Psalm 59 title).

> Deliver me from my enemies, O my God;
> protect me from those who rise up against me. . . .
> Each evening they come back,
> howling like dogs
> and prowling about the city. . . .
> But I will sing of your strength;
> I will sing aloud of your steadfast love in the morning.
> For you have been to me a fortress,
> and a refuge in the day of my distress. (Ps. 59:1, 6, 14, 16)

Pouring out his heart to God and waiting for God to work upon the broken porches of his life was David's normal approach. When he was hiding in a cave from Saul, or when enemies revealed to Saul David's whereabouts, or when Absalom his own son was trying to dethrone him, David chose candid prayers from his heart. He expressed through psalms the full range of his emotions, appealing to God rather than Herodian huffs and puffs to blow his enemies' houses down or to secure his own.[12] In response to very specific life situations that were overwhelming or devouring him, David chose God in prayer.

Exposing Our Temptations

Through prayer David entrusted to God not only specific situations of fear or trouble or danger but also specific occasions of his own sin. When David did choose sinful paths rather than God's ways, the wreckage he made of himself and others poured forth from his heart to God as well.

> Have mercy on me, O God,
> according to your steadfast love;
> according to your abundant mercy
> blot out my transgressions.
> Wash me thoroughly from my iniquity
> and cleanse me from my sin! (Ps. 51:1–2)

But David couldn't pray Psalm 51 regarding Bathsheba until a very long time after the fact. It was not until Nathan the prophet confronted David that his heart bent into surrendered repentance.

To "make psalms" means to become specific about our actual lives. To become specific in these ways means that we will have to experience very disorienting thoughts, uncomfortable feelings, and the knowledge that nothing will be fixed on the other side of our prayer until God does something.

Being specific, experiencing discomfort, humbling ourselves, and having to wait while the unfixed pain rages on—no wonder Herod's ways appeal more to us. With Herod's ways, we can rage but not feel sorrow. We can scheme and control and not have to feel fear. We can keep all of our thoughts intact and not have to wonder what to do or how to live an hour in the dark. No waiting is required. We do not have to acknowledge our own sin or feel the weight of what we did to another. We never have to appear weak or emotional or sad to anyone. Every sin is justified.

To spend time in a Jesus kind of psalm making feels like a mess. How can such messes prove to be a good use of time with all that we must accomplish for God? After all, few around us will value this. Many will want us to stomp about, get busy, and stop life from being hard to keep them from having to trust God and make psalms. For each of these reasons and more, I am still too slow to surrender.

I had memorized this catechism question, Question 98 of the Westminster Shorter Catechism, regarding prayer for ordination all those years ago:

> *What is prayer?* Prayer is an offering up of our desires unto God for things agreeable to his will in the name of Christ, with confession of our sins, and thankful acknowledgment of his mercies.

At ordination time, I was glad about taking my true desires before the Lord. But when I am standing on the porch with a girl curled pajama-ed in a ball, with a front door like a wall and an exasperated mother weeping on the other side, what does it mean to enter the conflicting desires in my heart? What does it mean to seek out which of those desires are agreeable and disagreeable to God's will, with a willingness to admit my own capacity for sin on that porch? What does it mean to find a frame of mind to give thanks for God's mercies even when I see nothing but painful flesh having its way in the moment? This calls me to humility, and I am often resistant to the endeavor. But this endeavor is the very means of power and peace that Jesus gives. His name rests upon the doorpost. This is his workshop. He calls us in. There is grace and power there.

And so psalm reading has taken up a partially furnished residence in my life. A historic Christian practice is to enter the rhythms of five psalms each day—early morning, mid-morning, noon, supper, and evening. In this way we all read the Psalms once a month.

At the moment, I usually seem to manage only one or two. But these prayers day upon day are gradually informing my own. The language that resists Herodian ways is fertilizing the soil of my soul.

Stolen Paintings

Psalm making reminds me of the poet who once explored the life of a stolen painting. He imagines such a great treasure tragically "stacked / in the warehouse somewhere . . . gazing at the back of the butcher paper / they are wrapped in," no longer able to see or be seen by "the rapt glad faces of those who love art."[13]

What then can such a treasure do? The poet answers by describing the inconsolable of the situation: "In their captivity, they may dream of rescue / but cannot cry for help. Their paint / is inert and crackled, their linen friable."

Is all lost then? For a moment it seems as if it is: "Only criminals know where they are. / The gloom of criminality enshrouds them." Hard questions therefore press in amid the ache: "Why have we been stolen?" "Who has benefitted?"

The poet then seems to surmise two options for how to live as a treasure stolen from its beauty and purpose. First, in our words, they "mount an offense even though the match is not theirs to win." "They have one stratagem," the poet says. It is "the same old one: / to be themselves, on and on." Second, while they remain what they were made for amid the cruel misplacement they face, rescue will not be required from somewhere beyond them. Someone "wise and kindly" is needed if such "disappeared excellence" is to be "restored to its throne."

The peace Jesus gives is meant to restore the disappeared excellence of God's Eden to its majestic place again. This is his to do.

Psalm making is an act of faith. Faith by its nature waits sightless amid the veiled and not yet. Inconsolable things are dumbfounded. For all of their criminality, faith will not quit. What faith is enough? The smallest ounce is enough. How alarming it must be to inconsolable things that a rebellion has been mounted against them—so small yet so strong. How much faith is enough? For the sick woman to whom Jesus said, "Your faith has made you well" (Matt. 9:22), all she did was appeal to Jesus. Like the Father whose daughter was healed, all he did was fall at Jesus's feet and implore him to come to his house (Luke 8:40–42). Those who were not healed by Jesus possessed the same mustard seed.

We unsettle inconsolable things when we act as if there is something beyond them whose power could bypass them, overcome them, and could reach us in spite of them. This is the unnerving little power that God revealed through Daniel, who, when faced with death or denial of his faith, chose death. God could save him, Daniel said. But even if God chose not to, God was still God and Daniel was still his, and not even death can change that (Dan. 3:8–16). The psalm making of faith is a sign on the porch that there is more there than the miseries we see and feel.

The signs are what we plant in the barren ground. Jesus did this with miracles. Lazarus raised was a sign that Jesus was the resurrection and the life. The blind man given sight was the sign that Jesus is the light of the world. The people fed was a sign that Jesus is the bread of life. As a result, every dying person, every blind person, and every hungry person has been shown that something more powerful than death, disease, and hunger exists. After demonstrating that power, Jesus humbled himself and made the cross a sign. All has been paid for; the tomb has emptied! Suffering traumas on the porch remain. But they remain on borrowed time and will not have the last word.

So, every act of faithful resistance to Herodian ways, every act of Jesus hope, love, patience, gentleness, and waiting in Christ, is a war cry, a sign hoisted in the shadowlands that there is more than sin and misery in the world. Herod's ways have met their match. Another way of life has more power than his.

These signs of Jesus that our faith posts throughout the cities and countrysides of our lives, lead us to psalm making on the porch.

> O Lord, all my longing is before you;
> my sighing is not hidden from you.
> My heart throbs; my strength fails me,
> and the light of my eyes—it also has gone from me. . . .
> But I am like a deaf man; I do not hear,
> like a mute man who does not open his mouth. . . .
> But for you, O LORD, do I wait;
> it is you, O Lord my God, who will answer.
> (Ps. 38:9–10, 13, 15)

We learn that shadows of death remain but that our fears don't have to remain with them. We learn that our enemies taunt us by moving in next door and staring at us as we step outside. But we also declare that the Lord comes and sets a table and spreads it with food and invites us to sit with him and eat. There we feast with the Lord in the presence of our enemies. And though rival kings assert their powers and raise their Herodian fists, causing mothers to weep for their children, there is a cup that overflows, an anointing that declares in the tyrant's hearing: surely goodness and mercy will not quit and will not die.

No matter what we face, all of our lives are traveled with goodness and mercy pursuing us. Soon enough, these and not Herod will have the last word. This is what we declare on the broken porches of the world with our faith as a sign and our psalm making as a way of life—tokens of the peace that Jesus gives.

Conclusion

This past year I received a letter from one of the elders who had stood with me on that porch that morning some thirteen years ago. Lori is a woman now. I learned from the letter that with Jesus she had gotten a handle on her anorexia. She was volunteering to minister to high school students at the church. She was getting married to one of the dear men who had also grown up in the church. Never in a million years would I have thought that those two would love each other and build a life of grace together!

What brought the peace to her life? To be honest, I'm not fully sure. One of the elders wrote an e-mail once a week to Lori throughout her trauma. Every Monday it simply began, "Good Morning." In it he spoke of the beauty he saw in her and the grace of Jesus that he prayed for her.

Another elder allowed Lori to live with his family for a while as her family sought grace to make it through. There was some counseling. There were lots of tears and setbacks. Psalms were cried and poured out.

A lot of time went by. Years of unfixed days with no seeming answers or remedies. So how did the healing come amid such inconsolable things? How will it remain amid the inconsolable things that are still hers to navigate?

I don't know fully. But I do know this: Jesus gives peace differently from the world. Jesus untroubles us differently than Herod and his strategies would. Jesus fixes things, but the power he uses differs from ours. The purpose and timing in which he does it differs from ours. It rementors us.

Scriptures return. Sins and miseries will not have the last word. Nothing can separate us from the love of God in Christ Jesus (Rom. 8:39). "O death, where is your sting?" (1 Cor. 15:55). We are more than conquerors in Christ Jesus (Rom. 8:37).

All I know, as I think back to that porch, is this: the match wasn't ours to win. It was his. And he did.

Calling for the Elders to Pray

When facing difficult and sometimes inconsolable things such as suffering and sickness, the prayers of the elders join our psalm making when we mount our offense. Jesus gives us this kind and powerful presence.

> Is anyone among you sick? Let him call for the elders of the church, and let them pray over him, anointing him with oil in the name of the Lord. (James 5:14)

Over the years, on Sunday evenings or Saturday mornings, every month or quarterly, we've set aside a day of prayer at the churches I've served. Alongside these regular public gatherings, sometimes the call comes and we gather in a living room or by a hospital bed.

"Let him call," James says. His words bring to mind the bent-boned and the eye-blind, forgotten by the sides of roads. News would reach these wheezy-lunged and sore-skinned. "Jesus is coming!" they heard. "Jesus is drawing near!"

Abrupt to find a voice, the blood-coughed tried to garble a word out or to knee-crawl on pebbled dirt to touch a thread of his garb. Either way, arthritic or tremulous hands finger-fought to raise the banner, "Son of David, have mercy on me!" With this we learn that in Jesus, the sick have a voice. Their call resembles nothing of nuisance or bother. The mentally harassed and body weary are not shoved to the outskirts of his community. So there is little surprise that praying for the sick asserts itself on an elder's job description. Elders are not Jesus. But Jesus has called out to them and placed a gracious vocation upon their lives. They are shepherds given to glimpse and resemble for others the presence, teachings, tone, and expression of the true and good Shepherd—that Shepherd who knows his sheep by name (John 10:3).

Sometimes there are two of us. Other times there are more of us elders along with friends or house-group members who tiptoe into the room, nervous with love for the one who suffers. Empathy. Intimacy. Compassion. Smiles with tear-drop eyes. These are like spring breezes brought into the stale air. The followers of Jesus step into the mud. They kneel into the grimy mess and take up the hand of the one who lies there.

This drawing near in itself reenacts how Jesus treated the worn-out ones. It signifies for the world that the sick one is cherished by God and that God's people not only rejoice with those who rejoice but also weep with those who weep. In Jesus we belong not only to him but, through him, to one another, such as we are. Whatever happens from this point on, the present love of Jesus has already been signified and manifest. Such presence is rare in the world. Linger here. Do not rush.

One of the elders, a maintenance man by day, reaches his dirt-creased knuckles into his pocket for the oil. He hands it to the pastor. The oil was bought at a local bookstore. It smells like incense. But any oil will do, for the oil is like the dirt in the maintenance man's hands. The dirt is not the work but a signal of the work that was done. Both the dirt and the oil offer no defense for soap. Neither can outlast the scrubbing. Both will release their grasp from the skin and wash away into the sink or tub drain that night. But though the symbol disappears, the work it revealed remains. Like Old Testament anointing, a setting apart has taken place.

The work to be done has to do with the name of the Lord. There is no incantation or spell here. One can recite the words "in Jesus's name" and still know quite little of what it means to pray in the name of the Lord. Name dropping is a tool used by the arrogant to show others what kind of resources, friendship, and connections the arrogant has. Among the humble, name dropping is rarely used except when a need rises that no other remedy can meet. Either way, one's name reveals one's character and work and ways. The elder's work or character or ways can do nothing to fix this inconsolable thing. They humble themselves, therefore. They appeal to the character, resources, fellowship, and provision of Jesus.

This gathering, in sum, is a sign of Jesus's active presence and heart. The oil is a sign that this person and this moment belong to him. The prayer in his name is a declaration that only Jesus possesses the wisdom, the resources, the provision, and the power to govern what ails us. (Even our good use of medicine and our active gratitude for good doctors and nurses are like shoes ultimately held together by the stitching and laces of God.)

The Prayer of Faith

At some point, one of the elders explains these things briefly to the one who has called. Then the one who has called expresses, if he can, what he is asking of Jesus. Then, amid flip-flops or loafers, coffee breath and sniffles, an elder dabs oil on his finger or thumb, touches the forehead of the sick, in silence or with words (James gives no directive). If with words, it can sound in substance something like this:

> Barbara, Jesus belongs to you. You belong to him. He alone can save you and mend you. Through him you were created. By him you have been rescued. For him you now live by his grace. You are a daughter of the King. We take up your cause with him. His throne is one of grace. Let us go to him in this time of need.

Then the prayers of faith begin. Different elders pray, quietly and out loud, in turn or all at once (according to cultural custom), as others in attendance pray alongside. A prayer of faith has no requisite tone of voice or body posture. God does not hear us because we are loud or soft. There is no amount or type of words. God does not hear us because we use enough words or the grandest words. Faith is "the assurance of things hoped for, the conviction of things not seen" (Heb. 11:1). In Jesus, elders pray with assurance and conviction, even if as only possessing a mustard seed of both.

But why must faith attend the elders' prayers? This is no last-rites kind of praying. The elder talks to the Lord as one who sees a future in Jesus for the sick person. There is another side to this sickness. It will not have the last word!

> The prayer of faith will save the one who is sick, and the Lord will raise him up. (James 5:15)

To believe that the Lord rules over the mud that mucks us up and can say a word to heal us challenges elders who see with their human eyes in that moment only men, women, and children who are sick-bent, thought-haunted, or brain-broken. When our only tangible piece of sacredness is a bit of oil that we bought for $5.95 down the street, it can seem that our words fall pummeled from the sky in a blitzkrieg of disease. After all, we who are praying just finished a burger and fries in the car on our way over here.

But "Elijah was a man with a nature like ours," James reminds us. "The prayer of a righteous person has great power as it is working," he assures us (James 5:16–17). Our faith is not in our words, our emotions, our worked-up agitation, or our limited and frail nature. Our faith is in the Lord, whose will and wisdom and power are able to sustain the loved one in their suffering or to free them partially or altogether from it.

I have prayed in this fashion for many people over the years (though not as many as I could have, due to my early fears about the spookiness of faith-healer misuse of such people and such texts). I am a Presbyterian. We Presbyterians are rarely known for our forays into the supernatural. We get quite seasick on the waters of such discussions. At our worst it is because we fear what we cannot control. We use doctrine to clearly state what we are against and sometimes forget to state positively what we are for. At our best we are tired of the misuse of people and the misrepresentation of Jesus that these kinds of biblical texts are often used to perpetrate.

With all of that in mind, I hope you can appreciate what it means for me to say that I have seen persons actually healed in the context of calling on the elders to pray. On one occasion, it was three weeks after the prayer. The doctors could not explain why the blindness-causing defect was no longer present. Healing can come minutes or years later. And yet on most occasions when I've prayed as an elder in this way, the prayed-for healing has not come. It seems to me that we pray with faith either way—faith that God can mend us with a word in an instant and faith that God can sustain us by his grace even if he does not remove our suffering (Luke 22:42) or leaves us with our ailment (2 Cor. 12:8–9).

Confessing and Forgiving

All of this has led me to appreciate more thoroughly the intimacy, promise, and soul-searching that such compassionate presence and prayer for the sick surface. No wonder James shifts gears from the healing of the body to the healing of the soul.

> And if he has committed sins, he will be forgiven. Therefore, confess your sins to one another and pray for one another, that you may be healed. (James 5:15–16)

While sickness can indicate on rare occasions the presence of sin as a cause (1 Cor. 11:30), on most occasions sickness has nothing to do with individual sin (Job 2:1–7; John 9:1–3) but rather represents the fact that Eden is broken and heaven is not yet.

But when sickness yells at us and taunts us like a bully and no one comes to rescue us, there in the mud we begin to see things in the thoughts and emotions of our inner being that we did not realize. Ugly things that reveal that we are not as righteous as we once thought. We see our need for a savior all the more. We begin to confess. The sickness of body or mind throws a brick at the mirror of our perfect image. We see our reflection shattered and find ourselves more needy for grace and the merit of Jesus than we ever knew when our joints and muscles worked.

This is probably why I have come to count such times of prayer when the elders are called for as among the most precious of my life in ministry. Rarely but in such moments does one feel the presence, the work symbolized, the faith, and the broken confession and humble appeal to the Savior as in these moments with Jesus's care for the sick.

It won't be long. Likely, I too, in time will lie beside the road scooted to the outskirts of community, crying out, "Son of David, have mercy on me!" With hope I imagine some young pastor and ordinary elders with their coffee breath and their Bibles coming to my bedside in the name of Jesus. I will hear them beseech my Lord on my behalf. Their presence, their empathy, their touch, and their tenacity to lay hold of that which I cannot see, their gracious reception of my newfound confessions of my true need for forgiveness, will lead me to Jesus. The throne of grace awaits. These sickened bones on this couch or bed on which I will lie cannot and will not keep me from it.

CHAPTER FIVE

Know-It-All

Walking through Decisions, Discipline, and Sin

"A man . . . has no choice but to be ignorant, but he does not have to be a fool."[1]

I gave up on the moon once. It was early evening. The clouds had taken the night off, and the moon had its opportunity. Commanding center stage, it boldly and confidently lit up the dark hemisphere. The kids and I watched the performance through our van windows. We were driving on Highway 64 toward home.

"Do you see the moon, Caleb?" we said almost in unison. Then we stretched our bodies into odd postures and leaned against seatbelts. We tried to gain a sense of little Caleb's car-seat perspective. We finally found it and pointed toward the side window as if we saw someone famous. "There it is, Caleb! There's the moon!" Caleb's two-year-old blue eyes adjusted to our pointing view. His gaze widened.

"I see dit!" he rejoiced. "I see dit!"

We all erupted with celebration. "What do you think, Caleb?" I asked. "What do you think of that moon?"

Caleb paused. He looked intently into the sky. The moonlight reached through the window and lightly touched his left cheek. Then little Caleb surprised us all.

"Broke, Daddy," he said.

With sudden urgency, he thrust his arm and pointed with his finger out the window. "The moon broken," he clarified.

We questioned one another with our eyes and a giggle. I looked again through the window up at center stage. The view before my eyes did not explain what Caleb perceived. I paused. I lingered. Then it began to make sense. The moon was not full that night. Caleb's young eyes did not take the partial dark of the moon for granted the way my eyes did. In Caleb's eyes, part of the moon was missing. "Oh, Caleb," I explained. "The moon isn't broken. It's a crescent moon."

Caleb did not understand the word *crescent* but it sounded monster-like. His face fell with seriousness. With furrowed brows he pleaded with me, "Daddy, fix it!"

We all laughed out loud. Caleb looked out the window again and then back at me. "Daddy can't fix the moon, buddy," I chuckled. "It's too far away and too big."

Without hesitation Caleb looked hard at me and said, "Daddy, go there. Daddy, go there and fix moon!"

As my eyes met the expectation in his, I was confounded. I had identified the moon as "crescent" and stopped further observation. (I later learned that my category was mistaken. It was actually a three-quarter, gibbous moon that we watched that night.) No matter, Caleb wasn't satisfied with the explanation of *the sort* of moon it was, whether crescent or gibbous. The luminary was shadowed, and little Caleb was trying to account for the shadow. What I called "crescent," Caleb called "broken." He wanted it to be made well again.[2]

Is this something of what it means "to know," to see through the description we give of a thing to the thing itself, and to respond with heart and will according to what the thing warrants? "If you had known what this means . . ." Jesus said to the Bible teachers of his day (Matt. 12:7). Is Jesus saying that "to know" must include making substantial contact not just with the description and explanation of a thing but with the thing itself?

The way I saw the moon, named its kind, and dismissed further attention from it (in contrast to how Caleb looked beyond its sort to the moon itself) causes me to think of the words said by the Bible teacher to Jesus. He and Jesus looked at the same woman but very differently. The woman cried tears upon the feet of Jesus.

> Now when the Pharisee who had invited him saw this, he said to himself, "If this man were a prophet, *he would have known who and what sort* of woman this is who is touching him, for she is a sinner." (Luke 7:39)

Knowing in Sorts

It is not that knowing in sorts is wrong. After all, this religious leader knew his Bible well. Proverbs, for example, identifies this sort of woman and the sort of man who will join with her. The people of God are taught to identify these sorts of neighbors and to seek the wisdom and grace to choose differently and more wisely for ourselves (Prov. 7:1–27).

Therefore, this Pharisee in Luke wasn't a bad student. He correctly identified the sort of woman. He also had chosen a life with a different prize in mind. He therefore had avoided the kind of relational damage that such sorts inflict. Sorting as a means of knowing can help us to identify different conditions of heart. It gives us categories for naming those conditions. The religious leader did well. The Pharisee was right. Jesus likewise had this knowledge. He too rightly identified the woman as a sinner (Luke 7:48). As it related to the sort, the teacher and the pupil were agreed.

But when left by itself, this knowing everything by its sorts harms us. Just as I looked no further with the moon after I had identified its sort, so the religious leader paid no more attention to the woman once he identified her sort. In contrast, Jesus's knowledge takes into account what it means to know not just her sort but her. "Do you see *this woman*?" Jesus asks.

Knowing in sorts not only has a tendency to make us impatient with another's humanity, but it also fosters blind spots in us. Though he is correct about the kind of woman she has been, the Pharisee:

- either does not have an equally good category for repentance, or he does but has no experience with applying it. True repentance is happening right in front of his eyes, and he does not account for it (v. 48).
- either does not have an equally palpable category for personal hospitality, or he does but cannot or will not apply it. His relational treatment of Jesus is profoundly impoverished (vv. 44–46).
- either does not have a robust way of sorting out forgiveness, or he does but is blind to his own inability to put it into practice. This woman is seeking forgiveness right in front of him, and he cannot see it (vv. 41–43).
- either does not have a solid category for sorting out what true love for God and neighbor is, or he does but has little of it in his own being. True love for God and neighbor is happening right in front of him, and he despises it while remaining blind to his own absence from it (v. 47).

Jesus seeks to teach him to see beyond the sort to the woman herself. She is not a theory but actually standing in his living room, within his capacity to act, needing a tissue as the tears roll down her face and the pangs of sin tear at her heart.

The Key to Knowledge

"Why I'm what some people call, 'a Calvinist.'" That was the title. It totaled about sixty or so pages. The spine that bound it was red or blue plastic, and the cover was clear so that the title was front and center for the reader.

I was the author. I was twenty-two and zealous. I was devouring a little book by A. W. Pink entitled *The Sovereignty of God*. I wanted those whose adult table I wanted to join to know the truth as I saw it at the time. So I sent this treatise to my family and friends. What better way to show Jesus's love to loved ones than by writing and sending a document they did not expect, to answer questions they were not asking, with a tone that was not warranted, in order to defend an argument that they were not engaged in or had heard of, and all of this by surprise without so much as a conversation?

G. K. Chesterton (whom I would not have read at the time because he was not my "sort" of Jesus follower) once said that there was a kind of thought that stops thought.[3] I've come to believe that what Chesterton said about this brand of skepticism in his generation at least partially describes what Jesus meant when he spoke to those who handled the Bible in his. By this time I knew that Jesus does not coddle church leaders who misuse his teachings to promote error. What I would later learn is that Jesus likewise does not coddle church leaders who use knowledge, even of good and proper things, as a tool for arrogance and spite.

> Woe to you lawyers! For you have taken away the key of knowledge. You did not enter yourselves, and you hindered those who were entering. (Luke 11:52)

Jesus says that the Bible knowledge the teachers communicated "took away the key" that others needed to actually know God. A key opens and locks a door. They described the door for people, but they had no way to open the door for themselves or for others. Make no mistake: when it came to door description, they were accredited experts. They spent their days gathering people to look at the door, to painstakingly memorize every line, crack, corner, color, and carving. The Bible teachers and the congregations possessed an expert (keyless) knowledge of an unopened door.

The problem was not the Bible itself but how it was being used apart from Jesus. After all, a light shone into our eyes is still a light that shines in the darkness, but it does not help us to see. The problem isn't the light itself, for the light retains the capacity to illumine. The problem is the way we are using it. Such light so used in our eyes actually blinds us for a moment. We blink and blink when the light is pulled away. We see spots. Exposure to such a torch certainly gives us an experience of light that is powerful and unforgettable, but this kind of power neither aids our vision nor clarifies our path. We stumble with squint amid the blur once we try to walk. Because of this, a wise old pastor was right: "It is possible for us to develop a false notion of knowledge."[4]

Forgetting Where We've Been

I had just given Eric his first Bible. He had shared with me what Jesus meant to him during these first few days of saving grace. We smiled a lot and cried some. There was awe and wonder and play. A sense of gratitude filled the room. He didn't know much of anything yet, concerning life in Jesus. But the joy of Jesus's Spirit can adorn a person even though he has never yet heard of the book of Habakkuk, has read only a few lines in the Bible, and has only prayed in Jesus four or five times in his whole life (and this in the last two days!). It does us good to remember this about God's ways with the lost and found (Luke 15:5–7).

But then a knock banged the door, and I opened it. Standing there was one of the elders at the church. He had stopped by to pick up something for Sunday school class.

"Hey Jason!" I said to the elder.[5] "I'd like you to meet Eric. Eric is a brand-new Christian. We are meeting for the first time today and celebrating together. I just gave Eric his first Bible."

The elder shook the new convert's hand and said hello. What he said next surprised me. "So, Eric," he said. "What is your opinion of Westminster Larger Catechism Question 109?"

Eric smiled blankly and looked at me.

I remember that long-ago moment. I look at it like a mirror. It warns me and raises a question. How come so much of our Christian knowledge robs us of joy, wonder, awe, play, dependence, and the need to learn and be humble? How do we get to the place where we forget that there was a time that we too didn't know what the Gospel of John was, much less how to find it in the Bible or how to read it when we did? What is it about how we Christians sometimes view growth in knowledge that enables us to belittle or demean or judge or confound or overwhelm a person who is opening his first Bible for the first time? The haunting answer is that the Serpent's temptation still whispers to us: "You will be like God, *knowing* . . ." (Gen. 3:5).

Like Adam and Eve, we too are tempted to know as God knows and to take his superior position of knowledge when relating to others. The problem is that even though God knows what we do not, and this to an extent that dwarfs us, he remains humble toward us. Tempted to omniscience, we fool ourselves on both counts. What we do know does not compare to God. And the way we relate with what we know often little resembles the humility of God.

In his compelling novel *The Idiot*, Dostoevsky describes those know-it-alls who strive for appearances among others in society. Sick in body with childlike nobility of soul, Prince Muishkin acts as a foil to the know-it-all way of life. "You know, I sometimes think it is a good thing to be odd," the prince observes. "We can forgive one another more easily and be more humble."[6]

By "odd," the prince meant an awareness of our own weaknesses, sins, insanities, limits, and societal imperfections. To those who were striving to hide such things by a continuous appeal to what and who they know, the prince observed:

> No one can begin by being perfect—there is much that one cannot understand of life at first. In order to attain to perfection one must begin by failing to understand much. And if we take in knowledge too quickly, we very likely are not taking it in at all.[7]

"If he had known," the Pharisee said of Jesus. He mistook Jesus's compassion for the woman as a lack of knowledge rather than as an abundance of it. Simultaneously the Bible teacher failed to understand that the sinful woman knew something substantially more about truth than he did in that moment. Her "oddness" and the "odd" way Jesus related to her revealed an understanding that the Pharisee, for all of his learning, had not yet learned. Jesus is setting before the Pharisee an opportunity to learn in a living room how the doctrines of the Scriptures are meant to live.

Keyless at the Door

If it looks like a duck and quacks like a duck, it just might be a goose. This notion likewise did not occur to Job's friends. To them, the "sort" was obvious. They defined Job and barged in. It would not have been hard. The Scriptures are clear:

> Whoever despises the word brings destruction on himself,
> but he who reveres the commandment will be rewarded.
> (Prov. 13:13)

> Disaster pursues sinners,
> but the righteous are rewarded with good. (Prov. 13:21)

But like me with sending my early treatise to my family, like the elder with the new believer, and like the religious leader with the woman, Job's friends did not consider how a particular individual's story could require more in God's name than merely finding the correct identification of a verse or a sort and then rendering our judgments and sermons. Sorts, when left unchecked, speed us up and make us hasty. The Scriptures also tell us:

> There is a righteous man who perishes in his righteousness, and there is a wicked man who prolongs his life in his evildoing. (Eccles. 7:15)

> There is a vanity that takes place on earth, that there are righteous people to whom it happens according to the deeds of the wicked, and there are wicked people to whom it happens according to the deeds of the righteous. (Eccles. 8:14)

Sorts overlook important contextual information. We forget that God gave us the maxims of Proverbs alongside the complexities of Job and Ecclesiastes.

Context and sorts remind me of beginning a six-week summer Greek class for seminary. During the lunch break each day, we went to the basketball court and played "hippos," the game of "horse" that we proudly converted with our newfound expertise in Greek vocabulary! After playing, we'd gather, sit on the lawn under a tree, share each other's burdens, and pray for one another before we went back into the afternoon grammar exercises.

Not many days into this routine, an upperclassman walked boldly toward us. His face was firm, his brow cocked. Sternly he began to rebuke us:

> Brothers, I warn you! You are obviously proud and stubborn. It is obvious that you want everyone to see you praying. You want the rest of us to see how spiritual and holy you are. I know. I too was once a new student like yourselves. I too wanted to show off to everyone like you do now. But I was wrong and so are you! Jesus calls us to "go to our closets" to pray. You are disobeying his teachings. You call yourselves future pastors? Stop praying in public. You are sinning. You are too proud. You need to repent!

If there was light for our path from the goodness of the Scripture our brother quoted, we had a hard time seeing it. His use of "light" made us squint our eyes. If there was something beautiful and redemptive about who he had been when he first started seminary and how Jesus had been changing him, we were too blurred in vision by his light to see what he was trying to tell us.

We began to object. We had never met him before. We were praying for each other because of the many stresses we all faced with the recent moves, family adjustments, and the challenges of Greek. We sat out under a tree because of the summer breeze and the blue sky. If it had been winter, we would have sat inside somewhere for prayer. We doubted the sort he assumed of us.

We also began to ask questions. "Is he saying that if we ever see someone praying in view of another on the seminary campus then he is sinning?" "Are we justified in passionately rebuking people without discerning whether they know any better or as if they have nothing to learn to help them grow?" "Is Jesus against anyone ever praying in front of someone else?" "If so, didn't Jesus pray in front of his disciples and in the presence of others?"

I'm not sure that his understanding or approach gave us the key to knowledge that our Lord is talking about. Likewise, I'm not sure that our responses enabled us (or him) to find it. In fact, for all of our mutual knowledge of the Bible, I don't think we helped each other to see very much at all.

This is likely because sorts, by themselves, tempt to the false notion that being wrong is necessarily and only a sin. God cannot be in the presence of sin, we surmise. So if you sin, you're out! Once we make this leap, we lose the capacity to give anyone room to learn or grow or make mistakes.

How different Jesus is! Though others may see only what they label you, Jesus sees you. This can frighten us. Few see us as we are, and fewer remain when they do. But there is a friend who sticks closer than a brother. He knows what you do not. He commands you to stop repenting because you do not know everything. He reaches for you. He points you to the sinner standing in your living room. "Do you see?" he asks. The asking is a teaching. What bounty there is to learn at his feet here!

Mistake Making and Room to Grow

Consider the apostle Peter's journey with Jesus. He makes so many mistakes and commits damaging sins. When would you say that Peter "arrived," or "got it"?

He walks on water but worries about the storm and sinks. Yet Jesus does not act as if Peter has no faith. He acknowledges that Peter's faith is real, but "little." Jesus then invites Peter into a dialogue for learning. "Why did you doubt?" The tone isn't harsh. The rebuke isn't demeaning. The relationship isn't over. Falling short and trying are part of the training (Matt. 14:29–33).

Peter later tries to stop Jesus from washing his feet (John 13:6–8). Peter is wrong, but this is no sin. Jesus tells us so. Jesus has room for Peter to encounter things that he has no category for and has yet to learn. Jesus says Peter is acting this way because he does not yet understand. Peter's need to grow and learn is further illustrated by his asking Jesus questions because he doesn't understand (Matt. 15:15).

Then Peter declares what no one else did or did as boldly at the moment: "You are the Christ, the Son of the Living God!" (Matt. 16:16). At that moment we think to ourselves, "Surely, Peter has now arrived! His knowing is complete!"

But immediately after this, Peter reveals that a correct and genuine profession of faith in Jesus does not dismiss folly from his life. "Get behind me, Satan!" are our Lord's words for Peter's boneheaded desire to keep Jesus from the cross (Matt. 16:23). Yet even with these harshest of words that Peter would hear from Jesus, Jesus did not separate from Peter, cast him out, or treat him as anything other than his true friend, follower, and brother.

Peter's follies abound when he declares that his faith is superior and his commitment strong (Matt. 26:33–35). He has no idea how terribly he has overestimated himself or how spiritually charged with satanic attack his circumstances. If not for the intercession of Jesus, Peter along with the others would have been sifted like wheat (Luke 22:31). And yet Peter keeps falling asleep when Jesus asks him to watch and pray (Mark 14:37).

He cuts off the ear of Malchus and receives Jesus's rebuke (John 18:10–11). Peter denies Jesus with cussing and blaspheming. The rooster crows, and he weeps bitterly (Mark 16:66–72). And yet Jesus pursues him, loves him, and keeps him (Mark 16:7).

Peter hurts and feels stung by Jesus's words, and yet these very words are restoring him (John 21:15–19). Even after the resurrection, Peter hides in fear after seeing the empty tomb (John 20:10, 19–22) and later requires Paul's rebuke because of how fear got the best of him again (Gal. 2:11–14).

And yet for all of this mistake making, folly, and sin, what Peter needed was gracious room to grow. Peter is neither Caiaphas nor Pontius Pilate nor Herod nor the Pharisee who in his home judged both Jesus and the sinful woman. Jesus saw mistakes, errors, and sins in Peter. This did not count Peter out and did not mean that he deserved the same response from Jesus as these others warranted. A question or two surfaces for us to mull over: "How do you handle it when other people get things wrong?" "Does anyone you serve have room to make a mistake?" In my biblical training, I learned the following question from the Westminster Shorter Catechism.

> *What is sanctification?*
>
> Sanctification is the work of God's free grace, whereby we are renewed in the whole man after the image of God and are enabled more and more to die unto sin, and live unto righteousness.

I learned that while positionally we are already made holy in Jesus, practically we progress throughout our lives in what has already been given us. I did not think about how the fact that "we are enabled more and more" should impact our knowing. To do something "more and more" means it is perpetually incomplete. So also is my knowledge in Jesus. I am at any moment in this life unfinished in what I know (and so are those whom I serve). Any sermon, any Bible study, any counseling moment, and any house group is an unfinished business.

Over the years, in the family of American evangelicalism to which I belong, it's been the rare environment of grace in which mistakes and sins are differentiated and in which the time needed to grow in relation to both is granted. We struggle to see that Caiaphas and Peter are not the same, that disciples who err may resemble but are not synonymous with Pharisees who fall.

Imagine "Rev. Famous Author." For a long while, he has written of the gospel of Jesus truly and helpfully to many. But in his latest book or blog post Rev. Famous Author, while trying to account for the gospel in our culture, seems to go askew on a fundamental teaching. This is a genuine problem.

Apollos had this problem. The gifted preacher of Jesus needed the gracious provision of Priscilla and Aquila to learn. They heard him preach. They gave thanks for it. They grew from it. But they at the same time invited him for dinner. They taught him things privately. They asked challenging questions personally (Acts 18:24–28). Apollos was given room in Jesus to grow. His good teaching was not made void just because he got some things wrong.

Sometimes I just want to ask, Can't we slow down a bit? Can we choose a meal and a series of personal human conversations as our means for helping each other grow when we get it wrong? Jesus has been so patient with us.

We are often less patient. We take on late-night banter, blogging attacks, and tweeting daggers as if Jesus, rather than the culture, teaches us this as the way of relating lovingly to our neighbors. So Dr. Well-Known Preacher and Mr. National Blogger immediately and publicly castigate Rev. Famous Author and relationally disassociate from him.

Then Long-Established Scholar and Dr. Conference Speaker offer an all-or-nothing response that acts as if, by making one error, Rev. Famous Author is all and only error. This sounds more like how Jesus dealt with the Pharisees than how Jesus dealt with Peter or how Jesus had Apollos dealt with. At minimum, wisdom teaches us that time is needed to determine which posture of heart the erring brother is coming from.

Exposing Our Temptations

There is something about our way of knowing that struggles to uphold two truths at the same time: (1) Rev. Famous Author is making a fundamental error by this aspect of his teaching; (2) Rev. Famous Author loves Jesus, has followed him faithfully for years, has helped the faithful, and needs our company and civil conversation in order to have a shot at growing. (Maybe by this kind of company and familial dialogue we might learn something too?)

A way of knowing that goes no further than getting the sort right will have no access to the kind of knowledge that Jesus is revealing for Peter and for us. Unlike Jesus we will forever tend to lump Peters and Pharisees together and treat them equally. But Jesus doesn't do this with us. We who were once Pharisees and we who are genuinely mistaken disciples are amazed and grateful to him.

When Jesus gives his "Woe!" to those who misuse the key of knowledge, Jesus highlights the signs we exhibit when we improperly stand on certain sorts and by this ignore others.

- Our Bible knowledge leaves us illiterate in terms of the interior workings of our souls (Luke 11:37–40).
- The schooling we gain leaves us ignorant of actual love for God (Luke 11:42–44).
- For all of our scholarship and erudition we remain unpracticed with neighbor love, humility, wisdom, and the deeds that truly honor God (Luke 11:45–51).
- We are intelligent with Bible passages but without know-how in terms of the sense or meaning of these passages as they are in Jesus. In fact, Jesus tells Bible handlers elsewhere that they know the Bible but not the One to whom the Bible points (John 5:39).

What this means for us in life and ministry is that what one knows and how one uses that knowledge is mine-laden with significant temptations, stresses, and pains. The ancient Serpent's temptation remains. Therefore, the quest to gain knowledge is a delicate matter.

Childlike and Childish Knowing

It is a delicate matter because this kind of keyless light gives us a notion that knowledge is meant to make us something other than childlike. This same Peter, who once declared that he would be what no other disciple would, calls each of us to embrace childlikeness.

> Like newborn infants, long for the pure spiritual milk, that by it you may grow up into salvation—if indeed you have tasted that the Lord is good. (1 Pet. 2:2–3)

Living with partial knowledge in a childlike (not childish) way makes us jittery though. Thinking of ourselves as children who need time to grow is not valued by the world around us. To turn all of the lights on and still remain partially in the dark agitates us as we try to minister to others with partial light. Therefore trust becomes prerequisite for the partially knowledgeable.

But trust is ugly. Ask anyone in a hospital emergency room. When the doctor diagnoses the thing, we are grateful to have a name for it. But regarding what it all means, we take her word for it. We also soon learn that just because we have something named doesn't mean that we understand it.

Now imagine what it means to trust when the doctor says, "We don't know what we are dealing with; we have to run more tests." Living with the unknown snatches the illusion of control from us. Panic attacks. We need a paper bag to help us breathe. We demand answers. But the notion confronts us that there are times in life in which there are no answers or in which the answers we have are incomplete. We must learn how to live when only God knows what is going on truly or completely.

But this also makes us jumpy because those who misuse others in the world often do so by veiling or lying about knowledge. Rarely have we met someone who creates safety for us by the way they handle our ignorance or theirs. Humility and love among the knowledgeable. So we learn that to make it in the world, one must become savvy and astute. The apostle says as much.

> When I was a child, I spoke like a child, I thought like a child, I reasoned like a child. When I became a man, I gave up childish ways. (1 Cor. 13:11)

It makes sense then why we reflexively agree with the slogan "Knowledge is power." Partial knowledge makes us vulnerable. We need insurance. We need protection. We need an advantage. We need an achievement. We need to become superior to another. No wonder Adam and Eve jumped at the chance to buy the product the Serpent was selling. "You will be like God," he said, "*knowing* . . ." (Gen. 3:5). To know as God knows would save us a lot of worry. It would ensure that we could control, explain, manage, and preserve any situation we face.

But when we act as if omniscience is possible for us, we run the high risk of becoming foolish. For though we are taught to give up *childish* ways, we are never to do so in a way that absolves us from being *childlike* in our posture of humble dependence upon God (Matt. 18:3–4).

Childishness includes throwing tantrums to get our way, boasting in what we know, laughing at others when we win, declaring that we can do it ourselves, resisting surrender to limits, defying the wisdom of benevolent authority, looking down on others as weaker than we are, pretending that we don't need anyone's help, and feigning that we are never scared. The foolish believe that the more we know, the more we will be freed to act in the above-stated ways. We needn't learn anymore. We become adept at airing only our own opinions and judging others by them (Prov. 18:2).

But Jesus teaches us the opposite. The more we know, the more able we are to wait when things do not go our way; the less we boast; the more empathy we have for the loss of others; the more appeal to grace we have when we win; the more honest we are about what we cannot do; the more able we are to be seen by others as limited; the more grateful we are for benevolent authority, and the wiser its guidance appears to us, because we see ourselves in the weaknesses of others, we cry out for help, and we admit that we cannot do it alone.

I've carried the subtle idea around with me that growing in knowledge will mean that I get to depend less and control more. But Jesus indicates the opposite, and this challenges the way we do theology and Bible study. To know God truly, we have to know that we are not him. In a word, Jesus teaches us that humility is the dominant quality of becoming like a child in order to see the kingdom of heaven (Matt. 18:3–4).

To capture this point in a kind of proverb, we might say it this way: "The humble knows the most and knows it not." Many of the leaders in the church of Jesus's day disregarded this kind of wisdom. They too succumbed to the ancient temptation—the temptation to assure others that they were expert in knowledge with no "oddness," the temptation to believe that they could know as God knows and to therefore treat other people as inferior.

Important for us to note is that Jesus corrects those who believe that childlike dependence calls for rebuke (Luke 18:15–16). What grace for us who still have so much to learn.

Puffing Up

A misuse of sorts is not our only challenge. A misuse of zeal also challenges the grace Jesus gives for knowledge. In America, potato chip bags are puffed up. They appear full. But when the bag is opened, it deflates. We look or reach inside and discover that the bag possess maybe half of the chips that it appeared from the outside to have. What looked like a full bag of chips was actually a bag filled mostly with air. The appearance of the bag is exaggerated; we overestimate its capacity to provide what it entices us to anticipate.

Common folk-wisdom has a similar maxim. We say that a person who overestimates herself is full of "hot air." As genuine believers in Jesus we are susceptible to becoming puffed up and full of hot air in these ways (among others):

- We inflate by displaying zealous preferences for certain gospel teachers over others and by allowing others to do this with us (1 Cor. 4:6).
- We exaggerate ourselves by zealously esteeming our daily disciplines or supernatural experiences as a means of feeling superior to others (Col. 2:18).
- Our zeal with our newness to the faith can exaggerate our knowledge and puff us up (1 Tim. 3:6).
- Our zeal for theological controversy, debate, and discussion to demonstrate our superior intellect or persuasive ability over others puffs us up (1 Tim. 6:4).

Dr. Well-Known Preacher was a pastor whom the Lord allowed to serve as an inspiring and faithful preacher in our generation. He often passionately preached with a prophetic edge about suffering for the gospel.

There was for a few years a contingency of students who fashioned themselves as disciples of Dr. Well-Known Preacher. They listened to his sermons, read his books, and attended his conferences (though to my knowledge none of them knew Dr. Well-Known Preacher personally except for a handshake at a conference). These young in the faith spoke often of suffering and martyrdom. With red-faced passion, they preached in Bible class about suffering. They sought to lead more ascetic lives on their seminary campus.

But by adopting just one aspect of their celebrity mentor's message without the context and personal experience of his years of pastoral travail for people, they actually hurt fellow students, misjudged professors, and strongly criticized both. They seemed blind to the fact that for all of their zeal, they had actually only preached four sermons in their lives. They glossed over the fact that they had never served a day as a pastor in a church. They dismissed the truth that what they had learned only yesterday in class, the professor teaching them had been seeking to live out in life and ministry before they were even born. Any of us are vulnerable to this.

As Jonathan Edwards noted, "There is nothing that belongs to Christian experience that is more liable to a corrupt mixture than zeal."[8] It is not that we desire less zeal. On the contrary, a life and ministry devoid of earnestness is like a heater that sits in a damp room on a cold day but does not work. We plug it in, all goose bump and tremble, frigid toes needing to be warmed, but no help comes. Thank the Lord for zealous young men and women!

But a fire can't safely warm us unless it has the proper distance from us. Get too close in the name of warmth, and we get burned. So our zeal is meant to be derived "according to knowledge" (Rom. 10:2). There is a sort of religious teaching, passion, and service for God that shines as a blinding rather than as an illuminating light. So there is a sort of blazing heat that does not warm us but scorches us. This kind of zeal that scalds without warming sparks from a misguided view of what it means to know as a follower of Jesus.

We may attend a local Bible study for years. We may finish a seminary degree or fulfill one year in a local-church apprentice program. But that does not mean that one is humble with childlike knowledge, able by Jesus's grace to illumine rather than blind, to warm rather than scorch. All of us eye-blinders and face-burners are called to Jesus for forgiveness and the empowerment to act out a different purpose for our knowing.

The Purpose of Knowing

And what but love is the purpose of our knowledge?

If I was on a desert island and in addition to the Bible I could have only one or two books with me, I would likely choose Augustine's *On Christian Teaching* as one of my books. It is not because I comprehend everything he is saying (particularly in the first half of his book). Nor is it because I agree with his entire theology. It's because of the subject: the book teaches us how to read the Bible and to communicate its message to others (hermeneutics and homiletics). There is nothing unique about that.

What is unique is that in order to teach us how to read, understand, and communicate the Bible, Augustine starts with describing true joy and genuine love. How rare! He asserts that the true enjoyment of God and the growing possession of actual love for God and neighbor in Jesus is the goal of any reading or teaching of the Scriptures. For preachers and teachers this question must arise for every sermon or Bible study: How does this text inform and promote love for God and love for people? However, to read the Scriptures in a manner that leads us to something other than greater enjoyment of God and embodied love in Jesus is to know without knowledge, to shine without illumination, and to stand at the door with no key. What is the sum of the law, the beginning and end of it, the entirety or grand total of what its knowledge produces but this double love for God and for neighbor in Jesus (Matt. 22:38–39)?

> So, anyone who thinks that he has understood the divine scriptures or any part of them, but cannot by his understanding build up this love of God and neighbor, has not yet succeeded in understanding them.[9]

The Scriptures in Jesus lead us toward "an epistemology of love, a way of knowing that is manifest in loving."[10] The elder with the new Christian, the upperclassman with our prayer group, me with my writing on Calvinism for my family—each of us had knowledge. The elder had knowledge of the Westminster Larger Catechism. The upperclassman had knowledge of Jesus's words regarding prayer in secret. I had knowledge of A. W. Pink's instruction about Calvinism and later an A in six-week Greek. But each of us struggled to relate soundly (i.e., with a resemblance of Jesus's love) to the people in front of us. We are like those young followers of Dr. Well-Known Preacher, who could quote his words, take up his cause, and imitate his vocal tones and facial expressions, but who knew very little of the experience and substance of Dr. Well-Known Preacher.

Sitting at the Adult Table

In addition to our sorting, our zeal, and his purpose for our knowing, we want to remember the kinds of knowing that each of us has quite apart from and often prior to our Bible training.

As a child I loved my opportunities to sit at the adult table. I enjoyed the laughter, the stories, and the talk about the work and weather of the day. It was in moments like these that I came to know things such as how the tree leaves turn their backsides toward us when the rain is on its way, how to butter crackers with your chili, current opinions on the state of Indiana basketball, who had to cut how much sheet metal for the job that day, or what Uncle Dave's farm was up to.

I know now to recognize this creation and providence kind of knowledge. It is this earthy, under-the-sun learning that we glean from experience or the news or local ways. Jesus often appeals to this kind of knowledge when he teaches. For example, "You know that the rulers of the Gentiles lord it over them," he says (Matt. 20:25). How do the disciples know this except by their observations and experiences with local life? From whom did the disciples learn to mend or wash their nets? On the basis of what knowledge did Jesus call Peter to take his boat and cast his net into the sea (Luke 5:2–4)? They did not learn the skill of fishing as children from the Torah in the synagogue. James and John learned it from their Dad, Zebedee (Matt. 4:21).

Sometimes as a child, when I sat at the table on Sunday afternoons in Henryville, the adults would begin to spell words.

"Is it time for Zack's N-A-P?"

This was before I knew how to spell, so their strategy was sound. Spelling made clear for the adults what they wished to remain hidden from my child ears.

As I learned to spell, however, it required more effort to veil that sort of adult talk, so I think they just quit hiding it altogether. "Zack, the adults are talking now, why don't you go find yourself something to do."

"Ack!" I would announce with protest. Then the dreaded refrain: "You have to wait until you are older." Because of this refrain, I think that I had this notion within me that all knowledge would be revealed to me when I became older. I couldn't wait for the day when I too would finally sit at the adult table and know it all.

I know now that adult talk sometimes just means "adolescent talk by adults," such as jokes about what happened when drunk or sex talk or self-trivia or gossip. This profane kind of knowing has come to many of us. The woman Jesus forgave, that kind of woman, probably had plenty of this kind of knowledge. On the playground in seventh grade, or in the car with friends when a junior in high school, or out on our own in college or with our first job—this kind of knowledge can feel grand. This exhilaration of saying and doing what our teachers would tell us not to empowers us. We grow up then, and as adults we too finally get to say cuss words and talk about body parts. We get to tell little kids that they need to go into the other room because the adults are talking. We get some thrill from this.

But after a while, if any hint of a meditated life begins to call out to us, this thrill fades. We begin to ask questions about our lives. Is this what I waited all of my life to finally be able to hear and do? Is being able to say the word "sh#@" or to put each other down with jokes, or having a puking story to tell, or touching the butt of a woman whose name I don't remember really what it means to finally get a seat at the adult table and to enter its knowledge? Is knowing second- or third-hand about what we heard might have happened to "you know who" the goal and achievement of adult talk? The shine wears off. The facade dissipates. At Jesus's feet we seek the new knowledge of forgiveness and restorative grace to a new way.

I look back and realize that when a child is told to find something to do, and that child goes and plays with Tonka trucks or Barbie dolls while this sort of talk indulges the adult table, the child isn't missing out at all. The religious leader with Jesus and the woman would see this talk and rightly sort it out. But his view of sorting would lead him to avoid the family. He has no knowledge of how kindness or grace or hope could rise from sitting his rump on the dirt and playing trucks for the child's or the family's sake.

But adult knowledge, so mysterious to a child, is more often than not an attempt to come to terms with what the adults themselves do not understand but must navigate anyway. More than earthy, more than profane, we wrestle with providences we cannot get our heads around.

Exposing Our Temptations

On Sunday afternoons I was sometimes asked to leave the table because the situations, along with the relatives or neighbors involved, and the level of brokenness that attended each, were too sensitive and too complex for a child to bear. The adults could not understand why cousin so-and-so shot herself, or how aunt or uncle so-and-such were going to pay their bills, or what it meant to have a baby at such a young age, or how to figure out church with some who go and some who do not—knowing a lot of questions with few answers.

At night, as the child of a single mother staying at Mamaw and Papaw's house, the knowledge of prayer came from Mamaw's lips. She sat by the bed amid those shouting days, and we prayed quietly to God. Knowledge of creation, providence, the profane, and prayer formed the bulk of my knowing prior to the Bible.

Over time the Bible would finally find me. The words, the divine words, were coming, sweet as honey. What a blessing! There is a kind of know-it-all-ism that has no love or patience for the words or teachings or doctrines of Scripture. One leans on his own understanding and feels no need to lean on the understanding revealed by God in his Word. With the woman who washed the feet of Jesus with her tears, I too am grateful for rescue from this empty way of knowing.

Nonetheless, with the training for the church world into which I would enter came the sorting and zeal ways of knowing. God's way of naming things would nourish and ignite my soul. But other knowings were coming too: the systematics, the denominations, the histories, the constituencies, the differences, the camps, the creeds, the confessions, the personalities, my own heart.

My view of what was required for one to sit at the adult table was about to change (and not all for the better). All of us were children once. Somehow my ministry ways of knowing were sometimes making that hard to remember. Jesus has no such amnesia. His grace will mend our broken knowings and heal us toward true knowledge again.

Conclusion

Paul's prayer, therefore, comes to mind for the know-it-all. By it we recognize that "if we are really to know anything about God it will probably be because God has chosen to tell it to us."[11] We pray on the basis of what God has revealed in his Word for the knowledge that God intends to lead us in (Prov. 2:1–8). We pray out of gratitude, knowing that anything true that we know of Jesus is his doing and not ours (Matt. 11:27; 13:11).

After all, just as there are inconsolable things that we cannot fix, so there are unknowable things whose mystery we must learn humbly to live with. With the psalmist, we consider the works of God and we say, "Such knowledge is too wonderful for me; it is high; I cannot attain it" (Ps. 139:6). We agree with the sage who tells us that no matter how wise we are or how much we seek, we cannot comprehend God or his works (Eccles. 8:17). And whatever we do know, we understand that these are "but the outskirts of his ways" (Job 26:14).

Therefore, in contrast to the Serpent's temptation to omniscience, by grace we take up the apostle Paul's testimony. "Now I know in part," the apostle acknowledges (1 Cor. 13:12). And so must we. In life and ministry, "Partial Knowledge" is the name of the street on which each of us must have an address and build our lives. Our hope is not what we know but what Jesus knows.

Prayer admits, therefore, that there is more than we can ask or think. It connects our growth in knowledge to the ministry of the Spirit in our inner being as our empowerment, and this according to his Word. It assumes that by faith we in Jesus are rooted and grounded in love, that what we are meant to know is the love of Christ that surpasses knowledge. With this recognition about knowledge, Paul bows his knees and prays for us

> that you, being rooted and grounded in love, may have strength to comprehend with all the saints what is the breadth and length and height and depth, and to know the love of Christ that surpasses knowledge, that you may be filled with all the fullness of God. (Eph. 3:17–19)

Decision Making

The hour is late. It is midweek. Bodies and minds are fatigued. Most of those at the decision-making table came to this meeting straight from work. They are on their fourteenth hour of a sixteen-hour day. But decisions still remain. When we are tempted to know it all, we can make decisions hurriedly and harmfully often with little awareness of the fatigue of our colaborers. When I think about decision making, my thoughts first go down memory roads of pain. And, for better or for worse, I think of pain from decisions made by others.

> Decisions made, they had no part in me
> But the consequences paid, they sure made it hard to see.[12]

Consequences sandstorm our lives; the choices pelt our eyes. This is why the decisions made by others are sometimes the hardest for us. These more than anything remind us that we are not able to control much in the world. No matter what we say, how logical our arguments are, how mistaken the reasoning of the other, someone else (and not us) takes hold of the wheel and drives, indifferent to our panic or plea. Our attempts at helming the wheel be damned.

There is nothing for us to do then but to strap on our seat belt or fling ourselves from the car. The other shows little interest in learning how the driver and passenger can work together in mutual mentoring. So we either click the belt, hold on to the seat, and let go of our hope of contribution, or we hike our thumbs looking for a different ride, our knees skinned from bailing out and stinging red. We try to stand at the road's edge, shifting weight to relieve the knees, while car after car passes us. We stand there bleeding, and we wait. We wait for friends, only to see some of them pass us by. We learn that people are separate from us. Our will is not theirs. Theirs is not ours. The songwriter Billy Joel captures this reality:

> So I would choose to be with you,
> that's if the choice were mine to make.
> But you can make decisions too,
> and you can have this heart to break.[13]

A child of divorce has to navigate these shifting dunes, their days the decisions of others. The abandoned spouse, the chronically ill, the employee, as well as the determined critic or disgruntled leaver of our ministries or our lives—these each remind us of this uncontrollable interaction with others' decision making.

Remembering how we feel when others detonate our lives with their decision making will help us remember those who are in our way and at our whim when the decisions are ours to make.

To help us make decisions humbly and wisely, to create paths conducive to our place and its people, Paul's words to Timothy in 2 Timothy 2:23–26 provide us three foundational questions to answer with respect to each decision.

- Is this the right thing?
- Is this the right way?
- Is this the right time?

With wisdom and humility, we will prayerfully seek an answer to all three questions before presuming to know what to do. Jesus will saturate our path with the grace of his wisdom and provision.

Is This the Right Thing?

Integrity and empathy as followers of Jesus call us to this first question. But answering this question is not as easy as it first appears.

For example, Timothy must teach the Word and correct opponents. Yet at the same time he must "have nothing to do with foolish, ignorant controversies" (2 Tim. 2:23). Do what is right but avoid unnecessary, irrelevant, and misinformed quarrels.

Controversy arises with a heated commitment to one's opinions, traditions, preferences, or speculations from one's priority and agenda.

Ignorance among leaders stems from treating these personal opinions and preferences as synonymous with "the knowledge of the truth."

Folly among leaders shows itself when quarrels form over these personal or speculative issues (v. 23).

How do leaders discern? How do they decide if a conflict arises from what God's Word says or from a misuse of God's Word to promote one's own agendas, speculations, or habitual commitments?

Imagine a scenario that concerns the pastor's parking space. Some deacons argue that the pastor ought to park at the farthest distance from the church. Other deacons argue for spaces closest to the church. The disagreement adopts biblical tones.

Exposing Our Temptations

One side argues that it is more biblical to park at a distance because pastors are to serve others and set an example. The other side states that it is more biblical for the pastor to park closer because honor belongs to those who lead. Though the Bible does not address where a pastor should park his car, both sides now believe that they are fighting for truth in their church.

In the end, however, gospel ministry is stalled, leadership is divided, relationships are strained, and families leave. Why? Because Christians disagreed about a parking space in the name of standing for truth in their generation.

Experienced leaders are familiar with these know-it-all temptations. Relational dynamics, decision histories, and emotional investment sometimes cloud our ability to distinguish what we prefer from what is biblical. For example, a dear man once said to me that "the church just isn't the church if it doesn't have a choir."

We all understand the feeling and commitment that a long life of church and/or cultural habit and assumption brings to our decisions. How do we untangle ourselves from these traps?

First, when trying to discern what is right, we must not assume that we can't be wrong or have nothing to learn. With that in mind, we must simply ask, Will our decision "add to" God's Word (Prov. 30:6)? Will what we decide bind the consciences of our ministry with something that God has not bound it? For example, someone requests the elders to declare that reverence in worship demands dressing our best, which means suits and ties. Dressing our best may or may not reveal a fine idea, but the elders need help to recognize that the person has imported white-collar, middle-class American assumptions into the definition.

When blue-collar folks dress up, they do so with different standards than white-collar folks. Unaware of this fact, the elders enact Sunday worship rules that require coats and ties, while jeans or khakis are dismissed. Subtly, one's reverence for God becomes tied to one's economic capacity. Reverence for God requires owning a tie. Over time, therefore, the church attracts and impacts only those who possess the income and the assumptions to obtain these kinds of clothes. When someone who does not have these kinds of clothes visits the church, she is frowned upon, even though the book of James reminds leaders that both rich and poor worship together and without partiality. To require otherwise is, with our good intentions nonetheless, to add to God's Word (James 2:1–13).

The second question that leaders can ask is if what they decide will take away from what God has required (Deut. 12:32). Coming back to the clothing example, if leaders suggest that immodest dress is appropriate for worship, they unwittingly remove something clearly stated (1 Tim. 2:9). If the elders pursue modesty of dress without gentleness, instruction, patience, kindness, and love, they also take away from what is clearly stated about the way we love our neighbors. Therefore, elders pursue modesty without requiring economic wealth or local cultural assumptions as God's standard for reverence, and they do so as those surrendered to the fruit and manner of Jesus's Spirit when doing so.

A third question that leaders can ask is if what they decide will promote love for God, for neighbor, and for enemy. Love is the sum of the law and the identifying mark of Christians. Leadership decisions cannot add to what violates love or remove what love would require.

Apart from these three questions, it will help us to recognize that we must make decisions in America about worship bulletins, paint colors, carpets, meeting times, ministry styles, choirs, and parking lots. Such "carpet decisions" are not explicitly a matter of following God's Word. Many of these matters require someone's preferences to surrender to those of the others. These kind of preferences, however, do not release us from treating one another according to Jesus.

So, both those who yield and those whose preferences win the day must recognize that they are bound together by a higher priority. Decisions about lesser matters should not separate those who follow Jesus. If you are on a leadership team, take a deep breath and remember that God can win people to himself whether the carpet is blue or green or whether the choir continues or disbands. Sadness or a certainty that "it would have looked better if" are feelings worth enduring so that foolish quarrels do not form. As leaders we must not bind the consciences of church members to what we might call our "carpet decisions." While people maturely yield, they are free to dislike our choices, and we are free to prefer them.

Likewise, though we prayerfully decide such things, it is a mistake to place these decisions on equal footing and authority with God's Word. The command to love one another and "God told me the church logo should be such and so" are simply not on the same plane. "The Lord told me that we are going to grow to five hundred people and then plant three satellite sites" may be a fine idea, but it is not the Word of God the way any book of the Bible is for the obedience of the consciences of Jesus followers. The know-it-all has a hard time on this, but by grace we must tenaciously uphold these distinctions.

What Is the Right Way to Do This?

Imagine a scenario in which elders study and affirm that divorce is a sin. Out of a genuine earnestness for fidelity to the Scripture, the elders write a fifteen-page paper in which they identify why divorce is a sin. They include arguments from the Greek along with exhortations regarding the liberal slide of our culture. The conclusion of the paper states that those who seek divorce or have been divorced are sinning. The elders send this paper to the congregation via mass e-mail. They state that the attached paper represents the official position of the church. The unintended result of the e-mail is widespread confusion, profound pain, and the fueling of self-righteousness in the congregation.

Why? Because while the paper states why divorce is a sin, the paper does not address how the gospel applies to those who are already divorced. Likewise, the e-mail did not take into account the varying and sometimes tragic circumstances of those who are divorced. There was no accounting for those who were abandoned for another, or who desperately did all they could to not lose the marriage, or who were physically endangered or misused. In other words, how the elders handled what they understood as the right thing caused unnecessary trouble in the congregation.

Know-it-alls will almost always identify negative reactions to their decisions as the cost of standing for the truth and suffering for the Lord. But leaders may not realize that they can wrongly wound people with the right thing. The right thing done the wrong way demonstrates a lack of pastoral wisdom and care.

This scenario introduces our second criterion for decision making. We are tempted to believe that our work is done once we have decided the right thing to do. But once we prayerfully determine the right thing to do, we must still contemplate the right way to do it.

Consider for a moment how elders can hurt one another by doing the right thing the wrong way. Imagine that two elders have trouble with one another. The other elders recognize this strain. So these other elders who recognize the strain schedule the next elders' meeting for 8:00 PM. When one of the strained elders arrives from work a little before 8:00, he sees the others already meeting without him. He sees among them the one with whom he is struggling.

As this one with whom he struggles leaves, the others call him into the room. They confront his attitude. They describe how he must pursue change if he intends to continue serving. This elder is now caught off guard. He responds defensively. He excuses himself and leaves the room. The result is that relational strain spreads to each of these men for the next several months. The others feel that he responded un-Christianly. They see his defensive response as proof that they are right about him. But this elder feels deeply wounded and betrayed. It looked like a secret meeting. The one with whom he struggles was a part of that meeting and, to his knowledge, was not also required by the elders to change.

The result? He feels ganged-up on by his friends. When he finds out that the meeting actually began at 6:00 PM, his sense of betrayal deepens. He has served the church for years. Even if he needs to change, how could these guys treat him this way?

Perhaps the confrontation was the right thing. The other elders rightly disrupted their passivity and moved toward the brothers to help them resolve their disagreements. Problems arose, however, because straightforward, gentle, and kind action was lacking. Coming straight from work with fast-food for dinner and no preparedness for these behind-the-scenes meetings forced the man into the position of answering the surprising moment.

For many of us, our first response in that situation is not our best. The surprise, hurt, misperception, and confrontation at that time of night make us grateful for a second or third or fourth opportunity to respond.

Doing what is right in the right way arises from Paul's point to Timothy. Timothy, while he must teach and correct, must also be "kind to everyone" (2 Tim. 2:24). Kindness includes thoughtful consideration of another person's situation and needs. Timothy must choose kindness contrary to what he may feel in a given moment. In addition, Timothy must correct those who oppose him. But he must do so "with gentleness" (v. 25). Teaching and even correction come with kindness and gentleness—the right thing in the right way.

Paul's words bring to mind my older son wrestling on the floor with my youngest son when he was a toddler. I find myself saying out loud to my older son, "Gentle! Remember to be gentle!" I mean for my older son to take into account the weaker frame of my younger son so as to wrestle without hurting him. Like this, Timothy must correct so as not to hurt. In fact, even though Timothy is avoiding folly and upholding what is right, he has no right as the Lord's servant to "be quarrelsome" (v. 24). Paul says that the Lord's servant must not correct others with an attitude that is ready to pick a fight or with a desire to rub another's nose in it. In other words, being right does not justify arrogance, intimidation, rudeness, or harshness. Holding the right position in the argument never justifies betraying the character of Jesus in our manner. Know-it-alls justify their mistreatment of neighbors in the name of being right. The Lord's servants must not do so.

A fellow leader once objected to this sentiment, reminding me that Jesus could crack a whip and turn over tables. The implication was that we have a ministerial right to do the same. It is true that some situations require a nonmalicious but forthright zeal from the ministerial leader. But the leader must examine which occasions may require this.

In the whole of Jesus's ministry we know only of this rare event. Cracking whips on tables was not the norm for Jesus. He certainly did not strike people. Nor must this posture describe our norms particularly in light of how our practice of love compares so poorly to Jesus's. Furthermore, Jesus cracked the whip in the temple for those who knew better. His hardest words were reserved for those who claimed to know and follow God but who persistently hardened their hearts toward him. In fact, Jesus never spoke to the woman at the well or his disciples the way he sometimes spoke to the religious leaders. Even with the hard-hearted and religious, the "woes" of Matthew 23 came after twenty-two chapters of reasoning with, teaching, disrupting, and inviting these leaders.

The rationale behind choosing the right way of patience, kindness, and gentleness resides with God, who "grants repentance and leads to a knowledge of the truth" (2 Tim. 2:25). A leader's coercion has no capacity to create what God intends. Even a leader holding a right position is still under the authority of God and waits upon God for God's purposes.

Sometimes, weak men use this appeal to gentleness and kindness to justify their passivity. Jesus, however, was far from passive. He actively pursued decision making. He disrupted evil. He exposed manipulative schemes and cultivated relational movement amid his fidelity to the Father's will. Gentleness does not equal or excuse passivity.

Conversely, others, in the name of leading strongly, resist postures of gentleness and kindness. Cultural norms and business environments often identify such fruit of the Spirit as weakness. Yet Jesus spoke directly without requiring an intimidating, harsh, or raging posture. This is true strength.

Still, some will say that doing right things in the right way will not work in the real world. "You cannot survive the boardroom with gentleness and kindness," some will say. "You do what you can to survive." But has the explosive gentleness or the forceful kindness of Jesus been tried in the boardroom? Who knows how the Lord might work through you to demonstrate his kind of strength to those you work with?

But even if it doesn't work in the world, it is the way of Jesus.

Others will say that gentleness and kindness are inefficient. Refraining from strong coercion slows things down. I recognize this and am reminded that efficiency, though prized as a Western value, is not always right in God's eyes. Perhaps God has already accounted for the slower pace and valued it. Still, even if God's way doesn't seem to work or seems to slow us down, the Lord's servants are required to lead differently than those who do not follow him.

This point highlights our need in life and ministry not only to pray for the wisdom to know what to do and how to do it but also to pray for God's work and glory among those we lead. Paul says, "God *may perhaps*" grant repentance. This means that the Lord's servants enter the uncertainty of God's design for decision making. They do so by entrusting him with the outcome. Paul is alerting Timothy to the fact that God may not grant change to everyone who opposes the truth. Timothy must gently uphold truth even so. Leaders, therefore, must concern themselves not with controlling outcomes but with doing the right thing in the right way. We are not in control. God is. Ours is to follow him and trust him with what is unknown to us—something a know-it-all cannot stand.

Is This the Right Time to Do This?

The third criterion for decision making forces us to consider the issue of timing. Timothy must patiently endure evil (2 Tim. 2:24). He must "reprove, rebuke, and exhort, with *complete patience*" (2 Tim. 4:2). We learn with Timothy that while we must not tolerate evil itself, we must live alongside of evil for a time. Timothy must demonstrate patience while he gently corrects that which is wrong.

Theologically, this brings us back to that question about sanctification, and how we are "enabled more and more." This doctrine reminds us that people are mixed works that gradually grow in holiness. It is helpful for us to consider what this mixture feels like and looks like on a Tuesday afternoon or a Sunday morning. Implementation of the right thing in the right way requires timing decisions with patient consideration of human capacity.

In John 16:12 Jesus says to his disciples, "I still have many things to say to you, but you cannot bear them now." These disciples required more truth than they presently possessed. Yet, their capacity was limited by their present season in life. Timing causes leaders to consider what people are able to presently bear. Our know-it-all temptation cannot bear to admit that there are things we do not know or cannot presently handle. Ministry leaders will remember that a failure to consider what people could bear forged Rehoboam's folly and divided the Old Testament kingdom (1 Kings 12:1–15).

Even the most experienced among us can demonstrate impatience. As we mentioned, sometimes our know-it-all-ism blinds us to where we ourselves have been. We forget the patience we have needed from Jesus to get where we are. Jesus has led us to the right things, in the right way, and at the right time. Others require the same grace from us.

Consider a board of elders that studies and changes its view on handling Sundays. They come to believe that it is right to rest from work on Sundays. They start to pursue a Sabbath rest. Will they have the humility to recognize the long in-house debate about this subject among equally knowledgeable, committed, and genuine followers of Jesus?

Will they seek the right way to introduce this view to the congregation with public and personal gentleness, kindness, and teaching? Now the question of timing arises. Several families have their kids in soccer leagues on Sundays. As members of the church they have participated in these leagues for the last five years. Will the elders equip parents with the same amount of time and access to the same resources that they themselves needed in order to arrive at these convictions?

Furthermore, will the elders help parents to remember that their older children may require equal amounts of time as well?

Someone will object that the thing is wrong so it ought to stop immediately. Besides forgetting what they themselves required from Jesus in order to know what is right, such persons also forget that many things exist that are wrong and need to stop. While God works with us on one sin, he bears with multitudes of others. He does this until the time when we can bear to hear from him on these other matters. Like Timothy, we must "reprove, rebuke, and exhort, *with complete patience and teaching*."

A know-it-all makes a decision and expects immediate obedience to that decision, blind to the time she herself has needed to learn and blind to the patience being extended to her in her many other mistakes and disobediences.

No Surprises

I was walking with Bryan, a seasoned leader who had just given some difficult news to a group of employees of a ministry organization. As we walked I asked him, "What is going through your mind when you prepare to lead a difficult meeting like that?"

"No surprises," he said.

I've thought about that a lot over the years and through many mistakes. To do our best to enable someone not to be surprised by the information and to have the kind of time needed to respond rather than react slows everything down. Businesses and organizations may find this difficult to implement. But for a church or ministry it is paramount that we try.

We need the time to walk through each question before major changes are made. (Taking this time will agitate the everywhere-for-all, the fix-it-all, and the know-it-all in each of us.) It will force us to wait upon God. What does this mean?

- Any major change more often than not takes one to three years.

- In order to give everyone the best shot of traveling with us, we will do the following:

- Drop the pebble of discussion personally and informally to leaders;
- Eventually bring this informal discussion to the formal agenda. Listen.
- Place it on the agenda for discussion but not for decisions. (Rarely decide anything the first time it is formally presented.) Listen. Learn. Pray.
- Eventually, when everyone is ready to decide (one way or another), bring it to a decision in the formal meeting.
- After the decision, reflect and process in personal discussions. Be willing to revisit the vote and revisit the discussion if things are unraveling or second thoughts abound.
- Now, begin this same process all over again with the primary ministry leaders and the volunteers whom these decisions will impact.
- Discuss, listen, learn, tweak. When ready to bring everyone as a whole into the decision making, teach, offer open houses for discussion, be available.

- By the time the thing is implemented, almost everyone feels ready and wonders what has taken us so long to do it. Those who leave do so not because they weren't heard, or we didn't give time, or we didn't listen, or they didn't have a voice, but because in spite of all of these avenues they simply disagree.

- Our decisions about most things do not carry the same weight for another's conscience as God's Word does. In such cases, people are free to disagree. The know-it-all will struggle here (and this is good).

Conclusion

When we are tempted to know-it-all, we can make decisions hurriedly or harmfully or both. One way to help us surrender to God's omniscience is to think of making decisions in church and family as creating paths rather than building roads. Creating paths moves with the landscape, is well familiar with the inhabitants and geography of the place, and provides movement while still leaving the place intact. In contrast, road building uses the place as a means to an end and sets dynamite to whatever stands in its way in order to get from one place to another.

> A path is little more than a habit that comes with knowledge of a place. . . . It is not destructive. It is the perfect adaptation, through experience and familiarity, of movement to place; it obeys the natural contours; such obstacles as it meets it goes around.
>
> A road, on the other hand, even the most primitive road, embodies a resistance against the landscape. Its reason is not simply the necessity for movement, but haste.[14]

Many of us in ministry and family leadership hastily dynamite our way through obstacles and people. We create well-respected and efficient organizations and homes but leave a trail of persons and places obliterated in our wake. Ironically, we often unnecessarily hurt people in the name of building God's organization and doing God's work. But pastors and ministry leaders and family members are not placeless people. "The road builders were placeless people," Wendell Berry notes:

> Not yet having devoted themselves to any part of it in a way that would produce the intricate knowledge of it necessary to live in it without destroying it. Because they belonged to no place, it was almost inevitable that they should behave violently toward the places they came to.[15]

Discipline and Sin

In my oral exams for ministry, I stood before the fifty or so elders and was asked the question, What is the purpose of church discipline?

Fresh out of seminary, with bits of Calvin and the Westminster Confession of Faith scribbled hastily on the flashcards of my memory, I answered something like this: "Our sin requires discipline so that, first, the character of Jesus is distinguished from ours so that his teachings are made clear in light of our often falling short of them.

"Second," I continued, "The protection, purity, and strength of those who follow Jesus is our purpose, like a shepherd who rescues the wolf-chased sheep and removes her from striking distance.

"So," I summarized, "the purpose of church discipline is to uphold the character and teaching of Jesus and to protect the welfare of the people of God."

No one said anything about this answer, and we moved on to other questions. But afterward a gentle brother caught up to me in the hallway and asked if he might suggest a fuller answer. This man had been a pastor for many years. "Sure," I said.

"There is a third purpose for church discipline," he said kindly. "That third purpose has to do with the welfare of the one who sins—'the reclaiming and gaining of offending brethren,' as the Confession puts it."

"Right!" I said. "I forgot about that one."

"Remember," he added, "how desperately we ourselves need this grace for recovery too. This third purpose is good news, not just for those we pursue as a pastor but for us too. It is God's grace to recover and mend us, and we, perhaps more than anyone, will give thanks that our Lord's discipline carries such a hopeful purpose for sinners."

When tempted to know-it-all, our decision making is not the only stick of dynamite we use to blast people. When someone is caught in a sin, we are likewise tempted to light the fuse and fling the explosive.

Relating to the Hardened

Sometimes our combustible response rises because the person who is sinning defends it. In my first pastorate a dear man who was a trusted leader both in our church and in our small town had an affair. For nearly two years I tried to meet with him, his wife, and his kids. I appealed to him with the two messages—the message that we would do everything we could to walk with him and his family through this terrible brokenness for the testimony in years to come that God could give them in Jesus, and the message that in time his continuous refusal to admit his actions as contrary to the gospel would put his correspondence to Jesus in question and require us to painfully say so. He eventually wrote this to us:

> Unless you consider man's laws to be of higher authority than God's laws, the adultery began in November 1979 and will end in 2000. My wife is not my wife, Luke 16:18. Referencing your meeting, I no longer consider you my church. For three years no one ever cared to approach me and talk to me about turning down the nomination for elder or trustee. Despite

> the fact that youth carry no importance in your church, no one in the last seven months has extended a hand to my children during this time. Jesus's response to what is the greatest commandment was, "You shall love your neighbor as yourself," Matthew 22:39.

We can struggle to enter the sins of others because, when someone refuses to admit wrongdoing, they use all of their reasoning to justify it. In this note, this sane and biblically respected and dear man actually called his marriage of twenty-one years an adultery. On the basis of Luke 16:18, he reasoned that to divorce his wife is to end the affair, and to keep going with his mistress is actually the biblical thing to do to please God. He reasoned that because his marriage was performed by a justice of the peace rather than by a pastor all those years ago, his marriage wasn't recognized by God, and therefore God would consider his marriage an adulterous relationship that he must end. In short, in his mind, the Bible supports his having an affair and leaving his wife. Someone using the Bible in this way can ignite our impatience.

We can also struggle because, when someone refuses to admit wrong, they take the moral high ground and believe themselves more righteous than others. In this case, he accused us as a church of loving our neighbor poorly. He attacked us for leading poorly while, as a church leader, he was having an affair and biblically defending it. He attacked us for not caring for his kids while, as a dad, he was cheating on their mom and separating from them. He saw potential specks in our eyes while the log in his remained undetected.

In all of that we can also struggle because blame shifting hurts. We wished our youth group was better. We were reaching out to his wife and his kids but felt terribly inadequate. We prayed and tried—made meals, went to coffee, sent notes. We were going slowly and trying to give him room and time to consider our appeals to him to remember our love for him, his identity as a follower of Jesus, and the hope that repentance in Jesus can bring. None of this effort to love seemed to matter. Our hearts can begin to fume. Defensive and justified, we light the fuse and hurl the combustible.

We sometimes respond in kind toward those who harden toward us, because we forget where we have been. We forget that the ground of truth upon which we ourselves finitely stand has been repeatedly seeded with grace and grassed with mercy. We too are quite capable of twisted reasoning, moral hypocrisy, and blame shifting. In the moment, this truth escapes us.

On the other hand, we can also react with trash talk because the event of another's sin can remind us of where we have been more than we desire it to. Maybe we are afraid of our spouse leaving us. Maybe we were the child of a dad who left our mom for another woman. Maybe we have been secretly thinking about the breakdown of our own marriage and eyeing the woman who sits two pews over every Sunday. Our emotional reaction can pull us by the hair. We swing our fists. We grimace and shout. His sin exposes a thread about to unravel in the stitching of our own lives. Seeing him causes us to look at things in ourselves that we'd rather not.

Others of us light the long fuse and then run for cover behind distant shelters. Our blasting of sinners is done through our neglect rather than our actions—what we omit rather than what we commit. Our business, we say, was elsewhere. We lit the fuse but were nowhere near the blast. We did very little, and, conveniently, there are others to blame.

Coming to terms with our humanity in Jesus, we need his grace to learn how to relate to one another in our sins. There is more to say than we can here, but let's turn to the apostle Paul for a moment to orient us, at least. The former Pharisee, both by his teaching and his example, helps us to trek with Jesus through the jungles of discipline and sin.

Watch Yourself

Let's look first and briefly at the teaching of Paul in Galatians 6: "If anyone is caught in any transgression," Paul begins (v. 1). By "anyone," Paul is referring to those who profess to follow Jesus. He expounds on this elsewhere:

> I wrote to you in my letter not to associate with sexually immoral people—not at all meaning the sexually immoral of this world, or the greedy and swindlers, or idolaters, since then you would need to go out of the world. But now I am writing to you not to associate with anyone who bears the name of brother if he is guilty. . . . For what have I to do with judging outsiders? Is it not those inside the church whom you are to judge? God judges those outside. "Purge the evil person from among you." (1 Cor. 5:9–13)

First, according to Paul, our task is not to separate from and judge our non-Christian neighbors. To do so we'd have to leave the world. It is God's role and not ours to discern the dealings of those who sin and do not know him. Therefore, the threefold purpose of discipline has to do with those within our fellowship who claim to follow Jesus (a lot of us get this terribly wrong).

Second, when Paul says, "in *any* transgression," our hearts are searched, for he includes any kind of stained thing that we might come across in someone's closet.

Prior to vocational ministry I coordinated a victims' assistance program, working with victims of crime in Blackford County, Indiana. I was unprepared for the kinds of transgressions that exist outside my window. The job pulled back the curtains of the world—murder, molestation, domestic violence, child abuse, drug use. In the pastoral ministry, the fact that these issues take place in churches too has often caught me off guard. A youth pastor who has sex with girls in the youth group, a man who fabricates the death of his son to his coworkers, a woman who bankrupts her family through habitually lying about and manipulating bank funds.

An individual may not have the grace to enter a particular sinner's plight (a molested person with a molester, a battered woman with an abuser), but as a whole, the Jesus community is meant to have the capacity to do so. A question arises: Is there any kind of sin that we would find ourselves unwilling to enter or unable to treat in a Jesus way? Our answer will show us where we need individual grace and a community in Jesus that can handle more things collectively than we can personally.

Third, Paul clarifies that entering the mess of a caught sinner's recovery is off-limits to most of us. How different! In my church experience, many people take it upon themselves and believe it their role and business to confront whatever they see in whomever they see it. But Paul says otherwise. Only those "who are spiritual should restore him" (Gal. 6:1).

By "spiritual," Paul references the context of the previous verses with which he addressed the fruit of the Spirit in contrast to the works of the flesh. If we intend or find ourselves confronting a caught sinner by using the tools of enmity or strife or fits of anger, for example, then we are not the ones to walk with the caught sinner. Someone else who is "spiritual," that is, given the grace to engage the sinner with love, peace, patience, kindness, and self-control, has this job, for such a sinner must be restored "in a spirit of gentleness" (v. 1).

Furthermore, it is a transgression or a sin that we are talking about. Church discipline (as with any kind of discipline, such as that of parents with kids) has to do with sins. This means that we have no cause to discipline because someone differs in opinion with us, has a different style of teaching, expresses a different temperament than we do, or doesn't do what we want them to do or within the time frame we think it should have been done.

We must also recognize the difference between the sins of a hard-hearted disregarder of Jesus and those of a wholehearted follower of his. The first denies Jesus altogether and seeks his demise or disregard. The second falls short but not out of hatred or deep-seated denial of Jesus. This distinction matters.

> If we deny him, he also will deny us;
> if we are faithless, he remains faithful—
> for he cannot deny himself. (2 Tim. 2:12–13)

Furthermore, not every weakness or struggle rises from sin. Imagine a parent with a child who spills milk. Sin is not the only possible cause of the spilled milk, and therefore the parent may have no warrant for treating the child as if he is in trouble. To begin, children (and adults) have limits. A two-year-old cannot do what a five-year-old can. A child has to be five before he can arrive at the age of ten. Just as we do not discipline a first-grader if she gets a fifth-grade math problem wrong, or because she plays the trumpet with all of her might but in such an inferior way to a junior-high student or a professional musician, so a two-year-old may spill milk because his hands and coordination are not yet what they will be. To treat limits as sins resembles nothing of Jesus's way with us.

Children not only have limits; they also have accidents. A child may have simply tried to pass the peas, and without intent or malice she knocked over the milk. In such a case, that we are frustrated is our own issue to take to the Lord and not something we can legitimately discipline our child about. Accidents can have greater consequences when they involve swinging a baseball bat or driving a car. A teen driver who, while driving the speed limit, does not see the toddler run out from behind a parked car has to face the nightmare of a situation he didn't choose. Those

who care for him maintain for his conscience that there is a difference between him and the one who tries to drive recklessly or even premeditates harm to a child.

Further nuance reminds us that, for adults, accidents can also stem from blind spots, particularly in relationships. Church small groups and ministry teams often encounter this. 

> Like a madman who throws firebrands, arrows, and death
> is the man who deceives his neighbor
> and says, "I am only joking!" (Prov. 26:18–19)

Often, adults will inflict pain on others by their relational words or actions and act surprised that another is hurt. The adult responds to the hurt they caused with, "I meant nothing by it," or "That was not my intent," or "I was just kidding." For the adult, this is true. They did not actively intend the hurt. Often, therefore, they assume the problem lies with the one who feels hurt. "She shouldn't feel that way; she has a problem," and the adult moves on. The "accident" is actually a sin that is present not due to intention but to lack of instruction.

The problem is that the adult is blind to the impact of her way of relating because she has neither seen nor learned the folly of what she is doing. So, without meaning to, hurt was caused nonetheless. While sometimes it is true that the offended one can learn to toughen and to grow less sensitive, it is equally true that saying, "I didn't mean anything by it," can act as an excuse. Help comes when these adults let the unintended wound transition from an excuse to a red flag. Constantly causing unintended harm invites the adult to pull off to the side of the road and take a fresh look at how he is driving. Perhaps a change by grace is in order.

A sin differs from a limit or an accident in exactly this: if the child holds up the glass and bold-faced glares at the parent in the eye, and the parent says no (assuming the child has learned what this word means), and then the child drops the glass and not the glare, now we are in the realm of an expression of sin.

And yet even here Paul teaches us that the wrong done does not justify our borrowing the works of the flesh in order to discipline the wrongdoer.

Finally, by way of a brief frame of reference, Paul teaches us to beware of taking the moral high ground as if we sit in God's seat. "Keep watch on yourself, lest you too be tempted" (Gal. 6:1). Have you ever heard yourself say, "I would never do that?" There is a trapdoor in that sentence.

When my pastor friend took his own life, several people in the ensuing months confessed to me that suicide was on their mind. Approaching the one-year anniversary of his death, one of those church members did, without warning, shoot himself to death. The broken church had to walk fatigued and numbed through it all again.

When my first marriage was imploding and I was scrambling desperately for help, there was one man whose repeated counsel to me was that a divorce wasn't so bad, that my future might be brighter, and that I should not feel so sad if it all ended. I found that I could no longer talk to this person about my crisis marriage. Such counsel was soured in taste. I was trying to save, not lose, my marriage. I later learned that his own marriage was deeply troubled, and that he had been contemplating doing something similar to his wife that my wife was doing to me. His counsel, rather than being biblical, was tainted with his own temptations.

Similarly, walking alongside the porn addiction of another, I remember a man sharing with me the porn sites he used. He did so as an act of confession to "bring it into the light." But for me, the web-address names taunted me to click on them for the next three days. It was like each site name was emblazoned in my thoughts.

Paul emphasizes this call to remember our own vulnerability and to resist measuring our sense of righteousness from others.

> If anyone thinks he is something, when he is nothing, he deceives himself. But let each one test his own work, and then his reason to boast will be in himself alone and not in his neighbor. (Gal. 6:3–4)

The Unavoidable Predicament

If we do not have this kind of footing, we have no business entering the wreckage of others lest we add to the damage.

The former leader ended his marriage and kept on with his new mistress. It was not a private kind of sin that could be dealt with in a merely private way. His was public, and everyone was watching. He was our friend. We were deeply pained. Some wanted swift action and vehemence. We resisted that notion. We would err on the side of giving too much time for him to come to his senses, if we were to err at all. Nearly two years of appealing, walking with, and attempting to help had passed to no avail. We had no success in gaining our dear brother (Matt. 18:15). He refused to listen (v. 17). We had to "let him be" to us as a "Gentile and a tax collector" (v. 17).

What did this mean? We considered how Jesus related to Gentiles and tax collectors. We would love this man. We would say hello and talk about the weather if we saw him at the store. Perhaps he would say, "Can we get together for coffee?" We would say, "Sure, but on my mind is the welfare of your heart. When we meet, can we also talk about that?" "No," he might respond. "We cannot." "Okay," we would say. "I pray for you and long for your good. Anytime you would like to talk about things, I'd welcome coffee with you. But, honestly, not until then. I need Jesus too. And I'm still hoping you will be able to admit what you've done with your family isn't what Jesus would have for us and that you will want to fall into the arms of Jesus's grace."

In other words, we treat him with love and dignity but not with pretension regarding what remains unfinished. When Paul says of the hardened sinner who calls himself a Jesus follower, "Don't even eat with such a one," he does not invite us to meanly shun or disregard or mistreat such a one. Such a meal would sit like a gift on our table if the person would see his need for forgiveness. We long for this. But we wait for it. Our love, longing, kindness, and prayers for him cannot take away the reality that in Jesus the man is now identified "as if" he is no longer part of the believing community. Our fellowship is neither what it was nor what it could be. Until admission of this clear wrong, we cannot pretend otherwise.

We recognize his marriage is likely (though not certainly) lost for good. The divorce is final. The consequences and the damage done still remain. But what joy and freedom it would mean to simply say, "I know I was wrong. I need forgiveness and change." The community could then join in with him with tears but also glad hope!

He could also still bless his kids with wise instruction. He could remove the crazy-making from them—the idea that Jesus says it's right for daddies to leave their mommies for another woman, the notion that such a teaching puts in their heads about who they are as daughters who will one day become women. He could tell them that "Daddy was wrong." Clarity could kiss his daughter's thoughts and take his kids' hands to walk down surer paths for their futures.

And he could still say it to his former wife, "I was wrong. Please forgive me." They may never return even to a posture of friendship. But simple admission can take the lightning and the thunder out of the storm clouds that will drape the skies of their mutual parenting as a blended family. Accusations that made what was right seem wrong and what was wrong seem right can finally receive an eviction notice from our consciences.

Most importantly, the honor of Jesus and his teachings would find clarity again in his public life for all who watched him. In his heart, before God, he would be reconciled. All that energy to twist Bible verses, to invert the moral high ground, and to blame shift can cool down. The muscles of each minute can relax. The heartbeat of each second can slow down. To be "gained" again in Jesus. To defend neighbor love and to find rest for the soul—these blessings would reveal the third purpose of discipline's bearing its sweet fruit in an ordinary life.

Relating to the Softened

Alongside this teaching of Paul we also have a case study through which we see his approach. Through this lens we see that sometimes our challenge regards not only how to walk with the resistant heart; we can equally and somewhat surprisingly struggle to relate to the one who says he was wrong and actively seeks forgiveness. Why?

To begin, we want the person who sinned against us or our community to hurt. We not only want him to *be* sorry enough; we want him to *feel* sorry enough. If he confesses his wrong too quickly, we can feel it unfair. Our emotions are just getting started. What do we do with them if we can't throw them at the offender?

Also, when someone is actually changed by grace, it requires us to change, not just them, and we do not like this. Imagine a husband and wife. The husband has struggled with anger for years. She has prayed for him. After all this time Jesus begins to change him. Her prayers are coming to an answer. During their next argument, she treats him as if he is expressing anger unlovingly the way he always has. The problem is, he is actually loving her quite well. He has turned down the flame on the stove of his anger. Suddenly, she is the one who is out of bounds in the way she is treating him in the moment. Now, he is the hurt one. She is the one who needs to ask forgiveness. Answered prayer for him now invites her to change too.

But she doesn't like this. He has poorly expressed his anger for years. She should be allowed to for once! Instantly she is tempted to remove the welcome mat from the answered prayer. It makes sense why. After all, she can no longer talk about her husband to the other ladies in the way she always has. Her prayer requests at women's group for her husband have to change. She no longer has a reason to avoid attention to her own issues. She can no longer legitimately see herself as "that wife" in the group but now has a new identity to find. All this time he was the defensive and impatient one. Now she finds that she is defensive and impatient—not because he is mean but because he is gracious!

Sometimes the joy, freedom, and thanksgiving such a change in him warrants find a cold welcome from the one who prayed for it. Going to a new place of gospel freedom together is lovely to dream about and frightening to take hold of.

Both of these responses surface when Paul writes to the church community in Corinth. A notorious sin headlined the newspapers of their hearts. Scandal was given a bed to rest on in the community. Paul was instructing them that they must avoid reading the news no longer. They must confront the sin.

At this point, our temptation leads us to picture Paul writing with rage in his mouth and fury in his pen. Surely Paul's eyes were dry with indignation, his heart filled with raw justice. And yet listen to how Paul writes:

> I wrote to you out of much affliction and anguish of heart and with many tears, not to cause you pain but to let you know the abundant love I have for you. (2 Cor. 2:4)

His posture is tearful, full of longing and concern for their well-being. They are dear to him. His purpose is expressly designed not to hurt them but to strengthen their sense of how loved they are in what they still have to learn and confront.

In fact, Paul initially regretted that he wrote to them, feeling he had hurt them wrongly (2 Cor. 7:8). He clarifies his thankfulness that they were not pained by him in the wrong way. "As it is, I rejoice, not because you were grieved . . ." (2 Cor. 7:9).

Exposing Our Temptations

What Paul teaches in Galatians 6, he lives out here. His intention is to restore those caught in sin and not simply to make them hurt.

In contrast, the know-it-all is tempted to become like the wrongful dad who spanks and spanks and spanks a child until he is certain the child has hurt enough for the sin committed. The know-it-all is tempted to act as if making someone feel conviction of sin is his and not the Holy Spirit's job (John 16:8–9). He does not want the person to ever forget what he has done (which translates into always needing to wear the grey overcoat of having sinned and never being able to dress in the bright clothes of forgiveness).

By this Paul points out that because the one who was caught in sin is actually being changed, they too must act accordingly.

> For such a one, this punishment by the majority is enough, so you should rather turn to forgive and comfort him, or he may be overwhelmed by excessive sorrow. So I beg you to reaffirm your love for him. (2 Cor. 2:6–8)

Punishment for the repentant does not go on and on. "Endless" is not sorrow's epitaph. We resist the excessive sorrow of the repentant heart with the gospel. Paul begs. "Forgive, comfort, reaffirm your love," he pleads. To do this, those who were the recipients of the sinner's harm may need true help. The community welcomes the forgiven one, and with sensitivity to the consequences that still remain, they likewise walk alongside those whose ability to forgive requires more than a few baby steps.

Forgiveness will not justify folly, however. There is no way that a person who hates the molestation he committed, even though forgiven, will ever have charge of the nursery. His place in the community will require his use of his gifts in other ways.

Similarly, forgiveness will not remove all consequences. Friendship does not always follow from forgiveness among those victimized. Though able to forgive by grace, the harmed one may attend a different church from the one who hurt her or vice versa. Rarely does forgiveness have a fairy-tale ending in the moment, but it does lead us toward a redemptive ending for everyone involved—an ending that heaven will fully mend into completion.

But why does all of this matter anyway? Because, according to Paul, how we handle the repenting sinner now is an act of spiritual warfare. These situations "test" us regarding the extent of our obedience (2 Cor. 2:9). Obeying by forgiving and reaffirming our love for the repentant one is necessary to fight against the "designs" of Satan in the community (2 Cor. 2:11). It is Satan and not God who inflicts excessive sorrow upon a repentant person, along with the absence of love, the neglect of comfort, and a punishment that never ends. At this point Paul reminds us, therefore, that when dealing with discipline and sin, we are tempted to reflect more of a devilish than a divine approach.

Discerning the Sorrows

Light a match for a fire pit while camping, and both gasoline and newspaper will ignite. Both are capable fire starters for dinner. Both are capable destroyers of the campsite. But one of them is volatile and not to be trusted.

Likewise, both the Devil and God talk about sin. But their impact differs dramatically. While the Holy Spirit convicts us of sin, never is the Holy Spirit identified as an accuser. Pause there for a moment. God is not the accuser of the brethren; Satan is. How does this fact alone instruct how those who are spiritual are meant to restore those caught in sins?

Paul identifies this difference by drawing two different kinds of sorrows on the marker board of our attention. The know-it-all has no time to pay attention to this kind of drawing. Categories, quotes, and first-draft thoughts form first judgments. Listening is overrated. Not so for Paul.

First, God's way of confronting his people in their sin Paul calls "godly grief" (2 Cor. 7:9–11). This kind of sorrow is given by God and accords with his character. This kind of sorrow for our sin is recognizable by three traits.

First, the grief produces not just tears or new resolutions. It actually produces repentance—which means a real turning point. The change is tender, it is new, and it is incomplete, but it is real.

Second, the grief from God leads the person back to a fresh acquaintance with the provision of salvation—the merit and mercy of Jesus. His sandals, the cross, the empty tomb, his present intercession and advocacy—these form a glad reunion in the person's being. The person knows that ultimately it is God he has sinned against and God for whom he comes home.

Third, grief from God purposes to send regret away: "For godly grief produces a repentance that leads to salvation without regret" (2 Cor. 7:10).

In contrast, there is a kind of sorrow for sin that has nothing to do with God. Over the years I have found that those caught in the sin of lying, for example, require the most active energy and time—particularly if lying has been a way of life.

Why is this so? On the one hand, a long life of this sin gives a person a very strong skill set with manipulation. Such a person is adept at tears, quoting the right verses, giving meaningful looks of the eyes, and saying what the person in front of him wants to hear. It is easy to conclude that someone has godly grief when actually he is feeling sorrow because he got caught and is simply trying to do what he needs to in order to get everyone off his case and to get back to normal.

On the other hand, when grace begins teaching a liar how to tie his shoes again, as with any other sin and sinner the change often does not come all at once but in fits and starts. This means that the liar requires time to begin to see how deeply she lies and how thoroughly words of spin saturate her daily life. For this reason, a person whom Jesus is actually changing will tell the truth in the same conversation that undetected lies are also present. A changing liar will state emphatically today that there are no more lies and mean this truthfully. But because her eyes to see this path are still new and squinting, she does not recognize the memories or strategies that will reveal themselves in a week or a month from now. It is easy to conclude then that a liar isn't actually changing at all, when, in fact, a powerful change is taking place. It just takes much more time than we want.

How do we know which kind of grief we are dealing with? Often we don't and must take our time walking through it, prayerfully waiting for God to show us. What we think one week will change the following week. Often, at least with those tempted to lie, we need a host of weeks in order to make this kind of determination.

In light of all this, this point that Paul makes has been invaluable. A grief that is self-generated and made mischief with by the Devil "produces death," Paul says (v. 10). That is, it sheds tears but does not turn; it makes resolutions and quotes verses. But it neither rests upon Jesus alone nor surrenders to God unless the consequences remain controllable and favorable. It also treats regret like a friend from whom we must not separate.

One method of holding on to regret is to relive and retell the story as if Christ has not acted on our behalf. We feel the same guilt and shame and sorrow as we did at the time, even though years have passed. We still tell the story in the first-person present as if we are still in the moment, that is, if we tell it at all. Godly grief will eventually turn our sinful secrets into testimonies of grace. Regret keeps secrets.

Also, grief that is not from God sometimes leaves out even temporary regret—the person does not adequately get what he has done. He moves on quickly, not just from guilt or shame but from adequately comprehending the sin itself. Or, at the other extreme, it makes regret a permanent fixture—he is never allowed to move on from the sin itself or from the guilt or shame.

In Jesus, a grief that is from God will deliver us, not always from our memory of what we did or its consequences but always from the guilt and shame of it. What was once our norm no longer is. The third purpose of discipline is having its wonderful way with us in Jesus.

Conclusion

I often think about Judas and Peter.

Both sinned terribly. Both wept bitterly.

Worldly and godly grief are put on display and set in contrast.

One grieved his wrong but did not turn. His was no depression, no diseased fit from chemical mismanagement. This was different. He hanged to his own solution for his sin. Regret, no salvation, the two hands that tied the rope.

The other man found more than weeping—splashed in the prayer and intercession of a Savior. Every day the rest of his life, roosters still crowed. Every day the foul reminders still screeched. But the cross stands. The tomb empties. The regret fades. Character grows. God holds the man.

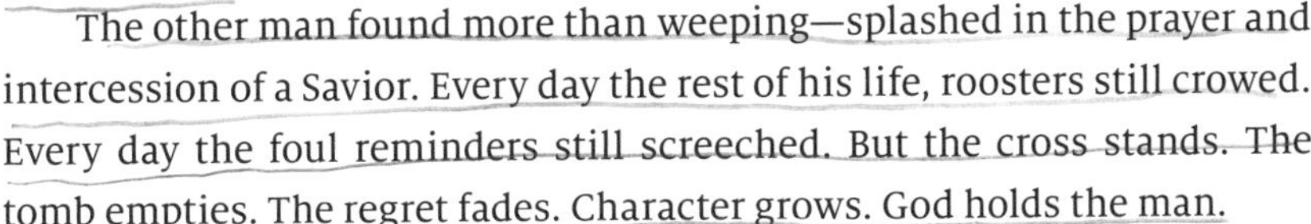

PART 2

EXAMINING OUR MENTORING

In this next section, we want to ask God to help us identify how our temptations to be everywhere, to fix everything, and to know everything are sometimes unwittingly bolstered by the influences of our families and ministry environments.

Two sets of questions await you.

The first set has to do with your physicality as a human being. Few of us are accustomed to asking such questions, and they seem awkward to us.

1) What makes you most uncomfortable, most thankful, or most tempted: being seen, touched, heard, or smelled by others?

2) What ministry situations do you least desire, are most tempted by, or feel grateful for: those that involve seeing people and their places up close, touching people, hearing people, or smelling people and their places?

In this next chapter, we raise these questions in light of our having been created with both souls and bodies. Then we take a practical look at how touching and hearing confront us in ministry settings.

The second set of questions invites you to consider the providences of your life. Who are the persons and what are the events that have most shaped you, positively or negatively? Persons and events, both in our families and in our ministries, have mentored us in ways that do not always resemble the gospel. This mentoring works within our blind spots and often acts as an unseen director for the ways we approach life and ministry. Becoming honest about these human and earthy providences causes us to seek prayer as our means of illumination as Jesus takes us by the hand, and by his Spirit recovers and rementors us. In chapter 7 Jesus shines a light on the providences of our lives.

The final chapters then expose how the goals of celebrity, immediacy, and advancement infiltrate our ministry environments. Jesus reorients us to our need to relearn how to return to obscurity, as only he is the famous one. By examining mistakes and challenges when haste runs our churches and our lives, we then find Jesus changing the way we look at how time is meant to work. Finally, with the lie of advancing ourselves in ministry on our minds, we end with a letter to a young minister.

Therefore, we take a candid look at how Jesus disrupts these attempts to deny our humanity. By doing so, he recovers not only our place but his. He alone is the famous one. Jesus values waiting, not haste. His views regarding what it means to advance often have little to do with changing positions, sizes, or geographies. How then do we find strength and joy for the long smallness we often endure and feel?

CHAPTER SIX

Physicality

Hearing and Touching in Ministry

> We have no home in this world, I used to say, and then I'd walk back up the road to this old place and make myself a pot of coffee and a fried-egg sandwich.[1]

In light of these temptations to be like God and for the purpose of reminding myself that I am only local and finite, I've picked up a strange habit as a pastor and as a man. Sometimes I find myself physically taking hold of the corner of my desk with my hand. If I'm out and about, it seems that grasping something firmly rooted will do, such as a tree limb or a car door. I suppose it is because sometimes my days in pastoral ministry suffer from vertigo—the day swirls, and I find no footing. Off balance, I feel I might fall. The ground is hourglass sand. The poet Czeslaw Milosz, a Nobel Prize winner, first showed me what the business of touching one's desk is. "Here I am," he writes:

> Here means on this earth, on this continent and no other, in this city and no other, in this epoch I call mine, this century, this year. I was given no other place, no other time, and *I touch my desk* to defend myself against the feeling that my own body is transient. This is all very fundamental, but, after all, the science of life depends on the gradual discovery of fundamental truths.[2]

To touch one's desk is a symbolic gesture, of course. It aspires to remind us that our lives, in contrast to God's, are necessarily physical and local. Faith, hope, and love—the matters of our souls—are tried, learned, and lived in close physical proximity to created persons and things within the limits of certain times and places. While spiritual wars rage about and while angels fly, I remain grounded. Battles all at once and everywhere outpace me. Here (and not everywhere) is where I must fight.

After all, I write these sentences with my rump on a chair in Webster Groves, Missouri. My fingers click these buttons on this keyboard. Colleagues in ministry shuffle past the door of my study. I hear my clock ticking. It is 9:25 AM. It is a muggy and blue-skied Monday in June 2010. How about you? Consider where you are as you read these sentences and contemplate their meaning. Compare and contrast your location and time with mine, and you will begin to feel the fundamental truth the poet yearned to reveal to us.

But long before this poet, a pastor, the apostle Paul, likewise taught this desk-touching truth. "The God who made the world," Paul said, "determined allotted periods and the boundaries of [our] dwelling place" (Acts 17:24–26). The ministry with its leaders and neighbors is boundaried and limited. This is fundamental.

But boundaried does not mean inferior. The poet touches his desk, not only to remember his physical and local limits but also to defend himself against the lie that he is meaningless and without purpose. As if that desk and his ability to touch it in that time and place mean nothing. As if he has no capacity to also participate with what is soulish and meaningful. The apostle likewise defends us. From these boundaried dwelling places, he says, we are meant with our neighbors to "seek God, and perhaps feel [our] way toward him, and find him," for "he is actually not far from each one of us" (v. 27).

As ministry leaders, we touch our desks and graciously proclaim, "Immanuel," God is with us (Isa. 7:14). Our calling includes helping our neighbors do the same.

Wendell and the Bone-House

I am one of Wendell's pastors. Polio has held Wendell's legs hostage for seventy years. Over those seventy years Wendell has also conformed to the regimen of diabetes, with its drill sergeant–like demands upon his daily routines. He pricks his finger to make it bleed before every meal. He counts calories and enters them into a machine that determines the daily insulin levels his sugar-confused body needs. Two bouts with cancer have also bushwhacked Wendell and sought to overtake him. The death of his wife ransacked his heart and made his bed too empty at night. His hands tremble. His voice sometimes slurs, revealing the effort Wendell exerts to converse.

It's a treat to take Wendell to lunch. Wendell's dog Chloe bountifully welcomes all visitors with tail-wagging glee. She is a joyful dog and encourages a room with her presence. Also, Wendell is a grateful man who likes to talk about the faithfulness of Jesus. Wendell is an evangelist. He has story after story of people he is praying for and with whom he has been sharing his faith in Christ. Lunch with Wendell blesses and instructs. It also humbles.

A motorized wheelchair mobilizes Wendell. He shuts doors, brushes his teeth, and lets Chloe outside from this chair. Within this chair Wendell talks on the telephone, cooks dinner, and cleans. It is from this chair that Wendell also reads his Bible, prays to God, shares Christ with others, and gives praise with tears to the One whom he says has been the faithful lover of his life all of these difficult years.

For Wendell, spiritual life happens within this chair with his atrophied legs and sore fingertips. Many of us learn that our main descriptor in ministry is "physician of the soul"; that is, "we work at the heart of things, where we are most ourselves and where our relationships in faith and intimacy are developed."[3] Ours is a life of soul care. However, to care as a physician of the soul for Wendell, one must account for Wendell's physical body. For Wendell, his walk of faith, hope, and love is worked out within the blessings and frustrations of his chair.

It is easy to grasp the physicality and locality of soul care with a person bound to a chair or who has chronic bodily riots. But I want to suggest that any pastoral ministry must account for the sensory and the physical of God's created world. In the words of the pastor-poet G. M. Hopkins, we are like a "skylark" in our "bone-house," the "rainbow" that stands upon "the meadow-down."[4] The skylark is our souls, residing within our bodies (bone-houses). They belong together, as do the stuff of heaven (rainbows) and of earth (meadow-down).

Early in pastoral leadership, in my desire to make a difference I imagined ministry as only benedictions for the skylark and caretaking for the rainbow. I gave little thought to what it would mean to give my life amid the bone-house and the meadow-down.

Examining Our Mentoring

Or, to put it another way, I knew that the battle I fought would not be against "flesh and blood" (Eph. 6:12). But flesh and blood would form the arena for this fight. I little accounted for the fact that this warfare with unseen principalities and powers would not negate my emerging need for reading glasses when taking up "the sword of the Spirit" (Eph. 6:17). Nor would this spiritual warfare negate the undeniable benefit of brushing my teeth prior to praying with members of my congregation.

The result is that I ventured to imagine difference making in ministry in such a way that celebrated the soul but underestimated the body. My imagination was too small. I forgot that both require my attention. I needed more mentoring in what the apostle John understood in his prayers for his parish: "Beloved, I pray that all may go well with you and that you may be in good health, as it goes well with your soul" (3 John 2).

Preparing Our Bodily Senses

What does this mean for us? Glorifying God with our lives and ministries requires us to prepare for the physical. When we minister to neighbors, we see. We see their facial expressions, their teeth or gums, the hair on their skin, their clothes and body shapes. We see their pictures on the mantle, the pine and oak that brood over their houses, their fences mended or rusty in their yards. When we preach, people see our saliva spurt out of our mouths with certain syllables. They notice our eyes, ears, and chins. The shape of our sweater or shirt or robe as it rests upon or over our bellies is not lost on them. Neither is the sweat soaking our shirts beneath our arms. We, too, see them as we open the Book and point to Jesus. We see their eyes, their noses, and their hair. We see them shift and settle, restless and contented in their seats, handing Cheerios to their children.

Life and ministry is a sensory vocation. To minister is to hear. We hear the human voice—female, male, childlike, and aged. We hear our grumbling stomachs, our humming melody, our groaning with sighs too deep for words. We hear the labored moans and stammers of those voices broken by disease. We hear noses blow. We hear cardinal and blue jay warble or a semi gurgle into a downshift on the highway.

We touch. We touch by shaking hands or giving hugs. We hold a glass of water. We receive a picture into our hands and gaze at the family resemblance. We touch apples or forks, bread or plastic plates. We touch snot and tears and scars. We hold hands and talk to God.

We smell. We smell breath and other bodily odors, both pleasant and less than pleasant. We smell after-lunch gas mixing with scented candles, baking bread and aftershave, cologne, or perfume. We smell manure in the pasture, ethnic foods on the city block, laundry in the wash, and all this while we hold our Bibles.

We taste. We taste the toothpaste or morning coffee or after-lunch mints in our mouths when we say, "Let's pray," or invite someone to "tell us more."

What I'm pointing out is that we minister to others amid the sights, feelings, and smells that come from the dampness, the breeziness, or the dryness of the place. On the park bench, in a restaurant for lunch, between office cubicles, or side by side in the seats of a Ford or a Chevy, in a rocking chair by a fireplace, in a metal chair by the hospital bed, in frosty grass, or below the clear blue at the gravesite, we sensibly minister the gospel of Jesus to ordinary persons in their particular places.

Jesus was seen, touched, heard, tasted, and smelled (1 John 1:1–3). To follow Jesus into significance is to settle into the physical. To mightily lead as a Jesus follower is to learn to rest among eyebrows, necks, and knuckles. Close physical proximity will force us into the landscapes of bodily and creational seeing, smelling, hearing, touching, and tasting.

Noticing Our Interior Scenes

Ministry not only befriends the physical but it also makes a companion of our internal scenes. We must learn to recognize the internal emotions and thoughts at work when we are in close physical proximity with one another.

Our dreams, our imagination, and our memories are like movies, like living films. But unlike a movie, our dreams or memories give us the apparent ability to smell and to touch. Sometimes we awake startled from a dream; we are unsure in those waking moments if what we feel in our bodies and in our souls actually happened. Sometimes memory makes us feel as though we have actually lived and touched the person or the moment again. Bodily senses accompany our interior lives. At times, they can adorn our souls with treasures and at times litter them with trash.

This is because the five bodily senses recline easily on the furniture of our imaginings, our dreams, and our memories. Ministry to others requires our attention to this interior reality. What people sense with their body or their interior being impacts how they interpret us and how we interpret them. Words or sights or smells awaken feelings and thoughts and perceptions within us both. We have to account for this when we speak.

For example, mention the word *Mamaw* to me, and my memory awakens. I hear her voice saying, "My lands," or, "He's a dandy," or referring to me as "Charlie Brown." I see her watching travel shows on television, wearing yellow short sleeves, walking in the yard picking up sticks, or sitting quietly with the unspoken meaning that sometimes danced and sometimes cried in her eyes at Christmas. I smell her perfume or the effect of sweat on her skin from the hours she spent cooking green beans with bacon. I see the dirt under her fingernails from her garden digging that planted and harvested those same green beans. I smell the soap from the shower, the musty wood from the stairs that Papaw built. I taste her macaroni with tomatoes, the chick-a-sticks she brought me after work when I was a boy, and the tears I kissed on her cheeks before she died. I feel her embrace on the porch when heading back to college. I feel her dark hair dried and surrendered on her forehead in hospice. To mention the word *Mamaw* in a flippant way, or even a harmless way, is to enter my story and stir my emotional waters. My being wakens with sense.

Mention *hospice*, and numerous pastoral memories both sad and beautiful cascade through the creek beds of my mind. Names, life stories, families, laughter, and loss begin to softly mist up from the land of my memories. I sit there in the enveloping shade of an oak tree and listen to the stream percolate and trickle onward. I remember my prayers. The smells. Singing *Amazing Grace* softly into the ear of one whose lungs labored and mined for each breath.

To talk of ministry and hospice in an only theoretical, detached, or academic way arouses irritation in me. I'm not saying my irritation is warranted or proper. I'm just observing a fact. Memory, imagination, and dreams shape the sensible responses and perceptions of those who minister and those who receive ministry.

Paul acknowledges this when he writes to Timothy. "I remember you constantly," Paul said to Timothy. "I remember your tears. . . . I am reminded of your sincere faith . . . your grandmother Lois and your mother

Eunice" (2 Tim. 1:3–5). Paul's words forge bodily senses with our memories and imaginings.

Pastors speak as those with skin and bones. People hear us while they sit their rumps on wooden pews. We are heard by those whose memories and imaginations constantly percolate their way into our conversations.

Entering the Awkward

Perhaps this talk of ministry as human and physical, not just as soulish, discomforts us. Something inside of us wants to protest! "Ministry is supposed to encompass theological books, not human noses," we might say. Divine sermons and not stinky human breath are our concern. To suggest that divine sermons have something to do with stinky breath, or that divine sermons are often given with stinky breath, may feel unnerving or irreverent.

Our personal fears can come into play. To enter the world of doctrines and facts is to enter the world of *truth and falsehood described*. To dwell with these descriptions is to feel safe, to have solid ground under our feet. The world is tidy. The rooms are swept. The floors are clean.

To enter the world of human beings, and creation, and the majestic deformities that present themselves in fallen Eden is to enter the world of *truth and falsehood lived*. Real life is much less manageable and much more unsettling. Our capacity for feeling and thinking and acting contrary to our own stated doctrines unnerves us when in the presence of persons and providence and creation. We want to flee back into the classroom where we are safe. Maybe you as a reader have never felt this way at all. Maybe I'm just projecting my own weaknesses, limits, and sins onto you. But if you do not struggle in this way, it will benefit you to know that many of your colleagues (like me) do.

Many of us fear what would be revealed if we were seen for what we are and others had to come to terms with what we are not. *Most of us have never had to ask questions about what it would mean for us that ministry is an act of neighbor love and that to love one's neighbor would require our close physical proximity.*

Attending the Jesus Seminary

Perhaps this is why Jesus trained laborers for ministry so differently from how we train. What I mean is this. Notice, for example, where Jesus leads his disciples after he asks them to follow him and says that he will make them fishers of men (Mark 1:17–45). As Jesus followers, they were meant to "fish" among the sick, the poor, the demon possessed, which included teachers, urban hipsters, rural folks, and mothers-in-law. At one point the disciples are surrounded by all the sick and demon possessed from the area. Imagine what it would have meant to follow and learn from Jesus in the midst of these tragic and putrid sights, sounds, and smells.

Jesus taught his disciples sound doctrine. Yet throughout the Gospels we consistently observe Jesus teaching theology in the midst of the psych ward. He took his disciples into the hospital, as it were; sat them down in the emergency room; and confronted them with the ghastly sights, grieved sounds, and rank aromas of actual human people in their diseases, their wrestling with demons, their disputes, their poverty, and their loss of spouses. He brought them near to ethnic prejudices, injustices, anxieties, and traumas, not to mention the joys, pleasures, delights, and longings of ordinary human beings. Disciples learned about God in the context of the bodily life situations that actually exist in the world, the sensory ramifications of an under-the-sun reality.

Imagine learning our doctrine of God by studying our best theologians while sitting in the ER amid anxious parents, traumatized children, gunshot wounds, and asthma attacks. Imagine reading amid the stale smell of coffee, amid the sound of tears and the sights of perplexity, trauma, and frustration. How would this impact how we process the doctrines and categories of God's omnipotence, omnipresence, and omniscience? Or what if we read our doctrine of salvation where mental patients spook the halls, where medications, prayers, and helpless parents wrestle with insurance, paperwork, and the pressure of strained budgets?

Perhaps Jesus purposefully taught his future pastors and ministry leaders in this fashion, "because any theoretical discovery of grace in the grotesque could be dangerous if divorced from the palpable experience of pain, the mundane smell of urine and despair."[5] It seems that with Jesus, we are meant to discover "an unlikely grace in a grotesque landscape of feeding tubes and bed restraints, wheelchairs and diapers, nausea and incontinence."[6]

Perhaps this is why Jesus so often chose metaphor alongside of his prose for his language choices. Jesus's language choices arose from a physical community. Jesus seemed unbothered by doing theology with earthy poetical language. So when Jesus wants to teach us about his divinity, he says, "I am the bread of life," or, "I am the light of the world," or, "I am the Good Shepherd." Jesus's language choice resembles the Old Testament pattern. When God speaks of himself, he refers to himself as a rock, or an eagle, or a strong tower.

Yet for those of us whose church stories have firm rooting in the seminary language of systematic theology or Western philosophy, the way Jesus depicts theology like this can sometimes confound us. Perhaps we sometimes assume that in order to demonstrate an aware and rich appreciation for God, we should speak with the language of systems, creeds, and confessions. We may even presume that theology with poetry demonstrates a watered-down and simplistic and less educated approach to God. We may feel that if a person really cared about God and knowing the doctrines of God, he would quickly abandon poetry. After all, to say that God is a rock seems childish. And when we became adults, we put away childish things, didn't we? More adult language would say that God is omnipotent. Right?

I value and treasure my theological heritage with its language. But I can't imagine that we are left more provided for if we say that "God is omnipotent" and resist saying that "God is like an eagle underneath whose wings we are sheltered."

To learn from Jesus requires a crash course in earthy and poetic language because Jesus used "the language of being there."[7] He spoke about birds, fields, pearls, and snakes. He did not minister as though everyone had his mind or his mastery of language and theology. He spoke among the grain fields. He talked about lilies. The bone-house and the meadow-down gave him speech. He "touched his desk" and helped us do the same, so that from here, God might reach us.

Touching

Considering the physicality of life and ministry also raises the practical question of touch. Let's pause for a moment before moving to the next chapter in order to expand our thinking regarding the role of touch in our

Christian walk. Taking on this subject reflects its reality in our lives—it is awkward and too complex for a small conversation. The following thoughts are meant to give us a few categories for the discussion and a few tools to use for our life and ministry practice.

I was twenty-eight. It was the second year of my first pastorate. I began singing songs and leading a weekly Wednesday morning Bible study at a local assisted-living facility for the elderly. After the study and the song, I stood up from playing the piano. The eyes of one elderly woman glistened with tears. She walked toward me, kissed my cheek (the way many of these older ones did), and thanked me. She was fifty years older than I was. I kissed her cheek in return. This was their custom, not mine, and admittedly I felt uncomfortable. But I gave her a hug and took a moment to pray for her. She gave thanks to God. I thought nothing more about it.

The following Wednesday after the study and the song, I rose from the piano and was dumbfounded to notice that a line of men and women immediately formed. Each one seemed to wait for their turn. The aged women kissed my cheek, and I then awkwardly kissed theirs and prayed for them. The silver-headed and balding men shook my hand, I shook theirs and prayed for them. Hugs blossomed. Smiles unfolded like petals; tears moistened and accumulated as if soaked by the dew of a sunlit morning. Strange!

Over the months, this kind of line forming for touch and prayer faded into a kind of normative community practice of holy kisses, handshakes, hugs, presence, and praying. Those Wednesday mornings, the many funerals that followed, this tender way of neighbor care and gratitude to God in Jesus—these became to me like the treasured drawings and pictures that persons sometimes magnet to their refrigerator. I'll come back to why this is and what Jesus teaches us about touch in a moment.

Prior to that, I cannot help but raise a contrast in ministry that sickens with the telling. Alongside those Wednesday mornings at the elderly care facility were Sunday mornings at the church I served. On these Sunday mornings there was a man who regularly gave "holy kisses" to various women in the congregation when he greeted them at the doors of morning worship. Over time, whispers of complaint began to find my ear. Two women in particular finally and awkwardly described how the kiss felt no resemblance to what is holy. As we began to gently but intentionally talk to the man about this, he defended his actions, stating that he possessed only Christlike motives. We asked him to stop, nonetheless. Later that year, his long affair with another woman surfaced, and his marriage did not survive.

In the New Testament, two kinds of physical touch are set in brutal contrast. The first is Judas's kiss of Jesus's cheek. This kind of kiss misuses physical touch in order to consume or preserve its own selfish wants, lusts, desires, or agendas (Luke 22:47–48). In contrast the "holy kiss" envisions a way for Christian community to recover in Jesus how human beings were originally meant to touch each other.[8] Physical touch is meant as a holy act. Few of us know in an experiential way what it means to touch or be touched in a sacred way. Profane touch has mentored and broken most of us.

At issue for life and ministry is that the close physical proximity of neighbor love and local life leads us into this territory of gospel touch and its counterfeits. More topography exists on this subject than we have room to map out in this moment together. But one thing is certain: in order to navigate this rocky terrain we need an expert guide. Jesus is our expert guide. He is our compass for navigating the touch of the sick, the touch between men and women, and the touch of children.

Jesus and the Touch of the Sick

Jesus touch of the sick begins by recognizing his frequent touch of creation. The contact of Jesus's skin with the stuff of earth dots the pages of the Gospels: bread and fish, a basin of water, a towel, a cup, wine, wheat, tree bark and tables, lilies in a field. Jesus is the one who gathered dirt into his hands, spit into it with his saliva, hand rubbed the brew into mud, and slathered the damp grit onto the broken eyes of a man born blind (John 9:6).

Jesus touched people. He touched bodies. But his was not the sexualized touch of a pornographic mind, a controlling cling, or a predator heart. The way of Jesus's touch graciously intends to reform our own.

To begin, Jesus touched the sick and often on the wound. Jesus touched the leprosy of the leper (Matt. 8:3), the ear of the deaf (Luke 22:51), the eye of the blind, the hand of the feverish (Matt. 8:15), and the tongue of the mute (Mark 7:33). This was *pitiful* touch (Matt. 20:34), the caress of pity.

To graze the bruise with pity reveals the intimate nudge of mercy. Pity does not avoid the gentle collision of comfort. It intentionally facilitates strong contact with true solace from the heart of an other-centered compassion that is resonant with the character of God. The sympathy of God in Christ, if only for a moment, exterminates with gospel touch the infestation of callousness that bores its holes into the foundation of the wooden seconds and rotted minutes of our painful bodily rafters. The moment of pity signifies that something beyond cruelty and hardship exists within these damaged walls and will outlast these unwanted pests.

No wonder that "all who had diseases pressed to touch" Jesus (Mark 3:10). Such touch, like a righteous army, thoroughly routs the abuse and neglect of enemy hands that intend harm to the infirmed. We the sick long for this Jesus touch that defends and comforts. Such touch either heals us now or meaningfully signifies the healing that with heaven will come. Though it may delay, in Christ healing will not ultimately falter. The touch of Jesus's pity preaches such hope.

For this reason, Jesus will lead us in our lives and ministries into the sickbed smells of medicated bones among muscles drunk with prescripted concoctions. The widow rooms and cancer wards of each community reveal for us where Jesus will surely visit. We the frightened or hardened need Jesus to take us by the hand and guide us toward the sick within our families or congregations or communities. Any adult whose life stage has transitioned her into the role of primary caregiver for her parent knows that we cannot care for the sick alone. Any family member who lives hours away or any pastor who can only be at one place at one time among an aging congregation needs help to remember that we are not Jesus, and our ability of care is more limited than we would like. There are too many people and too much ailment for our two shoulders. But in Jesus, a community of shoulders can substantially touch the sick literally and figuratively.

Where do we start? We start by recognizing our need for Jesus's grace with our own bodily ailments. Then we take our fears of sick people to Jesus. We ask him to grow us into the love that does battle with our fears. Ours may not be to touch the wound directly as Jesus does. And never would we touch anyone who would not wish it done. But when we pray for the sick, we can ask, "May I take your hand and pray?" Or for the critically infirmed we can gently lay our hand softly upon the head or arm. A gentle pat on the shoulder with a kind word or a hug can go a long way for those who can still stand.

In this regard, I remember Betty's mouth. It was covered with a mask that spoon-fed her lungs with breath. The steady beeping of an apparatus indicated the dripping of medicine into the taped tubes of her veins. She lay on one lone bed in a large bare room guarded by the machinery of remedy. I fumbled for a Bible passage to read, nervous with youth, unsure of how to glimpse Jesus for the eighty-year-old widow as she lay pressed beneath it all. I laugh now as I remember it—the laughter that flows from remembering grace and meaning. For, before I said a word, Betty raised her tube-laced arms and managed a sentence beneath her mask. "Shall we pray, Pastor?" She said this less like a question and more like a statement. Looking back, I now believe that this old saint was teaching me what my role for such a moment was meant by God to be. She was mentoring me. I took her hand and held it. I laid my other hand lightly upon her forehead. There together, in Jesus's name and with his present empowerment, I strongly raised my feeble voice to God.

The Touch between Men and Women

But touch not only walks down the halls of sickness; it also drives us onto the city streets of gender. As it relates to gender, I have been too awkward with touch where I needn't be. The occasional touch of familial Christian love is warranted among us. This challenges some of us who have a "never touch" policy. But, on the other hand, I have not been enough awkward with touch where I should be. There is less touch needed or wisely given than some of us who are younger in ministry seem to think. On both counts, maybe my awkward attempts to find my way can give you categories for the discussion you need in order to find your way in Jesus.

As it relates to making awkward what needn't be, before Betty raised her hand for prayer in her hospital room that day, she had already taught me something good about the occasional human touch between men and women who in Jesus are united like family. Admittedly, since I was fifty years her junior, I saw her as more grandmotherly than sisterly. But even here I had learning to do, and I think she saw that. To her I was her pastor—grandson-like, yes, but still a man of God sent to do her good in Jesus. Though I often secretly feared that I would be found out as somewhat boyish in the wise presence of the elderly, she saw me as the grown man that I was. She treated me according to the calling I had been given. This always humbled me. She was not one of those who used her age to look down on my youth. She called me "Pastor" and meant it.

Anyway, it was the anniversary of her husband's death. He had died over twenty years before. She asked if we could sit and talk for a moment. All of a sudden the dam broke and the tears poured through. She crumpled into the small couch there in the greeting area. We sat. She wept. My shoulder held her fatigued head and bolstered her heaving torso. I did not know what else to do. I prayed while she cried.

It turns out there was nothing else to do. I had not imagined before this how little a widow experiences touch as it is meant to be. Family members live at a distance and visit sporadically. Beyond the pokes of medical people, the elderly often enter a famine of touch as if dwelling in the desert years of their lives. Upon whose shoulder does a widow lean when she grieves the loss of the husband she loved? Only once was I that shoulder for Betty. And that is probably how it should be. But it reminded me of the role that we play for one another in community. My shoulder was safe and strong. For a moment it brotherly pillowed her genuine grief. I hope one day a gospel shoulder might kindly let me lean upon it amid my own fainting for the loved one I lost, as I too wait for heaven's glad reunion in Jesus to find me.

Not surprisingly, Betty was one of those in line by the piano early on. I look back now and recognize that I was too awkward with this touch of the right kind. Men and women formed a line because safe and brotherly human touch was like a rare gem. A handshake, a hug, presence, a kiss on a cheek, prayer—human touch the way a family is meant in Christ to offer one another, was a treasured commodity to take advantage of while it lasted.

In my case with Betty, Paul gives the category for us. Young men are to treat older women as mothers, which implies that older women treat younger men as sons (1 Tim. 5:2). The "mother" found a moment for the shoulder of a "son."

Gospel touch, then, is meant to resemble the touch normatively appropriate between family members. This is your guide. Therefore, abusive, neglectful, presumptuous, or sensual touch has no place in the gender touch of gospel life and ministry. (Those of us who have only such categories of damaging touch need the healing grace and mentoring of Jesus before we attempt familial touch in Jesus's name. Until the gospel rightly changes our use of touch, we are less ready for ministry than we realize, no matter how gifted we are to teach or preach or counsel.)

The Touch between Spiritual Brothers and Sisters

In this regard, there are other kinds of gender touch with which I was not awkward enough—particularly with women, whether younger or older, who were closer in proximity to my own age. I was not aware of how a seemingly godly man in the pulpit can cast a vision for the kind of man a younger single woman longs for or the kind of man a wife sometimes wishes her husband more resembled. Nor was I aware of my own way of relating that could invite or encourage such wishing.

Because of this, it is not that temptations to inappropriate gender touch never come in the form of overt sexual advances. They certainly do. But, at least in my personal and pastoral experience, there are temptations much more subtle in expression and readily more numerous in opportunity that offer an over-familiarity or inappropriate emotional connection between genders: the enjoyment of fixing our eyes on another or of having the eyes of another fixed longingly upon us, and this often in the context of our mutual regard for our spiritual gifts and love for Jesus. Augustine captures this more insidious way of sabotaging gospel touch:

> It is not only gestures of affection that desire between men and women is awakened but also by looks. . . . When impure intentions are allowed to appear not in words but just by exchanging glances and finding pleasure in each other's affection, even though not in each other's arms, we cannot speak any longer of true chastity which is precisely that of the heart.[9]

"We should pick our noses in public." That is what a dear colleague of mine and I decided we would do if we felt the gaze of a woman when we were teaching about God. We should be glad for a woman to do the same if our eyes should take a wrong turn down the dark alleys of a neighborhood we have no business in. The illusion busts with the picking of the nose! In truth, we both knew, only grace can bust the illusion.

Paul's words of grace in Jesus guide us again. Familial touch with those whose age is nearer our own is meant to be as adult brothers with their adult sisters and for whom our sibling interaction is guided not by intimate proximity, flirty tickling, or sensual embrace but by the glad purity of an older brother for his sis who respects her place in the family and seeks her good (1 Tim. 5:2).

When Jesus received the woman's kisses upon his feet, the Bible teachers rebuked him. They had no category for interpreting gender touch in any way other than as sexual and misguided, flirty and sensual.

In contrast, Jesus recognized the woman's use of a kiss as one of gratitude and from a heart for God. The presence of her kiss was not sexy but human and familial; it was localized to this one time and gave expression to her profound sense of forgiveness and gratitude.

Jesus rebuked the Bible teacher and not the woman. In doing so, he upholds a place for gender touch when it more resembles what it was created to be. The teacher, on the other hand, had a double problem. Not only did he have no category to make a right judgment about the kind of gender touch he was witnessing, but he likewise neglected the practice of such holy touch in his own relationship toward Jesus (Luke 7:45). Surely the normative expression of the hospitable touch of that culture resided more freely within genders (as it does in ours). Even with this, the Bible teacher misjudged the woman for doing what he himself had actually neglected.

Like the Bible teacher, many of us have no category for the boundaried place of familial touch between genders. We see the opposite sex only in terms of sensual use. We couldn't see each other with purity if we tried. So we misinterpret sibling or familial grace for intimate advance. We need a lot of grace to learn.

But most of us equally and wrongly excuse ourselves in ways that cost us and reveal either our naivete or our bent hearts. Among the friends and traveling companions of our Lord were several women. Rarely if ever do the Gospels picture Jesus as pursuing with touch or glances these women who were dear to him. To put it crassly, Jesus was not kissing the woman's feet. Even when Mary falls at Jesus's feet with the death of her brother Lazarus, Jesus calls for her and weeps with compassion for her and the others. Those who saw the scene testified to his love for Lazarus (John 11:28–33). But we are not told of touch.

This brings me to a short bit of counsel. Mary, a single woman, was not without community and comfort. She had plenty of shoulders to rest her head on as she wept. In the fullness of his humanity, it was not the carpenter, Rabbi Jesus, who himself was single, who would form the primary shoulder for Mary to rest her head upon.

As a pastor or caregiver, we are accountable and responsible to facilitate the care of those we love. But between genders it is rarely our place to take the primary role in this. Our role resides in the hub of facilitating care but not in the center of giving its most intimate expression. For example, single women have their closest female friends, their biological mothers and fathers, and their spiritual mothers and fathers to whom they pour out their hearts. It is the same with single men. Likewise, married women have a husband, their closest female friends, and their biological and spiritual mothers and fathers to turn to. So it is with married men. Our natural inclinations tempt us to knock over these boundaries and to disregard these community roles. But the gospel empowers us otherwise.

A Ministry Example

Our church outreach event had ended. It was late in the evening. By happenstance I walked out the door at the same time as one of the young women in the congregation I served. We found ourselves walking together because our cars were parked in the same lot. I noticed a sadness in her countenance.

"You seem a bit sad tonight. Are you doing okay?"

With that question, the tears came. She stopped walking, and so did I.

"No, I'm not doing well at all," she mustered as the sobbing began.

Earlier in ministry, in the name of being a pastor, I would have assumed that at that moment I should give her my shoulder. Back then, I would have felt chivalrous about it—protector-like. That masculine sentiment to come to her aid, particularly in light of my calling as her pastor, was right. But I believe I was mistaken in believing that chivalry meant touch and that shepherding gave me the permission to take a central role as a man in her life. If I had faced this situation back then, I would have put my arm around her. I would have told her that it will be okay. I would have asked if she wanted to talk for a while and assured her of my intent to listen. I would have nobly encouraged her that she was not alone and that in Jesus I would walk through whatever it was. That week I would have checked in with her.

But now, as this situation unfolded, I was able to see my role differently. I said to her, "I can see that you are going through a great deal of pain. Do you have anyone in your life that you are able to talk to about it?"

This is always my first question now. In most cases God has already provided a community of intimate shoulders to lean upon. We want to discern what God is already doing before we insert ourselves.

"Yes," she nodded. "I have a very good friend and my house group. They have been walking through this with me and praying for me."

"I'm so glad to know that. It seems that God is kindly pursuing you by providing a community of care that loves you," I said.

"Yes, I guess he has," she said. "I hadn't thought of it that way."

"Do you feel that you can drive home?" I asked. "I would like to make a call for you to one of your friends. Or do you know Jessica? I know she would be happy to give you a ride."

"No thanks," she said. "I'll be okay."

"May I pray for you?" I asked. "It hurts to know you have this kind of pain in your life. May I go to Jesus with you now?"

"Yes," she agreed.

At this point we have not touched. With the temperament and gift set that some of us have—or at our worst, because of the bent heart we possess apart from the gospel—everything inside of us may want to gently pat her shoulder, give her a hug, or take her hand to pray. But even though, through a gospel category, we may be free to do so, we almost never need to. She already has a community of care in God's hands. In addition, freedom to touch may not find its most prudent occasion there on the sidewalk at 9:45 at night in a restaurant parking lot.

So, at this point, I replace my urge to care with touch with the care of a prayer from my heart for her out loud to God.

After the "amen," in the awkward pause, I said lightheartedly, "My wife, Jessica, often says to me, 'Zack, you are a son of the King, dearly loved, so go get 'em!' May I encourage you with this same gospel truth that she encourages me with? 'You are a daughter of the King, dearly loved. Go get 'em!'"

An urge to hug strongly presented itself at this point. But again, the necessity for such touch hasn't changed. I have expressed care by facilitating her access to what God is already providing. So we parted. I prayed on my way home. I shared with my wife, and she prayed too. On Sunday morning at the service, I checked in to see how the lady was doing.

My point here is that I could have given my shoulder in that moment for her to lean on, and on occasion, assuming it is a gospel-healed touch, it may prove good and helpful. But nine times out of ten, I needn't do so because God is already providing those shoulders through others. And even if I do place my hand on her shoulder as we pray, it is as one who immediately after that will pass the baton of this kind of care off to others. Therefore, this kind of touch rarely rises to the level of need.

Those who have trouble with these last sentences likely need to take a look in the mirror of his grace. If you feel that without your touch in that moment the person in pain will not be cared for, you are possibly giving too much weight to your own presence. Remember, I am not talking about the absence of touch for her. I am talking about the absence of *your* touch for her. It could be that this says more about your need to feel loving than it does about her need to get the care in Jesus that will truly help her. Similarly, some of us are more concerned that she will think us distant than we are about facilitating the care in Jesus she needs. In this regard, there is really only one woman whose misconception of me in this way should concern me. That woman is my wife.

"But what if the woman had said that she had no one to turn to?" we might rightly ask. Again, our care in this kind of moment will often find aid with physical touch, but this doesn't mean that the physical touch must normatively come from us. As a norm, I will say something like this: "Don't worry. I know a very dear woman in our church. She is mature in years. The Lord has carried her through a lot. I know she would love to spend time with you. Her name is Carol. May I give her a call for you?" Then, as a norm, I would again offer her a ride home with Jessica or another woman.

As a rule, we do not want to be in the position of having intimate knowledge of someone that her spouse or closest friends don't have. Primary intimacy is their jurisdiction in God's community, not ours. On occasion this cannot be helped, and exceptions surely exist. Sometimes damaging circumstances require more knowledge from us and more moments of gospel touch. But because Jesus is usually already providing in other ways, it is less than wise and often costly to assert ourselves as central to the touch or care that someone of the opposite sex needs.

Jesus would not touch us the way Judas touched him. He would not touch the woman who kissed his feet the way men had handled her. Some of us have known the misuse of touch so profoundly that we doubt the possibility of receiving or giving the kind of touch that purity blesses us with. Jesus can mend us. Physical touch is not beyond the repair of his grace. In him our lives and ministries become living testimonies of this fact.

Jesus and the Touch of Children

Finally, I'd like to say a brief word about how Jesus's grace highlights the role of touch with the children we serve in life and ministry. This subject is profoundly sensitive because of the public scandal of misused touch with kids and because of the personal traumas that we ourselves may experience from our own childhoods. The Gospels tell us of Jesus that "the children were brought to him that he might lay hands on them and pray" (Matt. 19:13).

Jesus touched children in such a way that touch was recovered for what it was meant to be. There is no stranger danger here. His hand lay upon their heads, not their tummy or thighs. His words he spoke to bless them in their hearing, not to tempt them or misuse them for his own whims. His heart was for their good in God so that for them he raised his voice in prayer. All of this Jesus did in public, not in secret, before the eyes of all who watched. By his rebuke of those who thought to shush and shame them, Jesus set before us not only a picture of what the kingdom of heaven is like but also a statement about the dignity and love with which God blesses kids.

Each of my kids have known the strange but blessed experience of having Mr. Smart (my best man and mentor) bless them. Prior to leaving from a visit, he has knelt on the kitchen or living room floor and invited each child to himself in our view. He has placed his hand upon their head and passionately prayed for God's blessing upon them. Such touch and such prayer blesses.

When I greet children as a pastor, I kneel down so that we are at eye level (Bob taught me that, not in words but by his example). I pat their heads amid the crowd after or before the service. I speak words of blessing into their lives. When they play at our house as their families visit for dinner, I seek the same posture. More of us by grace need Jesus to empower us to do so.

This grace of Jesus teaches us not only to instruct but also to dignify, protect, and bless the children of our community. I pray that somehow these kids will grow up knowing that those who welcome them in Jesus's name are safe, wise, and full of love and hope for their good. In this regard, until we've been mended and taught such convictions by the grace of Jesus, we are not ready to touch the child of another (or our own), no matter how many gifts for public ministry we possess. First things first—when children encounter us, contrary to our natural inclinations, they are meant to catch a glimpse of how Jesus would welcome them and treat them. We cannot work this up. But Jesus has purchased this for us, and he will work it in us.

Mark Dalbey is a longtime pastor and dean at a seminary. Simon Kim is a youth pastor in the first years of his ministry. Jessica is a part-time director for children's ministries. But these three saints have one thing in common. Everywhere they go, the countenance of kids lightens. They are like kid-magnets for all of the right and wholesome reasons that Jesus gives us.

For others of us who have been misused or, by temperament, are slower to express a hospitable presence to kids, Jesus gives us such persons in our communities to give us a vision for what he intends. He helps us grow. By their presence he strongly denounces their opposites who degrade, shame, and consume children with touch and words. Jesus has the means to change our direction with children for his glory and in order to recover for them what touch was meant to be.

Conclusion

Spaghetti hands. It seems fitting to end with this red-sauce-on-knuckles thought. I received a phone call inquiring if I would make a pastoral visit to a middle-aged woman in the community. By "middle-aged," it was her biological and not her mental condition that was referred to. Mentally, she was four or five, though she had lived forty or fifty years.

When I walked through the door, there she sat. She was bibbed and trying to tackle a big plate of spaghetti. She smiled wide with wonder in her eyes as I sat down beside her at the table.

"Who are you?" she asked, covered with sauce and noodle pieces.

"My name is Zack. I am a pastor," I answered.

She immediately and excitedly responded.

"I have learned the 'Our Father' by heart," she said. "Wanna here it?"

"Oh, yes, I'd love to," I answered.

After proudly reciting the Lord's Prayer, she went right into declaring Psalm 23 from memory.

"Did I do good?" she asked.

"That was wonderful! You sure did!" I said.

"I believe in God. He loves me. I love him. He died on a cross for me. He will come and take me home one day." She said this quite seriously, staring straight into my eyes. It was as if she was assessing me. Then she suddenly dropped her fork on the table, held out her spaghetti-covered, saliva-sprinkled hand toward me, and said, "You wanna pray? Take my hand."

Hearing

The children's hymn warns, "Be careful little ears what you hear." But pastoral life in the broken world is rarely G-rated. Unless our ears are not working, physicality bumps us into sound. The sounds of body and soul reach our ears. Because of this, we have trouble sometimes when we try to decide what warrants the attention of our ears and what doesn't.

A story is told about a naturalist and his friend walking amid the frenzy of a New York City sidewalk. The naturalist suddenly stops as if he is listening for something. "Do you hear that cricket?" he asks his bewildered friend. "How can you hear a cricket with all of this noise?" the friend replies. "We hear what we are trained to hear," the naturalist replied. Then he pulled a quarter out of his pocket and dropped it upon the sidewalk. Immediately a handful of passersby stopped and looked down.[10]

While this story is fable-like, there is truth to recognize in the notion that "we hear what we are trained to hear." Jesus knows this. The widow among the rich puts in her two small coins. It is hard to hear her two coins amid the jingle and clink of the wealthy. Theirs drown out hers. Their voices fill our ears. Her tiny devotion, small, unnoticed, underestimated—it calls out and says among all the importance, "Look around. Listen. God is here." Jesus recovers the sound of the widow and her coins, and the disciples learn to hear again (Luke 21:1–4).

According to Jesus, there are two kinds of hearing. This is what Jesus means when he says, "If anyone has ears to hear, let him hear" (Mark 4:23). Jesus calls us beyond recognizing sounds to obeying or responding or discerning the meaning of the sounds.

To hear with the ear only is to recognize.

To hear with understanding is to discern.

To hear with the ear requires only that one's eardrums work.

To hear so as to understand requires that one's soul remain attentive and receptive to the goings on in another.

To hear with the ear one need only nod the head and shuffle the voice into "mhm" and "uh-huh."

To hear truly, however, one must ready herself to experience the life of another, and from that experience, to understand that other.

To hear with the ear only is to categorize, explain, and move on.

To truly hear is to name the nuance, to understand the meanings, to separate out what is consistent from what is not, and to let what is mysterious or confounding remain for another day.

To hear with the ear only is to quote the Bible.

To hear truly is to bend one's life toward the meaning of the quote in Jesus and by his grace.

Among the many sounds that reach our ears, let's briefly mention funeral sounds, the sounds of criticism, the Father's voice, and our theological cussing. Amid these sounds we are meant by grace to hear truly.

Funeral Sounds

A week ago, as I write this, seventy percent of Joplin, Missouri, was destroyed by a tornado that was a mile wide. The twister pummeled a hospital. Hundreds died. A local pastor rose from the church basement. He had huddled there with the youth group. Stepping outside, the storm was gone, but so was nearly everything he could see. While trying to get kids safely home, the pastor hears the sounds of misery. "A woman came out of a crushed house with a baby stroller, clutching an empty blanket. She was screaming 'My baby, my baby! Where's my baby?'"[11]

This morning my assistant pastor sat with me in our efforts to counsel a man. On the verge of losing his family, the man simply said, "Help me. Please, help me." Jesus heard the cries of human disease, suffering, misery, and fear.

> Lord, my servant is lying paralyzed at home, suffering terribly. (Matt. 8:6)

> Save us, Lord; we are perishing. (Matt. 8:25)

Examining Our Mentoring

> Two blind men followed him, crying aloud, "Have mercy on us, Son of David." (Matt. 9:27)

I think it was funerals that first confronted my ears with the kind of tearful soundtrack that life and ministry can sometimes play.

At the time, I actually had little acquaintance with the sounds of death. The years since have changed all of that. But I remember then how strange it was to encounter grown men and women heaving with pained gasps. Waves of sniffles like the tide sounded back and forth in gentle laps. Clichés hurried to put costumes onto the awkward silences. Questions about God or life whispered in embarrassment or raged into sudden bursts. I heard mints unwrapped and the crinkled leftovers. Laughter emerged often in the strangest places for a comfort that's not strange at all.

Pat had died. Her sister brings a story to my ears.

"Pat used to find stray cats and give them a home," she says.

I chuckle with this surprising introduction and begin to smile.

"It's the darndest thing," she continues. "Pat would not only give these cats a home, she'd also dress those darn cats with clothes—doll clothes!"

"Really?" I ask.

"Oh, yes!" she says. She begins to laugh as she thinks about what her heart knows of happier times. I begin to laugh too.

"So, here's Pat, with all these dressed-up cats, posing for a picture, and Pat smiling from ear to ear!"

We're both laughing hard now and depending on tissues to maintain decorum.

"Oh my, that Pat! She sure was a loon!"

We laugh hard for a moment and then take a deep breath into a sudden downshift. The storyteller now stares off and quiets into silence. Without looking me in the eyes, she says, "I'm gonna miss that Pat."

My very first funeral as a pastor was for a neighbor that I did not know. I hear the director come to me in the separate room. "It's time," he says. I hear my stomach growl and my bowels want to move. I hear the sound of my shoes on well-worn carpet. I hear myself try to patch words of life together for those who are mostly strangers to me. I hear myself begin to tremble a voice out into the devastated crowd.

That was the first such occasion that I heard the bagpipes sound. After the service, out by the graveside, the bagpiper stands as if ugly and holding a goose. He breathes in and out into a moaning that wheezes air into a haunting melody of "Amazing Grace." A swan of music emerges and takes flight. Sobs and whimpers accompany the tune with red eyes, along with tear-stained mascara bleeding on cheeks. The wind ripples through the fall leaves. Rented aluminum poles clank with rope and tarp. I hear the sound of flowers dropped on a casket. Other occasions nuance the grief. I hear talk of fried chicken and green bean casserole for the reception. A military funeral, the flag folded and given, rifles armed for different use; death bullets shock the silence to honor a life.

Yesterday I sat with a couple whose child has a drug addiction. I sat earlier with another whose daughter was raped. A month ago I listened on the telephone to two different women. The one has had an affair and thinks of ending her life. The other is contemplating an affair and is trying to find her life. At breakfast I listen to a combat veteran speak of Jesus amid memories of screams, killings, and firefights in the nightmare of another world.

We cannot control most of what we hear. Nor are we meant to. But in Jesus we can interpret the racket and walk through it. So can our neighbors.

Critical Sounds

Jesus also heard the personal accusations, criticisms, and the tauntings of devils and of men.[12]

> Two demon-possessed men met him, coming out of the tombs, so fierce that no one could pass that way. And behold, they cried out, "What have you to do with us, O Son of God?" (Matt. 8:28–29)

> This man is blaspheming. . . . Why does your teacher eat with tax collectors and sinners? (Matt. 9:3, 11)

> The rulers scoffed at him, saying, "He saved others; let him save himself, if he is the Christ of God, his Chosen One!" (Luke 23:35)

> But they kept shouting, "Crucify, crucify him!" (Luke 23:21)

The critical speech of persons attends the ministry. I was not prepared well for this. In my first pastorate I grew to learn how those you try to help can sometimes harm you—like the mother who sent a letter to the congregation when I tried to enter the life of her son who was having an affair. The son—a grown man—and I had several lunches. The mother misquoted things I had said in the pulpit and called upon the congregation to have nothing more to do with me. Thankfully, those sermons were recorded and my words withstood the accusations.

But my first real taste of how bitterly others can slander us or gossip about us, arrived also in the form of a letter. The letter was sent to my presbytery (about sixty elders and pastors) and arrived the day before we all met. Its three pages slandered my character, lied, mislabeled partial truths, and called for my removal from the ministry altogether. A man, who we as elders were trying to help and confront, sent the letter. His rage was getting the best of him, and he was damaging people in our congregation and community. Sometimes we are more committed to attacking the help than to surrendering to the change the help would bring to us. If the help we bring does more harm by our manner and timing than it does for good, resistance is warranted. But often, when graciously and gently confronted, resistance comes when the heart does not want to soften.

It is difficult to describe the pain such criticism can bring, especially when it isn't warranted, when it reveals more about the critic than it does about you. Jesus was criticized even when he healed or helped persons (Matt. 12:10). Sometimes you too will hear the critical voice for doing what is right or what would gently require the hardened heart of another to soften.

In contrast, critical voices come to all of us, because we regularly make mistakes and never rise above our need to grow and learn. In this case, "faithful are the wounds of a friend" (Prov. 27:6). It is unwise to make others walk on eggshells around us. We do ourselves harm when we make it hard for a friend to help us. None of us are above needing this kind of faithful wound for our own growth and for our better service of others.

It is just as unwise, however, to entrust equal weight to the critical voice of everybody. Nehemiah needed not to give credence to the tabloid rantings and slanderous headlines offered by Sanballot and Tobiah.

Instead, our friend, the one who knows us and who retains a memory of who we are at our best, even when he or she encounters us at our worst—this one's voice seeks our good and carries a weight with us that others ought not. We certainly take into account the criticisms of acquaintances and strangers, and these will be many for anyone who takes up a pastoral or ministerial call. Even the criticism of an enemy can have a partial truth to it.

But the enemy or one who acts like an enemy uses truth about your weakness to disadvantage you. The enemy characterizes you as if what is human or weak about you is the whole and sole truth about you. You are only what your weakness and sins are, according to an enemy. But we needn't take to heart the criticisms of those whose sole design concerns their interest absent a commitment to our own good and the larger good as well. Neither is it wise to spiral down into the gloom at the words of one who sees the speck in your eye but remains blind to the log in theirs. This includes acquaintances and strangers. They can help us see blind spots and sins. We listen and we learn. But they often do not have sufficient context and likewise mislabel some things. We can learn and listen, but we needn't fold or quit with such voices.

Rather, we learn to take to the Lord what acquaintances, strangers, and enemies say. We ask our closest faithful friends, whose wounds we can trust, to join us. The wound, the day of sorrow and repentant tears, comes from God's hands through the faithful friends he gives us. By grace, these who wound us do so for our protection and good. After they point out the blind spot, they sit with us in the ashes and cry with us. Then they rise with us through the strength his grace provides to give it another go.

While some of us struggle to let any voice, even our friends', call us out, others of us let every voice interpret us and have authority to name us. So while some of us struggle with pride that believes we need no help or have no weaknesses, others of us struggle with pride of a different sort, the kind that makes a god out of human opinion and bows, no matter who says what. This means that some of us are crusty, intimidating, and always carrying around a countenance that sadly makes clear that we are not to be messed with. Others of us are hollowed out, breached, and spiral down at the least hint of a critical word, no matter where it comes from. Jesus intends to counter both of us.

This brings us to a brief word regarding the critical whispers of devils. Imagine the nature of what a "messenger of Satan" would proclaim to the apostle Paul (2 Cor. 12:7). Satan's messages to God's servants neither encourage nor do they "wound" like a friend would. Satan's messages harass us. To harass, Satan makes false interpretations and accusations out of true facts. Paul has pain that does not end. He serves God faithfully and prays. But the pain remains. God doesn't answer the way Paul hopes, even though Paul has given his life for the Lord.

Satan's message isn't, "Don't worry, Paul. I know this is hard. But God has always been faithful to you. He won't fail you now. His purpose will prevail in your life. His love won't quit, and he will bring you to what is best. You are a son of the King. He will sustain you and have the last word in your life. His strength sustains you and blooms in what others deem and you feel to be weak. The presence of misery does not mean the absence of Jesus."

His messages suggest otherwise: "God has left you. What point is there in doing good and serving him? Look what it gets you! People despise you and malign you. Happiness has escaped you. Each day is pain and sorrow and hardship. After all you have done for God, your prayers mean nothing to him. He has passed you over. He blesses other preachers, but not you. He gives them honor and position and esteem among the crowds, but not you. He has left you, Paul. He has lied to you. Your life makes no difference. You make no difference."

Yet somehow Paul still hears the voice of Jesus amid this devilish bullying:

> My grace is sufficient for you, for my power is made perfect in weakness. (2 Cor. 12:9)

Our Listening Priority

Amid the slanders of men and devils, Jesus heard the voice of God, his Father:

> And behold, a voice from heaven said, "This is my beloved Son, with whom I am well pleased." (Matt. 3:17)

In this light, it matters to recognize that the essential nonnegotiable priority of Jesus's life and ministry was to hear the Father's voice for and in the midst of the audio of his life. His posture in a given moment was one of receptivity. While Jesus is fully God, in the fullness of his humanity we learn from him that listening to the Father preceded and determined what

Jesus spoke. Jesus didn't enter a moment determined to make things happen and knock heads. He entered a moment waiting:

> For I have not spoken on my own authority, but the Father who sent me has himself given me a commandment—what to say and what to speak. . . . What I say, therefore, I say as the Father has told me. (John 12:49–50)

Jesus didn't give us his first drafts. He didn't brainstorm in our presence or ramble on and on with unexamined chatter. The Father's voice determined and arranged all other voices, including his own. Misdiagnosis was not therefore part of Jesus's interpretation of persons, conditions, and situations.

We are not our Lord. Misinterpretation and misdiagnosis will not elude us. But, we needn't mishandle sound as much as we do. A minister who resists listening will eventually spew secondhand leftovers and hand-me-down thoughts from a hurried and cluttered mind. Or worse, we will offer others the words of impulse. We might even pass these unexamined word bursts off as the speech of God.

But in Jesus we learn that we are never the first to arrive on the scene. We enter the moment quieted to learn what has transpired there before we arrived. What has God been doing prior to our arrival? Once there, what is his intention for our presence? Our nervousness, our desire to do well, our past wisdoms and successes, our longing to have nice things said of us, or our leftover feelings from how we just handled our spouses or were handled by our deacons—these ought not guide our words and actions once we are on the scene.

A ministry leader will want to learn that sound is education. Sound mentors us with wisdom or folly. To hear truly is to have what is there breathed into our ears.

> An owl sound wandered along the road with me.
> I didn't hear it—I breathed it into my ears.[13]

Owls, roads, and ears all form an audio in which through Jesus I am meant to locate the voice of the Father lingering in another's ditches, settling in another's ashes, persisting through another's devastation, jubilant and dancing amid another's celebration.

Examining Our Mentoring

Therefore, one who has no interest in cultivating a habit of listening is not yet ready for what ministry in Jesus's name will require. Ours is a listening vocation. From a posture of attentive invocation we give language to what is there. As ambassador-discerners, we enter the stories of others and say each day to them and to ourselves, "Slow down. Look here, listen, God is revealing himself."

Cussing

With all of this in mind, may I say a word, with some fear and trepidation, about the cussing we hear in the world? To begin, I have grown up in a Christian world that tries to keep out unwanted or unspiritual sounds. While I embrace giving no credence to the language of the show-off and the shocker, it seems we must take seriously the foul language that often dominates the lives of our neighbors.

To begin, the neighbors we seek to minister to often cuss. In a sermon once, I said the expression "dumb butt." I wasn't quoting a late-night comedian or a movie; I was quoting how an abusive father spoke to his daughter. For the pulpit, I changed the quote. The father didn't actually say, "dumb," or "butt." He used synonyms that were much worse. I said as much.

I was contrasting the sound of abuse in our real world with the grace of God as our Father and how he enters our lives. After the sermon a man rebuked me. "I don't bring my daughters to church so that they can hear the world's speech!" he exclaimed. "I expect a preacher to keep the world out of his sermons, to protect little ears." (His daughters were teenagers.)

As a father of three I fully understand wanting to protect my children from the world in which they live. But it seems from the Wisdom Literature of the Bible that protecting involves preparing our young for the real sights and sounds of life under the sun in age-appropriate ways. Anyone who has entered the lives of abuse knows that for me to say "butt" is tame compared to what is actually spoken by adults and heard by children. How do we apprentice our congregations to handle what really sounds forth in the world unless we equip them with the gospel for it? Likewise, to speak without reference to what is real will cause our preaching to seem out of touch with any in our congregations who are in the helping professions or who themselves are under duress, addiction, or abuse.

Whether I should have said "butt" in the pulpit, you can decide. But the point remains. If we do not learn to handle the language of the world and in our hearts when we are together in Jesus, under his roof, as it were, having family instruction from his Word, then when and where do we? We can tell the world, "Don't talk like that." The problem is, it already has. So, now what? Jesus teaches his disciples not to cover their ears but to wisely know how to bring the gospel to what their ears hear. We can turn off the racy lyrics on the radio but the question of how to love and reach the neighbor who wrote the lyrics remains.

In order to help victims and criminals, law enforcement officers hear brutal things. In order to aid trauma victims, medical personnel hear difficult sounds. Counselors listen to painful descriptions. Why is it that ministry leaders rarely prepare for what they will hear should they attempt to enter the real world with the gospel? How is it that we believe that we can only enter environments of pristine language as rescuers of sinners?

The Cussing of the Irreligious

At this point, some of us feel happy to saturate ourselves with the foul speech of the irreligious. We believe that speaking in kind is the way to evangelize. While it is difficult to imagine that Jesus heard no cussing when he spent time with prostitutes, tax collectors, and sinners, it seems equally intolerable to believe that while with these dear ones, he took up the mouth of a drunken sailor.

One believer feels we should cuss in order to reach our neighbors. Another believer uses his neighbor's cussing to justify not reaching him. For both may I suggest some nuances or categories of cussing to promote discussion among us?

This feels a bit humorous to me, maybe even a bit silly. But it seems to me that there are three categories of cussing: (1) Using words to describe the horrors and tragedies we see in the world or the profound pain we individually feel. In this category a World War II soldier describes the atrocities of war as "fubar"; a songwriter looks at the corruption of the city and identifies it; a parent in an emergency-room trauma cries out for her child. (2) In contrast are those who use words to show off, be cool, or shock, such as dirty jokes, late-night television, music award shows, eighth graders on a playground, college pranksters. (3) Separate from both are those who use cuss words because those are the words they know for ordinary dialogue.

Examining Our Mentoring

Ironically, at this very moment, right outside my office window, workers from the pub next door are taking their smoke break. Four-letter words fill the air. But the cussing isn't flowing at this moment to describe atrocity or pain, nor is it being used to joke, boast, or shock. Two men are having a conversation about some difficulty the one guy is having, and the other guy is giving him advice. These dear men are using the language they know to try to help each other out.

We may not appreciate the language of either category, but I suggest we need to distinguish the first and third from the second in terms of the purpose and heart behind the words. As human beings trying to reach one another in the gospel, we can certainly identify with category 1 and we can, if we remember where we've been apart from Jesus, understand category 3.

For those who feel they need to take on the language of the culture in order to reach it, I suggest that category 1 may offer that opportunity to us, but not the other categories. If you disagree with me, the question still remains, How do you resemble the voice of Jesus if you only sound like everyone else?

For those who feel that we should never cuss under any circumstance and that we should separate ourselves physically from those who do, I suggest that this is simplistic. We act unwisely if we treat each category of heart equally. Even if you disagree with me on this point, the question still remains, How do we love our neighbor and enter their lives with the gospel of Jesus if we separate from anyone who does not get his language right?

The Cussing of the Religious

But the cussing of the irreligious is not the only issue for us to navigate with our ears. We religious must learn to recognize our own kind of cussing. Religious cussing often does not involve foul four-letter words. Rather, full sentences or silences that distort the character and work of Jesus forms our way of foul speech. Let's use Jesus's story of the two sons as a compass point for our discussion.

> Irreligious men praised the Prodigal.
> Religious men praised the Pharisee.
> Irreligious women flattered and flirted with the Prodigal.
> Religious women flattered and swooned over the Pharisee.

According to Jesus, to enter either's story is to hear mud. To heal the

Prodigal is to hear of usury, drunkenness, and the painful memories of multiple women. To heal the older brother, who represented the Pharisees, was to hear of power, manipulation, and arrogance. The Prodigal did his worst with open sheets on a bed. The Pharisee did his worst with an open Scripture on a place of worship.

Language, therefore, always comes in the form of resistance or repentance or mixtures of the two. We speak in defiance of God's having the first word. Or we speak in surrender. Or we wrestle toward surrender through the battle and flack of our defiance.

Language at its best is meant to express our always returning home from the mud to God. "Go, call your husband and come here," Jesus says to the sexually promiscuous woman by the well (John 4:16). "I have no husband" she replies (v. 17). With that admission, the language of homecoming begins to sing.

But sometimes our language choice expresses a heart unwilling to leave the hidden homes away from home that we have come to pine for. "One thing you still lack," Jesus says. The language of resistance hardens and saddens in response. We go away saddened by the language of homecoming (Luke 18:22–23).

At this our definitions of what it means to cuss get tangled. We assume that to hear someone say a four-letter word means he is resisting the language of repentance. We identify certain four-letter words but rarely include the four-letter words that Jesus identified, such as calling someone a "fool" (Matt. 5:22).

But Jesus makes no such mistake. Corrupt speech is that which says no to homecoming and distorts God's character. In this light, many of us, like the rich young ruler and the religious leaders of Jesus's time, are cussing every day while using sweet, socially acceptable, and even devoutly religious language. We refuse to listen to someone say "F&^%," while we accept the language of greed, pride, manipulation, self-centeredness, covetousness, rage, and folly. "I thank you God that I'm not like this sinner," we say. We seem deaf to how filthy this language is to God.

The older brother's language is as foul as the language his prodigal brother reveled in. Neither spoke from having heard the Father's voice on the matter.

Both sounds need the gospel of Jesus.

CHAPTER SEVEN

Seeing

Praying for Illumination and Relating to Our Relatives

> I must *unlearn;* I must believe
> you were merely a man with a character, and a past—;
> you wore them, unexamined.[1]

When a stray dog came onto the property, Papaw would burst through the screen door scrambling to load his rifle. As the scratched-up metal banged hard against the outside of the house and then slammed back into its place, Papaw, who was by now standing sock-feet and firm on the carport, aimed his gun and fired. He didn't mind the resulting yelp. In fact, he seemed to take pleasure in it as if he had just defended his family from a pack of wolves. He would try to hide a grin and would cuss the yelping mutt like it was a man taunting Papaw to fight. So when my Papaw told me one early Christmas that he was going to shoot Santa Claus, I believed him.

It was not an easy thing to possess a sensitive heart in that dear man's world when he was younger. "Drop your drawers and run, Mamaw! You are a lacy-ruffled-pantywaist." That's what Papaw taught me to say to my Mamaw when I was a little boy, and I did. I learned to see women not only by the way Papaw spoke to Mamaw but also by the *Playboy* magazines and the calendars with nudes that were no secret to Mamaw or to us, and were strategically placed in the house that he built.

At the dinner table, I learned that there was something called "niggers" in the world. I'm not sure at the time that I had ever seen such people. But when the adults played the card game *Rook* and drank Pepsi at the table, Papaw had stories to tell.

Preachers weren't much better in his estimation. The parsonage for the Methodist church was next door. Preachers were nothing but hypocrites, and Papaw had the stories to prove it. Stories were as much a part of dinner life as his homemade spaghetti sauce spiced with jalapenos. Papaw loved jalapenos. He'd shove a bunch of them into the pickle jar. Papaw felt that bread-and-butter pickles could be neighborly to jalapenos. After they sat together for a while in the fridge, Papaw would pop them in his mouth for a snack and then sit in his brown leather chair.

When I came home from elementary school and would talk, the first thing Papaw would ask me was if I had got into any trouble and if I had received any wuppins from the principal that day. When I would answer, "No, Papaw," he would laugh, slap me on the arm, and say, "My lands, boy, what good are you?"

Papaw never sat me down and conducted a class on how to see and interpret stray dogs, women, preachers, or nonwhite skin, but Papaw's way of seeing, along with the others in my young life, coached my own, and this is the point I want us to meditate on for a moment.

Ways teach. They form the primary classrooms of our learning. Ways are lenses. We step up and put in our quarter, and through these lenses we look out over the entire city. One requires no syllabus to learn about anger. Raging bursts after dinner with the dishes by the sink form a suitable curriculum.

The fact that we relationally learn doctrines by which we live is pointed out in the Bible. "Make no friendship with a man given to anger, nor go with a wrathful man," the proverb says, "*lest you learn his ways* and entangle yourself in a snare" (Prov. 22:24–25). For better and for worse, we learn to see the world and present ourselves in it for witness, not just from the creedal statements we learn in class but also from the relational mentoring of those we do life with (Prov. 13:20). "We learn through what happens to us from one moment to the next."[2] How we see the creation and providence of our days has a deep mentoring to it. I am naive if I believe my current ministry as an adult in St. Louis, Missouri, is a stranger to my Papaw and the ways he and I shared in our common life together in Henryville, Indiana. You too have had a visual mentoring.

Visual Mentoring

Consider the disciples. They had learned a curriculum of ministry ways long before Jesus first called them to follow him. Because of this, discipleship with Jesus meant unlearning and reinterpreting many of these sight instincts. When Jesus's disciples encountered Samaritans, James and John were ready to call down fire from heaven and destroy them (Luke 9:54). When the disciples saw children wanting time with Jesus, the disciples rebuked the children (Luke 18:15). When a woman broke open an alabaster jar to perfume Jesus with her adoration, the disciples were indignant when they saw her. They gave the woman grief (Matt. 26:7–10). When they saw Jesus talking to a Samaritan woman, the Jewish disciples were baffled (John 4:27). When the disciples saw Jesus on the verge of betrayal, they readied their swords to do violence (Luke 22:49). When they witnessed a rich man walking away from Jesus's invitation they wondered, "Then who can be saved?" (Luke 18:25–26). When the disciples saw a man born blind, they assumed that the disability was punishment for sin (John 9:1–3). When those who followed Jesus and ministered to others were not part of the disciples' group, the disciples assumed that the others' ministry should be stopped (Mark 9:38–41).

My questions for us to consider are these: From whom did these disciples learn to see the world like this? Who taught them to see Samaritans as second-class people worthy of mistreatment? Who taught them that children who want time with a teacher of God are a nuisance? Why when they saw a woman worshiping did they assume the worst about her motives? Who taught them violence as a justified reaction to betrayal? Why is it that they assumed the rich had preference in the kingdom of heaven? Why is it that when they saw disease in a person, they interpreted it as punishment from God for an individual or family sin? Why did they think that followers who were not part of their group were against them?

But this kind of seeing wasn't isolated to the disciples. The people who lived around the disciples had similar lenses through which they saw the world. For example, when they saw Jesus welcome a tax collector, "they all grumbled" because Jesus had "gone in to be the guest of a man who is a sinner" (Luke 19:7). When others saw that the tomb dweller was set into his right mind by Jesus, they asked Jesus to "leave their region" (Matt. 8:34). When tragedy struck and innocent people died, folks seriously assumed that tragedy strikes only those who are worse sinners than others (Luke 13:4).

From whom did these crowds of people learn that when you see a sinner, keep away from him; when unexpected divine healing happens, tell the healer to leave; when tragedy strikes, it must be because you are a worse sinner than others?

For starters, they learned such things from the pastors in their midst. This sobers us. After all, the disciples' and crowds' ways of seeing described in these last couple of paragraphs strongly resemble how the Pharisees related to Jesus. In addition, there was family lore and marketplace news. There were the jokes that were told in school about Samaritans and the way the men in their families looked at and spoke about women. The poor were overlooked, the rich were praised, and the diseased were talked about at the dinner table as having received the judgment of God for their sin.

Every pastor has such a mentoring history. Every congregation and community the pastor seeks to serve does, as well. To begin to see and perceive is to have the Spirit of Christ turn the lights on in the dark rooms of our mentoring. In order to help others see, you and I need him to show us from whom our seeing has been formed. Without such illumination, we may continue to pass on our blindness to others, all the while calling it sight from God. Giving our blindnesses to others and calling them God's way of seeing, will not do. "Can a blind man lead a blind man?" Jesus asks. "Will they not both fall into a pit?" (Luke 6:39).

Stories are tools to explore and interpret creation (the stuff God made) and providence (our voluntary and involuntary interactions with the stuff). The stories we know mentor us. So Jesus often tells stories that invert characters and reorient us toward sanity. At the dinner table, the disciples would have grown up hearing stories that implied the poor were in hell and the rich were in heaven. But in Jesus's stories a rich man is in hell and a poor man is in heaven (Luke 16:19–31). Likewise, with Jesus Samaritans are envisioned nobly as fellow neighbors (Luke 10:25–37). Repenting sinners are justified before God, and arrogant Bible teachers aren't (Luke 18:9–14). And children, far from being merely rebuked and silenced, are what we must become like in order to enter the kingdom of God (Luke 18:15–17).

So to be my Papaw's Christian friend or pastor is to help him to gradually relearn through Jesus to see and perceive animals, women, fights, persons with darker skin, and the hypocritical sides of church people.

To be Papaw's grandson is to need a pastor or friend that can help me learn the same. So it is with you, no matter how gifted or solid you are regarding the facts of your faith or the skills of your gifts. Each of us has a visual mentoring that ministry in Christ will expose and that the grace of Christ must alter. 

Take a moment and make a list of the key figures in your life. Ask yourself regarding each person you list: "What about seeing the world did this person teach me?" If it helps to become more specific, consider the specific sight lines that Jesus disrupted in the disciples. Recognize that he will intend these same disruptions in your own perceptions of things. Now ask, "What about seeing men, seeing women, seeing money, seeing children, seeing the sick, seeing tragedy, seeing race, seeing church hypocrites, and seeing sinners did this person teach me?" What stories will Jesus tell to unlearn your blindness into sight?

Men with Fists

I was twenty-six. I was in the first year of my first pastorate. Holding a Styrofoam cup half empty with Sprite, I stood motionless. The Christian education meeting had recently ended. His wife suddenly bolted out of the room. Then it began. The spit on his lips was white. It jumped onto me in parachutes, landing on my hair, nose, and shoulders for invasion. He was all teeth, eyes, and voice. It was my first encounter as a pastor with a raging man. This man, thirty years my senior, started with "Don't you ever . . ." For the next couple of minutes he let me know how I had no calling from God, what a disgrace I was as a pastor, and that as a man I was only worthy of disrespect. Dipping into the rated-R movie dictionary, he chose words to let me know that if I ever crossed him again, I'd be done as a pastor (a threat he later tried to keep). My heart raced. Anxiety flooded my veins. "A soft answer turns away wrath," I remembered (Prov. 15:1). So, I tried and it didn't. "I'm sorry," I gulped.

He scowled down closer within head-butting range, raised his tense finger, and threatened, "I'll be watching you to see if you mean it." After a long pause, he burst out of the room. I made my way to my office, fell into the floor, and cried like a baby (or did I cry like a man?). For the next year I did what many of the leaders around me and before me did with this man. For a while, I played the coward while he trampled about on his midnight raids into people's lives. To confront him was to protect others. To avoid him was to leave others and himself to his worst. Eventually, we would have to collide again. But that is another story.

It is enough to ask the following questions: How could a man who sacrificed so much of his resources and time for the gospel, a man for whom the grace of Jesus was so dear, a man who had done good to so many—how could such a man itch for a fight like that over what he saw?

Likewise, how could I crumble like that? I look back and recognize that he was not the first Hulkish man I had known. Many of the men mentoring me throughout my life resembled him in that way. But the fact is, no matter what I had learned in seminary, or the nature of my calling and identity, when the storm blew out of nowhere and the spit started to rain down, I may as well have been an eighth grader in the hallway of my stepdad's fists in Clarksville, Indiana.

Did the other leaders who had cowered before the man when he was at his worst have such eighth-grade hallways in their lives too? In the moment, what our hallways had taught us seemed to overrule whatever we might have learned in the classrooms of our Bible studies and the gospel in our hearts. It was like the moment splashed the windshield in torrent. My frenzied windshield wipers couldn't match the pace. I couldn't see. I had to pull over. I was a pastor called by God to do this man and the congregation good by resisting his worst and seeking his best in Christ. But all I saw at the time was an abusive man doing what abusive men had often done in my life. Who I was as a pastor was profoundly entangled with the mentoring I had known as a boy. I couldn't see this man and me in our own moment. Rather, I saw in him hundreds of moments I had witnessed before. They all crowded into the room at once. Boyish fear stole my credentials and hid them in the closet somewhere. I couldn't find them amid the tantrum.

Did such things form why Nicodemus came to Jesus at night and not in the day (John 3:2)? Some men struggle all their lives not to crumble. They control loss by means of silence and gaze shifting. These are the in-between men, who have no opinions of their own. They hide behind the majority or decide always on the basis of what will best maintain their current peace. For a while, Nicodemus was not alone in this kind of boyish fear that rightly adorns a boy but is a misplaced coat on a man.

> Nevertheless, many even of the authorities believed in him, but for fear of the Pharisees they did not confess it, so that they would not be put out of the synagogue. (John 12:42)

Boyish fear is not the only snapshot of my mentoring history, however. This vacillation between timidity and violence, this difficulty with finding a different kind of ground distinct from both to stand on, was true for the disciples as well. The same men who locked themselves behind doors for fear could be known as "Sons of Thunder." There is a reason men are told not to provoke their children to anger (Eph. 6:4).

The stories men told in my family often had to do with our being smaller but tougher. Men were lenses for fistfights. Even my dad and grandpa entered the ring. My family was not above bruising each other's faces. My stepdad and I boxed with open hands; the red slap marks across the cheeks and the tears they produced were meant for my toughness.

Therefore, I too would have my own version of a Hulkish tendency to contend with. The first time I heard myself ask, "Do you want to mess with me?" to a man not at his best in line at a furniture store, I felt surprised and sobered. But the first time I asked my son, "Do you want to mess with me?" it caved in on me that I was little different from the men I'd tried to outrun. I was undone. I began a series of confessions to my family regarding what we all now refer to as my "scary eyes." I wonder if Paul needed such rementoring. Or Peter's taking up his sword and cutting off the ear of the servant? These, like the Sons of Thunder, were men with fists. Jesus rementored their tendencies to punch.

Before Jesus met me I had learned to think of men in terms of fists; either as a child abused or as a boy in the ring. To receive Jesus and to minister to others compels me to account for both. To account for both matters. Otherwise, I pass on my hulkish or boyish tendencies with varying men and call it sight. Those I mentor therefore learn ways of seeing that Jesus calls blindness.

To enter the ministry is to remember that Jesus intends to teach us how to see men differently. Why? Because as a gospel minister I see men every day, and so will you. What do you make of the men you see? From whom have you learned to see men like this?

Examining Our Mentoring

Do You See This Man?

A man knows his own voice. That is, until on chance he hears his recorded speech. At that moment he discovers anew or again how others have heard him each day all these years. Similarly, a man who is forty-one or eighty-three imagines, as he stands to choose apples in the grocery store, that he appears as he was when he was twenty-four. He is reaching, as it were, for those same apples in that same store the way he has always done over the long years. But down the dairy aisle he catches his reflection in freezer doors made of glass. How he looked to the woman and child who passed him in the cereal aisle now slaps and shakes him. He discovers again how he actually is to himself and how he appears to those around him. And yet for all of these knowings, imaginings, and discoveries, a man remains only hazily known until he is at last heard and seen by Jesus. Jesus's sense of us is the cool drink a man truly needs.

Matthew was a tax collector. Men are often known and measured by what they do and the titles they have or do not have. "That boy better make something of himself" captures the idea. Matthew is no exception. When Luke tells us about the time Jesus called Matthew to follow him, Luke identifies Matthew by his job. Jesus "*saw a tax-collector* named Levi, sitting at the tax booth," he tells us (Luke 5:27).

But Matthew was also a son in a family. Men are often known by who their family is and what place in that family they have. Are they the good son or the bad son, the forgotten son? This too was true of Matthew. When Mark tells us about that same moment, when Jesus called Matthew, Mark identifies Matthew by his pedigree in his family. Jesus "saw *Levi the son of Alpheus* sitting at the tax booth" (Mark 2:14). I wonder: did it heal or rust Levi's heart to be Alpheus's son in that community?

I don't know. What I do know is that Matthew tells us about that same time when Jesus came to him and called him. When he does, it is Jesus and Matthew that he remembers. Matthew mentions nothing about his family and keeps his job in the background. It is as if Matthew stares off in the distance for a moment and then looks back into our eyes. He pauses. Then he tells us, "As Jesus passed on from there, *he saw a man* called Matthew sitting at the tax booth" (Matt. 9:9).

Mark saw Matthew's family. Luke saw Matthew's job. Jesus saw Matthew as he was. Jesus saw a man. Jesus sees men not through the lens of this fallen "life under the sun," as the preacher puts it in Ecclesiastes, but instead through the lens of Eden as it once gloriously was. He will teach us to see men in this way too, not as men with jobs, not as men with trophies, not as men in relation to the dads to whom they must prove themselves, but just as men.

I wish I could have been a fly on the wall that moment when Papaw was recovering there in Clark County Hospital. He had worked there as a maintenance man for years. Now he was the one needing repair, a repair that he would outlive for a while until it would finally catch him ten or so years after. But at the moment his heart was older than his body. It was tired and wanted to quit early on him. When Papaw saw the man who lived across the street, you remember, he saw only a preacher, a hypocrite. When Papaw saw dark-skinned men, he saw only "niggers," good ones and bad ones. That's why it must have been something for Papaw that day when a stranger came to visit him amid the tubes and monitors that were chained to his arms. That someone? A black chaplain. Who knew, deep into his middle years, that such a man would sit with Papaw and ask him about Jesus? Oh, the marvelous return to old and ancient things, to those Eden things, that Jesus intends to see us into again. What a shrewd move on Jesus's part to see men so differently from Papaw and to put in front of Papaw this different vision. It is like the kind of parable Jesus told in which a Samaritan is the good rescuer of a Jew in need. Jesus rementors our sight. Scales fall from the eyes. Human, we see and are known.

Eyes with the scales left on cause men to see in comparisons. We compare biceps and bulges, paychecks and professional titles, and we tally points scored whether with siblings, sport, business, or our prowess with women. Some men compare penis size, other men compare church size—there is little difference between these games. Both are false measures and are of the same genre of self-misdirection. So Jesus calls men to places where glad-handing does not work and advancement in the company has no merit. Jesus looks grown men in the eye and tells them that caring for children and those equally dependent and overlooked will make us great (Luke 9:46–48).

Likewise, when wealth and a powerful position seem to cause a man to believe that he will lose out if he loses both, Jesus says in essence, "Let me strip you of your money and your position so that you can know what true life, true wealth, and true happiness as a real man with God can be" (Luke 18:18–30). When Peter wants to know what John is going to do for the kingdom with Jesus, Jesus crushes this competitive and nosy comparison. "Stay in your place, Peter," he seems to say. "Let John be in his. Both of you doing what I call you to in the places I have called you to is enough for a good life. What is it to you what I do with John? You follow me. I'll take care of you both" (John 21:21–22).

To follow Jesus and to minister to others requires asking yourself these questions: Do I know that I am a man created and regarded by God? Do I know that whether I compare favorably or unfavorably as it relates to other men or women is a false measure and is irrelevant to my actual worth, contribution, and need for grace?

As Matthew lists the who's who among men, the Jesus way of seeing has begun to change him. I think about sports statistics and our placing every man in a category either as the worst or best at the game. To be the maker of the list would tempt Matthew to buy into this way of measuring men. But something has happened to the tax collector, the son of Alpheus. To Judas and to himself he ascribes a descriptor. But besides family references, he does this to no other man. What I mean is that when Matthew lists Peter, for example, he tells us that Peter is the brother of Andrew, but he mentions nothing about Peter being a fisherman or about Peter denying Jesus. So it is as Matthew tells us about each of the other disciples.

But of Judas, Matthew recalls the thirty pieces, the murderous kiss on Jesus's cheek, and the absence of return for forgiveness. "Judas Iscariot, who betrayed him," Matthew says. And, as if to stand out in some way, not with the others, but alongside of and with Judas, Matthew lists himself as "Matthew the tax collector" (Matt. 10:2–4). Matthew lists himself alongside of other men for all to see. In Christ, he has been freed to list what those in his day would value least. Matthew lists what to himself was a life of sin against others and a misuse of his calling for his own selfish gain. How is it that a man could ever come to the place in which he could name himself alongside other men as having a disliked job and a sordid past? "Jesus *saw a man* named Matthew." Matthew was never the same.

Paul, that staunchly Jewish man, echoes this grace applied to the eyes. The Jew becomes an advocate and servant to Gentiles. "The love of Christ controls us," he says. "Therefore, we regard no one according to the flesh" anymore. Rather, he seems to say that we see people as Jesus sees them, as they are in Christ or as they are with defiled dignity apart from Christ (2 Cor. 5:13–21).

This rementored vision educates us not just regarding our ways of seeing men and race but also for our ways of seeing women. We who minister to others have such a mentoring.

Our Game Playing

I am a pastor now. But I was a boy once, a young man. I remember that we spent the night outside. I looked forward to it. I enjoyed the freedom of hanging out with friends after our parents went to sleep. Not that the night promised wild abandon. The tents, after all, were in my backyard. My friends and I would wake the night and invite it to play just a few feet from my parents' bedroom window. But still. I loved the summer. I enjoyed my friends. I imagined the jokes and the laughter. It would be fun to camp out together. I was fifteen. The girls who were my friends would stay and then go, and the rest of us guys would continue cheering on the night.

At this point I had not thought that anything else but the simple companionship of close friends in the company of trees and breezes was necessary for a good time. Maybe that is why I seemed surprised when embarrassment and shame determined to crash our party. A familiar voice broke through to brashness. "Let's play 'Truth or Dare,'" it said. Boys and girls glanced at one another with knowing. Others of us looked down at our shoes or bare feet. We looked down and felt that someone had just invited a boastful stranger into our group. Safety fled. Fun and friendship unbuttoned their shirts and sheepishly walked out onto the stage. I wonder: was this the Vaudeville act that mentored Samson and hollowed him out with women? Like Esau who gave away his birthright for his lust for food, so Samson would give himself away for the shape of a woman's body and voice, no matter what her intentions toward him.

I think my awkwardness revealed the questions deep within me. Why must we make a game of kissing? Why must we make sport of our bodies? I couldn't have named it then, but I felt that I'd have to give myself away for use if I wanted to remain cool and accepted among my friends. I had felt none of that through all our activities to that point. Being together had been sufficient. Laughter and play was enough. But now I felt it deep.

Examining Our Mentoring

The intimacy of friendship or the promise of genuine romantic love didn't satisfy my party guests. Friends couldn't rest without benefits. I'd have to become something I'm not in order to be something they want.

Karen must have felt the same way. We both chose the dare. But we did so with painted-on smiles amid the catcalls of our friends. Danny boasted about what a man I am. Jeff shamed me with jokes about how I wouldn't know what to do with a woman if I had the chance. I don't know what Karen's friends said to her. Or what it felt like for her when Danny and Jeff talked like this in front of her. What I do know is that she and I both laughed as if joining our whistles to the jeering chorus. I also know that we both avoided each other's eyes. Karen wrestled with whether she would stay intact or give way. So did I. But we both chose to breach. To gain admiration among friends was preferable to honesty about my reluctance or lack of interest in this particular game.

The dare? French kissing in the tent for at least five minutes. We unzipped the tent and went in. Our friends became voyeurs wanting a good show. Whatever dreams of true love with a boy that Karen had, and whatever thoughts I had about what it would mean to truly love a woman as a man, were taunted. I chanced a bold move. I mustered the courage to say, "We need our privacy." I winked at the boys. I led them on in their imaginations. They winked back. "Allll riiigghhhht, Essswiiinne," they flaunted.

It worked. I zipped the tent. Karen and I sat close on top of sleeping bags with legs crossed. Our knees touched, but nothing else except our breath. We felt each other's breath on one another's faces. Doritos and Pepsi. We breathed heavy with fidget. She looked one way and I looked the other. We were close enough that her looking away was blurry to me. We held that position like statues for our allotted minutes. Our mouths inched toward each other, but never touched. Both of us longed for a kiss. But not like this. We unzipped the tent and boasted with lies about how awesome we were in our "making out."

Women with Bodies

What does that have to do with who I have been becoming as a pastor? Well, that was not my first dance among the catcalls. But more often than not, I went into the tent and pretended. I was the one who held one beer throughout the whole night. I looked like I was drinking, but I wasn't. I looked like I was French kissing, but I wasn't. (Instead, the kind of pretending and equally damaging game playing that I would increasingly choose was religious and self-righteous.)

For the moment, however, I want to reflect that for many of my friends, kissing in tents for entertainment and acceptance soon mentored their maneuvering in bars, their learned tactics for parties, and their justified ploys for Christian singles nights. *Friendship* became defined as "those who stick with us as long as we lose ourselves for them." We want to stop at one beer. But our "friends" cajole us and demean as a joke until we join them for more. We introduce "friends" so that they can hook up for amusement. Girls feel the power of their bodies and learn to exploit it. Boys feel the power of their words and their drink. Boys and girls begin playing "Truth or Dare" as a habit of being. What starts as a game becomes a way of life. A way of life mentors how we see each other.

As this mentoring happens, we start a strange reasoning that this dismantling of neighbor love actually helps us to have fun. We verbally and physically striptease and applaud. The woman knows she wouldn't talk to him unless she was drunk. He knows it too. They manipulate conscience and each other into what they have learned to call "acceptance." We flirt, tease, joke, and touch necks and thighs. We invite another to use us for her pleasure and let us do the same with her. We call this "freedom" or "love."

We trespass with hugs or glances or intimate speech and then pat ourselves on the back for how well we kept our boundaries. We cheer each other into hazard. We destabilize one another and call this "community." A woman can no longer watch football without seeing tight pants. A man can no longer live any part of life without such views. Over time, the dreams we left under the sheets of another's bed or in another's bottle call out to us. Shame becomes a way of living. We no longer try to silence it. We tell ourselves that we've lost everything anyway so it doesn't matter anymore what we continue to give away of ourselves.

We remember the innocent and meaningful drink and intimacy offered us in Jesus's house. We remember that words could be spoken and touch given that was an end in itself. Such words and touch required nothing further of us. Words and touch weren't used as tools to get us into bed. We once knew that. But we forgot.

Or maybe we've never known this. We remember or we imagine now and groan. We are unworthy. We are too many gropings down the road, too many empty bottles to go back. We deserve the food of pigs. We resign ourselves in slop. There with the poet we finally confess the rut: "We don't know what we're doing. So, let's do it again. We're just amateur lovers with amateur friends."[3]

I remember my stepgrandparents' *Playboy Channel*, the *Hustler* porn magazines under the sink cabinet in the upstairs bedroom. I think of Papaw's closet. I am crushed with a realization. I cannot see or minister to women until I learn the grace to see through her body to who she is. "Sightless, unless the eyes reappear," a poet says.[4] I write some poetry of my own.

> You hid your *Playboys* in the closet
> along with everything else.
> You hid me there too
> and that's what we became.

Do You See This Woman?

So, when Jesus says, "Do you see this woman?" I'm humbled by his rementoring (Luke 7:44).

I'm humbled because the pastors only saw the "sort of woman" she was. All they saw was her body and her sexual ability in life. In this, they were no different from the men she had slept with. They too, though they were not pastors, saw only her body and her sexual ability. I should say, rather, that most of her body went unnoticed by either kind of man. The religious men and the irreligious men had this in common: they looked at the woman, but they did not see her. Edenic eyes gave way again, poked out amid the haze. The religious denounced her. The irreligious desired her. Both were blind.

I'm also humbled because Jesus isn't looking at the men when he asks them this question. The poignancy of this escapes my words. He has been looking at Simon and his friends, speaking to him and to them. But now, before he asks this question about whether they see her, he turns toward the woman. They no longer receive his gaze. She does. He speaks to them but looks at her as he asks, "Do you see this woman?"

I wonder what it must have been like for her in the presence of Jesus's gaze. There was no lust in his eyes, no use of her behind his smile, no flirtatious familiarity or flattery in his tone. Her given beauty was noticed and cherished; her heart and mind were understood and known. Had she ever in her life been looked at by a man with such delightful purity, the sheer enjoyment of human company? And, in turn, had these men ever known that they could learn to look at a woman in this way of grace?

I walk through Lleywellyns Pub on a Friday night with my bride. Hand in hand we walk. The men turn and grab her with their eyes as we walk toward the back for our table. They don't care that I'm hers and that she is mine or that our covenant before God is sacred and happy for us. I've come to learn that she has had to learn to live with this all of her life. She has had to live with the "Do you want to get drunk with me eyes" of men.

I suddenly remember June. She was known for "putting out." I remember her offering herself to me in eighth grade. "Zack, if you see something you want, you should just go for it!" she teased. My friends cheered. I remember seeing June three years later. I had transferred schools. My friends and I were at McDonald's. June was there. She was drunk. "Heyyy, Zaacckkk," she called out. My friends were different, but the situation hadn't changed. "Get her in the car," one of them said. "Get her in the car!" I wonder where June is now. Has she ever come to know the gracious dignifying rest of the pornless eyes of Jesus? Do I possess such eyes as I open the Bible or pray or eat food in the presence of a woman?

I've rarely thought of my mamaw by her name and apart from her role in my life. Grandsons can forget that mamaws are women. Her name was Pauline. As a girl she and Papaw had dated and flirted and kissed. His name was Bud. She had put on her best dress and touched her neck with perfume, hoping his fingers might gently touch her there too, I imagine. I like to think that she saw a change in Papaw's way of seeing her near the end. I know that we all saw it in him after Jesus saw him and she was gone. There was a gratitude, a tenderness, a longing in his eyes as he spoke her name or recounted her presence that once sat with him in the living room, peeled potatoes with him in the kitchen, lay womanly before him in their bed of years. I think in the end he saw her, and the years of *Playboys* had their eyes poked out. I like to think that the woman who knew and loved this man of fists found her aging prayers for him answered, and tenderly his fists opened. They relaxed and caressed, rather than used her again, in the bonds of an old promise and a long love.

I think what I'm trying to get at is this: just as men have been mentored by the bent world to compare anything and everything, a woman too has her trials with comparing herself to another. The way men rank bodies has made this so, but in her own heart the damaging desire to be the unique woman among women is her own. She was made to be cherished (Eph. 5:28–29). Mostly she is handled.

I think of Judy sitting in my office. "You need to leave him," I said to her about her abusive boyfriend. "I know, but I can't," she said. I paused. I had already spoken of Jesus and his provision for her. I had already committed our time and presence to help her. She was still resistant. I knew her. I prayed silently in my head. I saw the shame in her face. I risked a statement in the context of our knowing. "I'm guessing that the sex isn't even that good," I gently said, almost as a whisper.

Her facial expressions all stopped for a moment. She looked down. After a moment, hardened cheeks softened. Tears began to fall onto her knees. "No, it isn't," she finally said. "I feel so dirty afterward, the things he wants me to do. I take showers," she said through the tears. "But I can't get clean," she reflected.

"Then why are you still with him?" I asked. A longer pause lingers. "Because at least for a moment," she says, "at least for a moment, I feel wanted."

It is no wonder that whereas Paul cautions men about provoking others to anger, he cautions women about a tendency to gossip (1 Tim. 5:13). For men, the desire for respect (Eph. 5:33) gets tangled up, delayed, and confused, and the fists are used to take it. For a woman, the desire to be wanted means she will use anything at her disposal to wrestle it from another. Not just a bit of skin, but a bit of news and suddenly she is wanted. "Tell us what you know," they say, and at least for the moment, she is desired. But thirsty for water, she finds none to satisfy until she is seen by Jesus and known and cherished.

When that happens she will go and tell men and women what he has done for her. Among the men she used to flirt with and the women about whom she used to share bits of news (or bear the brunt of), she now has found a different way of relating. She will find again that glorious intimidation she possesses as a daughter of the King. Foolish men will frighten away as she sees right through them. Tongue-twisted women will go elsewhere. Old lovers will face the gospel in the new mentoring of her Jesus eyes toward them. No longer will she say, "Come and see me." "Come and see him," she now says. "Come see the one who told me everything I ever did" (see John 4:1–45).

If Jesus teaches us to see through the fists to the man, he will teach us to see through the bodily shape to the woman. To minister to either will require both. This is why Peter shares with women that it is not their bodies or attention to their appearance that will ultimately win their wayward and defensive husbands, though this will be a man's or woman's default, because of the mentoring we have been discussing. The man might enjoy the view, but his heart cannot change by that means (1 Pet. 3:3). Instead, it is a woman's character, a woman who is loved and defended by Jesus, that will win the day (1 Pet. 3:4–5).

Men with fists want to take Peter's words and bow women into slavish submission in the name of God, not realizing that Peter is actually rebuking such men. Trying to help a woman whose husband is wayward, he tells her not to trust her body to do the job (1 Pet. 3:1). "That kind of heart in a man with fists can only be changed by God," he seems to say. It is as if Peter says, "Appeal to him and wait upon him with the quiet dignity you possess as the dearly loved woman of the Lord that you are." When Abraham was out of line, it wasn't Sarah's body that could bring the repair. It was her waiting upon the Lord for Abraham (1 Pet. 3:6). Make no mistake: her waiting was not to Abraham as her ultimate lord. She appealed beyond his pay grade and put her hope not in her man or her clothes or her body but in God (1 Pet. 3:5).

Then, to emphasize that a man is meant to see this beauty of holiness and be frightened by it from harming her, Peter points the wayward husband to what God sees in the woman. She is a co-heir of grace, meant to be understood and honored. Her bodily strength, though it often may not match a man's bodily strength, is meant for cherishing, not misusing. And if the man cannot gain such eyes with which to see the woman, God will begin to oppose the man. A husband who will not see beyond the body to the woman will soon find that God will no longer answer such a man's prayers (1 Pet. 3:7).

"Do you see this woman?" Jesus asked as he saw her. She left that night back into the wolfish world of religious and irreligious men, back into the world of gossiping women with bodies. But she was different. She had known the gaze of his love. His way of seeing her gave her a new mentoring to take with her among the tents of Truth or Dare that lay waiting in the night. Poetry comes to mind:

> I could see everything but what you wished . . .
> show me where to look . . .
> Instruct me in the dark.[5]

In Jesus, we learn that to see is to know. To be seen is to be known. Perhaps this is why Jesus suggested that appearances make poor judges of us all (John 7:24). By this he seems to say that explaining the appearance of a thing does not mean we have seen the thing as it is. To lust diminishes. To ignore veils. Quick labels make easier what should not be easy. To say that I am a Presbyterian allows easily for dismissal or embrace. Yet wisdom teaches us that we should neither dismiss nor embrace a human being on the basis of such surface information. The problem is that this is our tendency, even in ministry, for we have been poorly mentored in the art of seeing Christianly.

Beyond that, our hearts are sinfully seeing-impaired. Left to ourselves, we would naturally look at appearances and choose the wrong man for the job of king, leaving David in the fields tending sheep. In Jesus's words, therefore, with appearances before our eyes and judgments made in our hearts, we can be those who "see but never perceive" (Matt. 13:14). We are easily lied to and hastily unobservant. So we are beckoned to awaken. "Look, I tell you, lift up your eyes, and see," Jesus says (John 4:35).

Praying for Illumination

For this reason, Jesus teaches us that our attempts at seeing must be accompanied by equal attempts at praying. Nights in gardens of betrayal can fatigue our ability to see. It hinders our ability to rightly interpret what marches our way with mutinous torches in the night. "Watch and pray," Jesus notes (Matt. 26:41). Both to see and to pray is like Bilbo and Sam heading necessarily toward Mount Doom. The one will not succeed without the unwavering friendship of the other. Many of us are often stumbling over the uneven sidewalks of our ministries because this friendship has yet to be forged. We pray without watching. We watch without praying. We keep separating a necessary fellowship.

So a question arises. In light of how you have been mentored to see, how blind are you to what is there? To answer this question is to take notice that even if our physical eyes remain unbroken, our ability to see well has not escaped wreckage. We enter ministry as human beings "who have to act on the basis of what we know," and yet, "what we know is incomplete."[6] To see only gibbous is to miss much of the moon. "For now," says the apostle, "we see in a mirror dimly" (1 Cor. 13:12).

The fact that we see dimly means that "the question of how to act in ignorance is paramount."[7] Therefore, I must learn to start each day in ministry with this admission: regarding every person, bit of creation, and circumstance that I encounter today, I must say to myself, "I am in the dark," or, "I've been mentored to distort what sits before my eyes." Therefore, I must remember that when I enter the pulpit, stand by a hospital bed, take a walk, or sit in my chair to counsel another, I physically see people and things always as one at dusk.

This is why the eyes of our hearts need the divine aid that prayer facilitates (Eph. 1:18). We have no kingdom sightings apart from divine provision (John 3:5). What we see of God is binoculared. We are like those who stand at the "outskirts of his ways" (Job 26:14). Therefore, we are helped to learn how to attend every moment of ministry activity with this pilgrim prayer: "Lord, I can't see, please open my eyes." This necessary friendship holds true for everyone to whom we seek to minister his grace. We have no power to open their physical or soulish eyes. Only Jesus can do such deep things (Acts 26:17–18). Anything wondrous we hope our parishioners or counselees to see must come from his illumination.

If this humility chafes, take note. Like a woman who strikes a match to light her way through the jungle, is a person who believes that seeing with her eyes will illumine all things. The famed Welshman Christmas Evans was a one-eyed preacher. The point is, in some ways we all are. We squint through our days. It is time to acknowledge the fog through which we drive. The world is braille. There is a reason that business must discuss what it calls "risk management." Because "even the very wise cannot see all ends."[8] Therefore, ministry begins with a cry that becomes a prayer to Jesus.

> So I try to be like you, try to feel it like you do
> *But without you it's no use,*
> I can't see what you see when I look at the world.[9]

Prayer as sight leads us to a praying and seeing community. This fact explains why Jesus not only lectured and preached to his disciples but also had them do life with him. His teachings included his footsteps. His ways teach. To see his ways was to see the Father (John 14:8–9). So Paul could say to Timothy that he had passed on not only his teachings to Timothy but also his ways (2 Tim. 3:10).

Jesus gives people to us. We spend time with those people. They are farther along the road of grace than we are. They have more of Jesus's eyes as they look at persons and minister to them. I have needed such sight mentors in my life. Prayer and doing life join to renew our prescriptions.

Conclusion

I was leaving the Guernseys' Thanksgiving gathering. My papaw called out to me. It had been thirty-five years or so since he told me he planned to shoot Santa; six or seven years since the arrival of the black chaplain; and six or seven years since I had written that letter to him telling him of my love for him and of Jesus, that letter that he called "a keeper." It was a year or two prior to Mamaw's death and to Papaw's unblinding beneath the gaze of Jesus. It was after fifty years of Mamaw's praying.

"Hey, young man," he said. Silver-haired and thin. Long gone were the once strong sideburns, dark and full on his now sunken cheeks. As I turned around, he pointed to me, and with all seriousness from his piercing blue eyes he said, "Not many people know what's inside this old man."

"Yah?" I asked.

"Two years ago, this old man began to give thanks to God every night," he said. "A few months ago, this old man started going back to church."

I was stunned with the sacredness of this moment. I foraged through my keys toward the empty deep of my jeans pockets trying to find words. "What is that like for you, Papaw?" I mustered.

"Well, I don't go along with all of it," he said. "But to tell you the truth, I've missed it."

He inched toward me with the awkward makings of a hug.

Then he said it, "You never know what will happen to this old man, do you?"

"You never know."

Ministry and Our Relatives

Internally, I was feeling exhausted. Pastorally, the stresses to our church budget, our staff, and many of our families had been converging. I was waist-deep in a bog of weighty decisions and the traumas of others. Criticisms from church members waited restlessly for me in my e-mail inbox. They also found their way through messages given to my elders but not spoken to me. It was one of those valley seasons within the ebb and flow of doing ministry as a family together.

At the same time, as a parent, my kids' ages and stages had me concerned for them. I was humbled and feeling inadequate to father them well. Blended-family challenges were daily pounding on my door. Then, as a neighbor, I had also just received an anonymous letter asking that we trim our hedges from the sidewalk. Added to this, I had regular e-mails from a critic who told me I was a cult leader and that the church I served was a cult too.

My wife, Jessica, and I were in sync, by grace, but feeling our need for prayer. My Sabbath rhythm of weekly rest toward God had gone missing for months.

So I found myself plopped on a blanket with a packed lunch, my Bible, and some paper, nestled between the shade trees of one of my favorite Sabbath-rest places. It was a Monday afternoon. Looking down the long hill to the fountained waters of Forest Park, I tried to find a bit of quiet. I opened the Bible. I needed to turn the knob through the mishmash of fragmented frequencies playing within my thoughts till I could hear something of God's voice instead of mine or everyone else's.

During that time of reading, praying, and listening, what kept coming to my mind was something more than the church decisions or my kids' situations. It felt silly and surprising at first. But what hounded me, among other things, was a recent statement from a relative of mine. It was critical in nature. Before I knew it, there in prayer with the opened Bible in the park, I recognized that I was worrying and pained regarding the varied thoughts that my varying relatives and step-relatives had of me (or that I imagined they had of me). I felt I would spiral down.

So, in the park, I began to write down every role I have in my extended family alongside of the other hats I wear. I needed to separate them out and seek illumination regarding each one from the Lord. I wrote the following:

man	grandson	uncle	author
husband	ex-husband	pastor	counselor
father	brother	neighbor	house-group leader
son	stepbrother	friend	professor
stepson	half-brother	mentor	
son-in-law	brother-in-law	nephew	
former son-in-law	former brother-in-law	cousin	

What list would you jot down? Each role represents a host of relationships. That I am human, limited in time and emotional capacity, represents my boundaries or shortcomings or sins associated with each word. Some roles bring pain as I think of them. Others bring a sense of joy. Which ones do this for you?

All of them together forge a strong reminder that I am not God. All of us will need Jesus amid our limited abilities of time and energy and life season to care hospitably and adequately for one another. It also means that priorities will give less and more time to some roles than others.

In that light, I began to think about how extended- and blended-family members can often relate to those in ministry in ways that cause pain, and how we in ministry sometimes do the same in return.

Marveling, the Few, and Going about It

I have to admit that for most of my time in ministry, I have wrestled with various kinds of legitimate and illegitimate guilt as it relates to my extended and blended families along with my hometowns. I am the one that "moved away." Many of us in ministry have.

In his own hometown, as long as Jesus was "the carpenter, the son of Mary and brother of James and Joses and Judas and Simon" along with his sisters, Jesus was welcome. He was a member of the people and the place. He grew up there and had a trade like everybody else (Mark 6:3).

But once Jesus "began to teach in the synagogue," and once he began to read and interpret the Scriptures along with naming his own identity within them, the welcome mat was removed by most. "They took offense at him" (Mark 6:1–8; Luke 4:16–30). Ironically, it was only where Jesus grew up that "he could do no mighty work there." Only among his former teachers, pastors, playmates, and family members would he marvel "because of their unbelief" (Mark 6:6).

Jesus says about this that hometown offense is not unique to him. Actually, Jesus's experience reveals a truism. When God calls us to speak of him, we can expect that many among our relatives and in our own household will not get what we do, will mischaracterize us, and will seek to minimize our life's vocation (Mark 6:4).

My way of handling my small resemblance to what Jesus experienced has sometimes made it worse. I've brooded over my own experiences with pain wondering why I'm picked on, singled out, or misunderstood. I've defended myself by trying to instruct or explain or blame. I've said, "The heck with this," and just disappeared or avoided people altogether for a while. But our Lord handled hometown offense in a very different manner. He handled it by marveling, laying hands on a few, and then going about. What does this mean?

First, Jesus marveled (Mark 6:6). He honestly assessed the rebuff, felt its sting, and shook his head in saddened disbelief. To refuse the grace he could give makes no sense. It's like a humble philanthropist offering five million dollars for the poor, the downtrodden, the schools, and the local businesses of a town, and the mayor saying, "No, thanks, we don't want it." The absence of sense making causes a shrug of the shoulders, a scratch of the head, and sadness from losing the good that could have been. So Jesus marveled. But he didn't pout or blame shift or stomp his feet and tantrum about. He didn't go on a marketing campaign or go door to door to explain himself. He named it, ached about it, and let it be. Jesus shows us the grace to marvel too, when relatives and hometown folk disregard our gifts and calling.

Second, because Jesus "could do no mighty work" among his relatives and in his childhood community, this did not mean that he could do no work at all, nor did it mean that everyone tritely or angrily overlooked him. "A few" had the grace to see Jesus for who he was. They looked to him for healing, and they found it (Mark 6:5). Imagine a pastor at his family reunion. Many at a family reunion will go no further than small talk, on the one hand, or avoidance or rebuff, on the other. Blended-family realities can add to the strangeness.

But the pastor can learn the grace in Jesus not to leave or huff and puff. Rather, Jesus will show the minister that someone there needs Jesus and is looking for Jesus. Someone there knows that Jesus has called you as a minister in his name. Linger, watch, pray, bear with the jokes and the avoidances; enjoy the small talk and the memories. And trust that Jesus will give you grace to humbly love everyone and the eyes to see the exceptions. For with a few, you will find patches of conversation in out-of-the-way moments in which Jesus will minister through you to your family and through them to you.

Third, Jesus then "went about among the villages teaching" (Mark 6:6). Disregard among relatives doesn't keep Jesus from the calling he was given. He taught and sought to care for people in the gospel, regardless of how his relatives may have interpreted him. The rejection of some, even though that rejection hurts because it comes from those so dear, does not negate his obedience to fulfill his calling. Though we hurt or wish things were different back home, Jesus will take care of those matters. Meanwhile he bids us to get on with the grace he has given us for the people he has called us to.

The Painful Adjustment

Sometimes the critical voice or implied disappointment comes from a well-meaning disposition. Our family misses us and wishes we were home. After all, for twenty-six years Christmas Eve at Mamaw's was a given. Now the Christmas Eve tradition at our new pastorate puts that in jeopardy and requires a choice. The church has never had Christmas Eve without its pastor leading them in worship. The Guernseys have never had a Christmas Eve in which their son/grandson/nephew/cousin wasn't there. Like in-laws adjusting to the fresh routines of their newlyweds, sometimes leaving and cleaving is not what a pastor, a church, and his extended family feel ready for in ministry. The change and the grace to give room take time.

Jesus and his family began early to navigate this changing use of time and purpose. It started when he was twelve. The call on Jesus's life announced by the angel those years ago was starting to assert itself. Even though Joseph and Mary had experienced the miracle of virgin birth firsthand, the implications for what this would mean regarding their family life with Jesus had not yet set in. In fact, Jesus's relatives were sincerely perplexed.

"Son, why have you treated us so?" (Luke 2:48). Many in ministry have heard this question. Jesus's family feels hurt by Jesus. His actions and his purpose that differs from theirs have stung them. "Behold," Mary adds, "your father and I have been searching for you in great distress" (Luke 2:48). Jesus's earthly father and mother didn't know where he was or what was happening to him. He had left them without his presence and in silence regarding where his calling was leading him. Their accusation, their pain, and their desire that he should choose differently overflow into family confrontation. They feel that Jesus is wrong.

Jesus asks a direct and gentle question in response: "Why were you looking for me? Did you not know that I must be in my Father's house?" (Luke 2:49). The young Jesus seems to imply that they all knew what they were getting into when Jesus was called. He seems to suggest that they can be okay even if they are not physically together and even if there is silence about his life for a few days. What his calling requires is something that he expected would be understood.

I wonder what it was like for Joseph to hear that Jesus had to be in the house of a different Father, and that this Father was not Joseph and did not include Joseph's provision or dwelling. The twelve-year-old had a purpose that included but was larger than what his immediate family desired.

As Jesus and his family began this painful adjustment, his family "did not understand" what Jesus was trying to reveal to them (Luke 2:49). They would have to ponder these things in their hearts and chew on it all for a while (Luke 2:51). Jesus would relate with respect and submission as they each came to terms with the change that was coming (Luke 2:50).

We gather from this that even for those who love the Lord and love each other, it is not easy to surrender our children to their God-given purposes. Likewise, it is not easy for the young to remain respectful and submissive when those we love the most don't understand us or illegitimately shame us. Jesus shows each of us the grace we need as parents to let go and to support, and the grace we need as pastors to respect, to graciously bear with the misunderstanding, and to give time.

At other times, however, passivity, or envy, or disdain reveal themselves, and some relatives simply avoid us. It is assumed by these that our holiness renders hidden our humanness. Likewise, for others, once we became a minister we resembled those Christians or churches that had caused hurt in their past. Their soreness with those others finds a place to roost with us. Year after year we receive the looks, the tone, and the words meant truly for those other "hypocrites" but with nowhere else to land. Our every visit becomes our relatives' runway. They release their wheels with speed and steer into us with screech and bounce and force.

These challenges seem to rise because extended family members are sometimes tempted to expect more of us or think less of us or both. For example, if we were maintenance workers or sales directors, normal family communication such as phone calls or texts, along with the normal pain and resolution of limits and sins, would ebb and flow. No family member is always at his best, and we each need each other's forgiveness. Forgiveness is a way of life. When living miles apart from each other, or on frequent job projects, or with the ordinary demands of parenting, our texts and e-mails can wax and wane. Most families understand this.

But when our vocation is so explicitly tied to God-stuff, somehow our human limits and sins, not so different from our cousin who is in sales or our sister who has kids, seem larger and cause more pain. Our calls or texts appear artificial, whereas his or hers just makes sense—after all he has to travel to support his family, and she is in the midst of those parenting intensities. This dual way of looking at others when compared to us is rarely done consciously. After all, those serving the vocation of ministry are human beings—a child to somebody, a grandchild to someone else, a nephew and a cousin to others—a spouse or parent. But not all family members have the grace to extend in this way. Such grace when it comes—heals.

Admittedly, often we clergy do not help matters, like Joseph with our coats strutting about. We wear our calling like a robe, our degree like a scepter, and our church like a throne. We act as if our calling excuses us from being human and home.

But even when we are humble and human, it takes adjustment for family members to see that God has called us such as we are to give our lives as shepherd companions for his people somewhere else.

A Time to Stand

Eighteen or more years later and Jesus's parents and siblings still did not understand his call or what it required of his life. This meant more pain.

For example, one of the most important moments in Jesus's ministry flowed out of all-night prayer and flowed into choosing the Twelve. Crowds were responding so powerfully to the grace of God in Jesus's ministry that Jesus had very little time to eat. He chose to use the house he was staying in for ministry in such a way that the roof was carved out and a lame man was lowered into his presence. The response of his family wasn't to bring him food for his hunger or a hammer for repairs or to encourage him that the Lord, who called him, would sustain him and be faithful to him. Instead they looked right into the good Jesus did and disparaged his character. They wanted him to stop his ministry and to come home with them.

> And when his family heard it, they went out to seize him, for they were saying, "He is out of his mind." (Mark 3:21)

In fact, when Jesus persists in mentoring and ministry, his family tries harder but not to join him or to stand with him. In fact, while others gather to learn from God through Jesus, "his mother and his brothers" stand outside (Mark 4:31). They send public messages that draw attention to their protest. They let everyone attending know that they are not with Jesus as teacher, and they want him to come back home with them. They assert their family position and imply that Jesus needs to leave at once. Maybe they want him to leave because he has responsibilities at home, or perhaps because he should be a carpenter, do more family things, and not embarrass him or the family any further.

We don't know. What we do know is that in that public moment Jesus is slandered by his family. They refer to him as a man not in his right mind.

Humanly speaking, there are very few critiques more painful than those leveled at us by those who have known us the longest. Sometimes these wounds of a friend bless and heal us. But when those who have known us the longest look down on our calling and then attribute ill motives or qualities to our character, the wound goes deep. Some of us will have to learn by grace how not to quit on our calling or how not to despair in the pain of family members who always stand outside and say that we are out of our minds. We will need grace day by day to brave the implied criticism that we are hypocrites who do not live what we teach.

At this moment, no longer twelve, but more like thirty, Jesus gently but profoundly makes an unnervingly direct statement. He asks all listening, "Who are my mother and my brothers?" Family and calling are about to be redefined.

> And looking about at those who sat around him, he said, "Here are my mother and my brothers! For whoever does the will of God, he is my brother and sister and mother." (Mark 4:31–35)

It was time. From the age of twelve Jesus had submitted to and respectfully loved his family, even while they did not understand him. But now at thirty, while he still loves and respects them, he will fulfill his calling, whether they understand it or not. There are things that even they must learn from God. They cannot continue to pick at him like this. The manipulation, the name calling, and the use of guilt to shame has to stop. They publicly draw a line in the sand and force Jesus's hand. In that context, the result is clear. He will no longer indulge their mischaracterizations of him or their interpretations about who God is and how God's ministry is supposed to work. The family and Jesus must surrender to God's purposes for them and not the other way around. Jesus will go on in his calling now, whether they want him to or not, whether they are embarrassed by him or not, whether they don't think he treats them well enough or not. This moment in Jesus's life floors me.

The family must have gone home that day furious and pained. They would have been tempted to view his words and tone not through the lens in which Jesus meant them to, but through the filters of their already-made judgments about him. Likely, Jesus only confirmed their suspicions. He is out of his mind. They are right to stand outside and not join in.

Maybe they genuinely believed that he cared more about those people who came to him than he cared about them. Maybe they felt disrespected because he spoke so plainly and honestly. Maybe they thought what a selfish and proud man their son and brother was, who loves the crowds and the fame and the attention. "Head in the clouds," he no longer eats meals with them, doesn't check in the way they'd like, and has left the family business of carpentry for others to pick up.

What we know for sure is that while Jesus gave himself to the Father's business, Jesus did not stop loving his family (John 19:26). In time, his mother would come to understand all those things that were prophesied and had been treasured within her heart. In time his brother James would affectionately bow to him as Lord and Savior. But we do not see them all together very much. Maybe some reading know what this is like.

My point remains, however. Extended-family perceptions, hometowns, and ministries are a mess—it was this way even for our Lord in the fullness of his humanity.

While none of us is Jesus, there often comes a time in every extended family and hometown when the vocational pastor has to say, "I love you, I need you, I want to do life with you. But if you choose to continue to stand outside and send messages of disdain and critique and shame to me, I will, by grace, declare that my first allegiance is to God, as is yours, and that our family is larger than ourselves; we have brothers and sisters and mothers in Christ to whom we must attend."

For some of us, it is time to throw off this illegitimate guilt, learn how to endure its pain by grace, and get on by grace with what our lives in Christ have been called to. Some will never think accurately about us. Jesus will teach us to live with that and go on.

Putting Up with Us

But others of us have legitimate guilt to bear. We have related with little of the humility and grace of Jesus or have refused his authentic directness. We've bullied, made pronouncements, and acted as if following God means that we have no responsibilities as human beings to those we love and to those who, in God's providence, have loved us. We need forgiveness for this, at least from the Lord, and as far as is possible from others.

Why? Because when we misuse the ministry to try to forget where we've been, it feels to those who were there with us as if we are trying to forget them too. We act like we never once fell crashing through ceiling tiles into the high school band (I think it was the horn section). That's right! Up there in those rafters we slipped while trying to peek into the girls' locker room while skipping class as a junior. We wear a collar now, but that was us then, make no mistake!

When trying to pray or say something of spiritual meaning, family members will not let us forget such things. This can bless us. We can laugh together. We can take the vocation but not ourselves seriously. When such memories of our folly are called to mind with this kind of grace, and when they are meant by relatives to encourage us in our discouragements, we are helped to remember where we've been, helped by family to remember that it was only by grace that Jesus called us in the first place, and that his grace will lead us on.

Sometimes our family members refuse to respect our prayers, refuse to humble themselves to learn from something in the Lord that we might be able to share. It does not occur to them that regularly we meet with people just like them at their age with their struggles, doubts, questions, and happinesses and that there are actually people in the world who come to us with their most intimate requests for help.

I think the memory of our worse or foolish moments will not let some relatives envision this help God intends for them through us. They feel glad for a plumber in the family when the pipes break, or for a hairstylist for free haircuts, or the 20 percent discount down at the retail store through Aunt Barb. But they rarely think of the blessing that a humble minister in the family can provide. They do not recognize the sting we carry with us because of this.

But maybe too, if we are honest, perhaps we in our virgin zeal for the Lord and within our earnestness for our newfound calling have often been less than wise or kind. Maybe we have acted as if our calling is more noble than theirs. Maybe we've paid as little attention to Aunt Barb and her retail discount or to Uncle Ed's offers to plumb our house as they have to our ministry. Unlike our Lord, all of us in ministry can be selfish. We can treat our ministries as if our significance resides there, as if significance has no room among our relatives. Maybe we've caused unnecessary wounds—added insult to what is already difficult to adjust to.

Likewise, some of these dear ones cannot yet see how Jesus has grown us over the years, humbled us and changed us for good. But just as possible is that we can't see how he has been working his grace in them. Forgiving such things takes time and grace from God for each of us. Some will never want this or see their need for it. But forgiveness in our extended families can start with our acknowledging that we have made things harder than they needed to be. After all, we don't walk on water. They already know that, and maybe it is time that we do.

So how do we assess this? When our relatives tell us we have hurt them or when they attribute ill to our character or motives because we have related to them with little of the Spirit's fruit and little of those qualities that describe love, then we have legitimate guilt and need his grace to pursue and restore and recover. We have much still to learn. They need time and grace to trust us again in our newfound repentance and change.

However, when family does not like what we do in Jesus, or our conviction about it or what such a calling requires of us on a given day, and then casts their dislike into moral categories by distancing themselves, calling us names, or attributing ill motives to our character, then in Jesus we learn to weep but not to quit. They have much still to learn, not from us right now but from him.

There are some relatives who, until they can see us as human beings who possess a mixture of both strength and weakness and sin and beauty, will interpret even our kindest action through the worst filter, will see our most honest mistake as a willful manipulation.

Therefore, we make psalms in our pain, but we get on with the grace and the calling we've been given. We entrust our family to Jesus's empathy and timing and healing grace. We hope in him and wait upon him for a future of better hometown days. Meanwhile, until then, we take each day at a time now. We learn what we can of grace, and in Jesus we seek to help others do the same.

CHAPTER EIGHT

Celebrity

Practicing How to Return

These eyes—holes of a mask.[1]

"What do you want to be when you grow up?"

Mrs. Canter had written this question on the chalkboard for us all to ponder. I stared at the question. I was eight years old.

"I want to be a fireman," one of my friends called out.

"I want to be a baseball player," another cheered.

One by one, the classroom buzzed with future plans. One by one, Mrs. Canter wrote them down on the board. "Baseball player, truck driver, a mommy, a nurse."

I sat quietly. But the more I stared, I couldn't help but feel that the question was somehow staring back at me. Maybe what I felt were my teacher's eyes landing to rest their gaze upon me. Either way, the first stirrings of a call from God upon my life arrived, almost by surprise, to me there in my second-grade chair.

"And how about you, Zack?" Mrs. Canter asked.

I was nervous. I felt in my heart an answer that I feared would cause my friends to laugh. But Mrs. Canter's eyes were kind. Courage found me and I spoke up. "I, I want to be a priest," I said. "I want to be a priest when I grow up."

I don't remember if anyone laughed (though the teasing about my being "Father Zack" weren't long in coming). For the moment, I just remember seeing Mrs. Canter patch two words together for all to see.

"Zack—Priest."

I had not yet associated serving God with the love of money (Luke 16:14), the networking for position (Matt. 23:6–7), the lust for power (Acts 8:18–21), or the advancement of my own name. I did not know that serving

God could be used as a means to try, in line with the Serpent's old whisper, to become like God (Gen. 3:5).

When I was eight, my desire to be a servant of God had no hint of fame to it. Misguided ambition was simply waiting for its moment. I was already ambitious to be the best at kickball or Wiffle ball in my backyard among my friends. I aspired to get a baseball card that would rival Nick's or to paint my army men as good as Chris, my next-door neighbor.

Desire

At some point, I did positively learn that an inward desire to serve as an overseer for the Lord's people was commendable. In fact, to have such an internal desire is a prerequisite to the external call that comes from a community that knows my way of life (1 Tim. 3:1). Through fits and starts, U-turns and crashes, this good desire hung around. A good desire is a gift and strength. It looks us in the eyes and says, "Hold your ground," when everything else in us wants to quit and run.

It wasn't a priest I was to become. But the pastoral call still found me.

As a college student I began to receive some recognition as one who studied the Bible, prayed, saw conversions to Jesus through my life, and wrote songs for God. Maybe the first weeds of a breach began there.

By the time I was a seminary student, I interned as a youth pastor at a small local church. Because of the seminary presence over the years, our city had become saturated with our denomination and churches. The pond was big, and lots of fish swam in it.

As a young man, I remember going to a regular gathering of the pastors and other elders in our region. My pastor, Scott, had care of one of the smallest and struggling churches.

Scott spent hours with me. He gave me multiple opportunities to preach, to lead worship, and to attend leadership meetings in order to help me learn. Scott patiently put up whenever I acted like I'd known some bit of information for years (even though I first heard it in class the day before) and would point out how Scott and the little church were doing things wrong. He prayed for me and listened to me as I brought a deluge of pastoral questions to him.

But as we walked into that first meeting of pastors and church leaders, Scott and I entered quietly. He said hello to two or three other pastors (each of which also had small and struggling churches). He introduced me. Then we sat down. We talked with each other and waited.

Meanwhile, I noticed that as we sat there, other pastors periodically entered the room to a kind of fanfare. A crowd gathered and a lot of folks wanted to shake these pastors' hands and say hello. I know those men now. They were the large-church pastors. Some of them had written books, moderated assemblies, and preached for thousands. Though years later I would know something of that kind of fanfare, Pastor Scott never would.

By the time I was twenty-six and finishing seminary, I wrote these song lyrics. The purity of my desire to serve God for his own sake was fading, and I knew it. I wrestled with what it meant to remain an unnamed mountain among the regular attention and opportunity for influence that a named one could receive.

> I've been searching most of my life
> For a stage that I could make my stand on
> I've been yearning for a spotlight
> To display some page of me
> That history would write on. . . .
>
> What makes for greatness in a man?
> To be known to the world
> or have a home in the promised land?

An anecdote shared between the famed Richard Foster and his son, Nathan, comes to mind. At the time, Nathan was eager to quickly conquer the famous mountains of Colorado. While resting on the rocky side of one of those celebrities, Richard pointed his son to the beauty of an adjacent mountain:

> Nate, see that mountain? It has a stunning ridge. That's a perfectly good peak. If it stood a few feet higher, you would know its name and want to climb it. As it stands, it's an unnamed mountain that no one bothers with.[2]

Already Discovered

To figure out what to do with this corrosion of desire, we look to Jesus. Our Savior was confronted with the temptation to celebrity. "Everyone is looking for you" (Mark 1:37) became words common for him to hear.

Examining Our Mentoring

Any of us aspiring to follow Jesus into neighbor love and ministry must humbly acknowledge the tempting invitation of these words. To have the attention of everyone and to become the object around which others spend their minutes and energy (looking for you) is called "fame."

Fame associates with pride and is no friend to humility. Fame as an ambition has flirted with us, flattered us, and gotten us drunk enough to undress ever since the garden Serpent whispered the words, "You will be like God" (Gen. 3:5). It is as if the Serpent said, "Get ready to have a fan base! You deserve it!"

What I did not take seriously enough is that fame as an ambition is no stranger to churches, clergy, and Jesus followers. A Jesus follower has to be honest about the fact that fame is not a bad lover. It comes through on many of its promises. It bestows status, identity, privilege, pleasure, and stories to tell. We get to be the conference speakers or over the coolest small group in the church. It advances and enlarges our borders of influence. Who we know and whom we follow become our ticket to importance. We can use it to access esteem in comparison to others even in the church (1 Cor. 1:11–12). The apostle Paul painfully knew all too well that "some indeed preach Christ from envy and rivalry" (Phil. 1:15).

Think about that for a moment.

Some of us are ministering the gospel right now because we want to have the esteem that someone else currently has (envy) and because we competitively desire to receive more praise or credit than someone else does (rivalry). And why not? Who wants to live an overlooked life? So, as the disciples did, we banter about and concern ourselves with competitive questions such as, "Who among us will be the greatest?" (see Luke 9:46), and, "Who will get the best seats with Jesus?" Our fame orientation irritates our fellow laborers. Theirs flusters us. Annoyance with one another lingers.

My point is this: in a celebrity culture, fame works as a way of life and ministry. It is no wonder then that many of us have felt in our being what Francis Bernardone once spoke out loud: "You will see that one day, I shall be adored by the whole world."[3] Something dark in us can want this too.

I remember being part of a team that offered an annual conference for pastors. The year we tried to resist a celebrity mind-set in ourselves and for our constituency, we barely funded the conference. The reason? Our speakers were made up of longtime, veteran ministry leaders who were nonetheless unknown. The registration for the conference was woeful.

The next year we had to go back to getting the big names so that people would come. Sure enough, the next year we were packed. In our land, a pastor's experience and wisdom has little monetary value unless we know his name. Where did that idea come from?

Whether we are attempting to have the most online social networking connections, trying to be the best-dressed person in the room, proving we can handle the most Jell-O shots, jealous for our team to win, or secretly rattled if we are not thought of as the best preacher, coach, mother, or counselor in town—this desire to be the unique one endures in us and in those with whom we do life.

Having wrestled with this desire gone foul in my own being makes me more fond of my lifelong mentor and his ways of being that I have tended to overlook. I was a long-haired college kid earnestly seeking Jesus and beginning to minister to others. I was becoming restless to make a difference. My older friend Bob, who at the time was a campus minister with the Navigators Christian ministry, regularly invited me to come with him for prayer. I remember him kneeling in a small and oft-forgotten chapel near campus. As usual, no one else was there. There, he would pour out his heart to God as I sat on a piano bench playing with the keys. I look back now and marvel that Bob saw this as no waste of time. It was his way of teaching me something fundamental about life and ministry. After a couple of hours, we would sit together to talk. One time, Bob looked at me.

"Zachary," he said. "You are already discovered."

"What?" I asked.

"I want you to know that you are already discovered. Jesus already knows you. You are already loved, already gifted, already known."

I think back now. Did I pass that wonderful truth on to my unnamed mountain of a pastor in that little struggling church among the large pond with big fish that day in the pastors' meeting? I wish I had. A cynicism seemed looming like a gray cloud over his horizon.

I likewise wish that I had remembered this message myself when I faced another early taste of how a celebrity mind-set mentors us. I was nominated for the homiletics award at the seminary. Preaching Jesus became a contest. To know that Jesus had known and loved me already, before I ever went to seminary or preached a sermon, was somehow beginning to fade.

"Everyone is looking for you," they said to Jesus. Jesus had become the unique one. Jesus was living the dream. Like Nathan in the mountains, I was beginning to forget that I was once delightfully unnamed.

The Fame-Shyness of Jesus

But how could I forget this in light of Bob's practice of taking me to forgotten prayer places? By it, he modeled for me that being already known in an unknown place of prayer with Jesus was enough. Is this why Jesus often could not be found? I have that question: Why did they have to *look for him*? After all, conventional wisdom would agree with the counsel of Jesus's family. "No one works in secret if he seeks to be known openly. . . . Show yourself to the world," they urged (John 7:4). They did not understand why a great worker for God would choose a manner of life that could be characterized as working "in secret."

I'm not sure that I, or most of the church communities I have served, have understood this either. I've spent a great deal of meetings, time away from home, money, technology, and energy on this "need to go public" assumption.

But, how could Jesus's brothers legitimately describe him as one who had no ambition to show the world what God had given him to do? After all, so public was the buzz about Jesus that he could not openly enter a town (Mark 1:45). Creating a buzz matters, right?

Yet, it seems that these brothers recognized something about Jesus that irritated them. As I begin to see it, it irritates me too (in the sense of conviction). Jesus is fame-shy.

His family was not the only one to recognize this in him. Jesus seemed drawn not to the spotlight but from it. Disciples and friends had to search. He wasn't tweeting. His blog lay unattended. His e-mail responses were not immediate. Where they often found him was alone and in desolate places praying (Luke 5:16).

In fact, it seems that just when Jesus was at the right place at the right time, and the opportunity to advance his work through greater celebrity called out to him, he intentionally allowed the call to go to voice mail and disappeared for a while (John 6:15).

Jesus would have driven any publicist and congregation mad. After he would do something great, he often asked that no one say anything about it.[4] I was taught that Jesus asked no one to speak partly because it was a marketing ploy of false humility. Entertainers do this when, with one hand, they indicate that they do not want our applause, while, with the other hand, they simultaneously encourage it. A more plausible explanation is this: it would have been impractical for Jesus to freely minister to others if everyone had known who he was. We see this analogy with rock stars and celebrities of our own day who have to travel at odd times or wear disguises when in public.

But as I revisit these explanations, I wonder: what if Jesus's reason for quieting the talk about himself is rooted in something more profound and fundamental? What if Jesus's desire to work in secret, to cultivate a hospitality toward desolate places, and to ask for silence among those who want to draw public attention to him reveals the stated conviction Jesus has about how we are to do what God calls us to do? Jesus simply may have been living what he taught. "Beware of practicing your righteousness before other people in order to be seen by them," he said (Matt. 6:1).

Jesus taught that our practice of doing God-glorifying things is somehow diminished when we "sound the trumpet" so that all can see us and give praise to us (Matt. 6:2). He believed that doing great things for God is done best with our left hand not knowing what our right hand is doing—in other words, God prefers that our practices for him go unnoticed and unacknowledged by the press, the church, and even those closest to us (Matt. 6:3). A thought occurs to me: do I possess a stamina for going unnoticed? Can I handle being overlooked? Do I have a spirituality that equips me to do an unknown thing for his glory?

What if Jesus was trying to teach this to those he healed and asked not to tell? What if he wanted them to know that they could possess this kind of sweetness with God without pandering it or selling it about? After all, there are some things so profoundly tender that to share them willy-nilly cheapens them. This is why a husband and wife in the love of long years know nothing of locker-room talk when with others. Or when their children ask what the initials they write on their love notes mean, the parents smile knowingly at each other and say, "That is just for us." No wonder Paul waited years before he told a soul about an experience he had with God. He wouldn't even tell it as his own. He told it like it was someone else's story to deflect attention from himself (2 Cor. 12:2–4).

Jesus's rationale is that in secret, when unnoticed by the gaze of others, we remain beneath the gaze of our Father, who sees in us what no one else does. To have no praise but that which comes from the God who sees and vindicates us is a reward that, for Jesus, outmatches any competing trophy or praise.

He doesn't deny the promise of fame. There is a reward that we gain from another's applause. But when the applause dies, so does its provision (Matt. 6:5). The shining moment fades into the empty theater of our lives where the fundamental questions still remain for us to live and answer. So three times, as Jesus catalogs the righteous things we do, he compels us to consider "your Father who sees in secret" (Matt. 6:4; see also vv. 6, 18). In so doing, he recovers a sense of Eden. We were meant to live beneath the gaze of our Creator for his glory and freed from seeking fame from others.

What if Jesus sought the desolate place alone, was indifferent to hype, and was desirous that people would not publicize him because he knew that celebrity praise and public buzz are not what God values? One can have the public praise and privately not love his neighbor. One can also love his neighbor apart from and irrelevant of public praise.

Some of us preachers get confused on this point (Phil. 1:17). For example, Paul's way of life led him into prison. The ways of some other preachers in Paul's day allowed them to preach freely and publicly. They and others seemed to assume, therefore, that God must have given them the greater blessing. I say this because of how they criticized Paul in light of his imprisonment. To them, Paul's relative silence and fade into obscurity seem to prove that they were the better men and the better preachers that God more fully owned. Yet it was Paul's letters and not theirs that God inspired. What do we make of this?

A troubling thought comes to my mind. How does the fame indifference of Jesus inform the way we go about growing our ministries or fashioning a life with Jesus? Are we willing to forego what works in the world for what Jesus teaches us to trust?

Jesus's Ministry Schedule

Have you ever noticed the Jesus way of strategic networking in Luke's Gospel? It is almost nonexistent (at least, as it relates to being in the know and connecting with those who matter). Jesus seems intent on noticing and orienting his schedule around the unnamed mountains in his range. He makes personal visits to the physically and spiritually ill that include a mother-in-law, a leper, a paralytic, and a tax collector (Luke 4–5). Then there was the man with the withered hand, the sickness of a Gentile's servant, and a widow and her dead son (Luke 6–7).

Jesus finally spends time with hundreds in a crowd. But within that crowd it is not the well known, the rich, or the connected that Jesus seeks out. The sick and the troubled remain his focus (Luke 6:17–18).

Even John the Baptist, who has been unjustly placed in prison, is confused. Jesus's way of doing a day seems strategically off. "Are you the one who is to come, or shall we look for another?" John asks (Luke 7:19). Isn't it strange that a life of loving unknown people in their miseries should cause others to consider overlooking Jesus?

But assuring John through the Scriptures that this way of spending time is exactly what God would have Jesus do, Jesus met with a sinful woman and then with several ordinary and broken women. And then miles away there was a man who howled naked in the tombs among the Gentiles (Luke 7–8). Jesus sought him out too.

At this point, some crowds become confused about Jesus's behavior. They ask Jesus to leave them alone (Luke 8:34). Jesus grants their request. He then spends time with another sick woman, and the sick daughter of a synagogue ruler (Luke 8:40–56).

Herod the king now becomes perplexed and desires an audience with Jesus. Jesus seems to have no interest in changing his schedule to make such an appointment (Luke 9:7–9)! Instead, Jesus sends his disciples to spend time with those who are physically and mentally troubled. Then he begins to talk about dying and to talk also about a cross that must in time become both his and theirs (Luke 9:21–27).

Finally, Jesus reveals himself as the very Son of God, greater than Moses and Elijah! But he limits this view to only three people, and no one is to speak of it (Luke 9:29–36).

In fact, throughout this whole time Jesus continues to withdraw to desolate places for extended times of prayer (Luke 4:42; 5:16; 6:12; 11:1). After spending time with some Samaritans and two obscure women who were friends of his (Mary and Martha), the disciples (who were recently wondering which of them would become the most famous, Luke 10:46–48) finally notice Jesus's way of life, and they say to him, "Lord, teach us to pray" (Luke 11:1).

And with this, Jesus at long last begins to engage the well-connected and influential persons of his community. But these conversations are anything but diplomatic. They end with a highly respected lawyer saying to Jesus, "Teacher, in saying these things you insult us" (Luke 11:45). And as for the elite Bible teachers and leaders in the community? Their response to all of this is to lie "in wait for him, to catch him in something he might say" (Luke 11:54).

Jesus's idea of doing great things for God meant a daily routine that looked something like this:

In particular:

- Early morning and late evening: disappear often and pray.
- After breakfast to just before dinner: seek out the unknown and scarily broken people around you and give them the bulk of your time. Set aside times to teach publicly and to debrief privately with those you are mentoring.
- Early evening after dinner: spend time together and enjoy each other.

In general:

- Eat and sleep.
- Help those other leaders who are for you to understand from God's Word that this way of ministry is from God and is no waste.
- Bear with people whom you help but who distance themselves from you because your way of life and ministry scares them.
- Don't worry that your true glory is veiled to almost everyone around you.

- Don't schedule too much time with those who believe themselves to be pillars in the government or the church. Remember that they too are just people. They have their own sins to repent of and their own callings to fulfill. They are not more important than the broken and the lost for whom you're called.

Causing Friction and Getting Stuck

Withdrawal to prayer? Prioritized time with the physically and mentally ill who have no clout? An active indifference to those who do have clout? Jesus's way is not the celebrity way. So why is his way of ministry so generally foreign to what is expected of me each week as a pastor?

I spoke with a pastor at lunch today. The church this pastor serves is large and long-established. The pastoral staff is worn out and trying to figure out why. He explained, "Over the last several weeks I've been working with our staff to identify the currently practiced values of our church—not the values we hope our church has, but the values revealed in the complaints, the ways, and the desires expressed among those who attend."

He paused, looked down, and shook his head.

"We determined that our church culture values professionalism, excellence, and the Bible. Professionalism is interpreted in such a way that transparency or relational honesty is suspect and a sign of weakness. Excellence means that it is hard to be human. Any mistake is quickly or harshly criticized constantly. Our stance on the Bible, as interpreted through this view of professionalism and excellence, means that Bible information is prized but not if it exposes or melts us and not if it is taught without the highest academic standards."

He continued: "We tried recently to invite folks for dinner and then spend time together with no agenda other than to get to know each other. Eighty-five percent of the folks left immediately after dinner. Many of the rest told us that, as pastors, we were wasting their time because we gave them nothing to do but sit with people."

As I listened, my heart was pained. This dear pastor was worn out with the years of constant pressure to veil his heart, to make no mistakes, and to have constant and new information from the Bible to pass on. In this environment in which cultivating relationships is viewed as a waste of time, I said something about a quote from Eugene Peterson's book *Under the Unpredictable Plant*.[5]

"Yeah, I've read all of his books. But, I don't read Eugene Peterson anymore," he said with a pained smile. "He draws out my longings for what a community of Jesus followers is supposed to be and how my time as a pastor is meant to be spent. But then I face my actual day in this system, and I cannot get from here to there and still keep my job. Our Lord knows I've tried."

Then he said something insightful: "In order for this church to grow in health, it will require a culture change. But that would mean we'd probably lose several hundred people. As soon as we imply that the gospel shows strength in weakness, grace for our mistake making, and biblical truth as having a relational context and a sacramental view of time, many will be agitated and leave. We'd no longer bow to their assumptions and would finally try to pastor them into more of a Jesus way."

Then he smiled with irony. "But here is the rub: even though those who would stay would join us in trying to replace our celebrity mind-set with a Jesus one, our community as a whole would see the loss of people at our established church and conclude that we as pastors are failing. We'd be known as the ones on whose watch the church went from two thousand to fifteen hundred members. Because of that, I don't think our elders have much of a stomach for this redirection. We are stuck, and so am I."

My friend's quandary is very real. We know that if we had been walking with Jesus at the time, according to Luke our "office hours" would be prioritized around the three ideas of prayerful disappearance, time with the broken unknown, and spending life together.

Most visions of professionalism do not value a disappearance that causes people to wonder where we are. Many ideas of excellence do not value the messiness of spending time outside of the limelight with the scarily broken. Put together, neither tends to have a category for doing ordinary life together without seeing it as a waste of our time and energy—particularly if no explicitly didactic element is present.

When my children were little, there was a time when they preferred McDonald's strawberry shakes to Dairy Queen's. The kids were so accustomed to the artificial flavor at the one that when they tasted actual strawberries at the other, they had no taste for the real thing.

Similarly, many of us are genuinely unaccustomed to what the real ministry tastes like. So when it is offered to us, we grimace with dislike. We prefer the imitation to the real fruit because our categories for discernment are marred.

If my friend and the staff allow the church to stay the way it presently is, with its critical and relentless pace, the graceless expectations, and the degradation of ordinary human relationships, it will continue to squeeze the pastors and persons into a machine-like approach to people in Jesus's name. They will burn out. And yet if a pastor leaves altogether, he feels he is abandoning a sense of call to a people he truly loves and longs to see grow. The problem is that if he stays and tries to slowly restore the ministry, he will likely put his job in jeopardy. My friend is at a crossroads. Many of us are.

Let's be clear though. Some churches make the opposite of professionalism and excellence their mantra. But even ideas such as "organic," "edgy," and "casual" can likewise become celebrity measures by which we compare ourselves, judge others, and keep our followings. As I've traveled a bit to partner with various brothers and sisters for the gospel, it is fascinating to notice a small bit of continuity. Maybe you've noticed it too. Those brothers and sisters who struggle with Jesus's challenge to the celebrity of professionalism and excellence generally dress alike: business formal or business casual. Those brothers and sisters who struggle with Jesus's challenge to the celebrity of organic and edgy likewise generally dress alike: slim jeans, obscure T-shirt, large watch band, thin-rimmed glasses.

In both of these cases, we have to acknowledge the elephant in the room—we give detailed attention to how we appear. For many of us, we possess little resemblance in our way of life to the fame-shy approach to Jesus that Luke showed us.

How does Jesus approach us and those we serve when we are practicing a celebrity way of life in his name? What path does a pastor or leader find when trying to lead his flock out from underneath this mind-set?

I See Right through You

"Do not judge by appearances, but judge with right judgment," he said (John 7:24). The who's who of the government and the church recognized this about Jesus and mocked him for it. We often mock in Jesus what would graciously undo us into healing.

Examining Our Mentoring

> And they sent their disciples to him, along with the Herodians, saying, "Teacher, we know that you are true and teach the way of God truthfully, and you do not care about anyone's opinion, for you are not swayed by appearances." (Matt. 22:16)

To be swayed by appearances is to make our decisions as a recognizer of faces. We avoid some and choose others on the basis of the apparent recognition and influence that one has over the other. "What will people think?" forms our central question. We keep in mind those whose opinions we want to rest favorably upon us and whose favor we feel we cannot lose. Name those opinions in your head right now, and you will discover whom you are tempted to resist Jesus for.

Jesus had mentored his disciples in this by giving them practical examples. When they wanted to rebuke children for interrupting Jesus's precious time, Jesus corrected his disciples and gathered the children to him. When a poor widow gave her coin unnamed amid the well known and well-to-do who were writing their large donor checks, it was her and not them that Jesus directed his trainees' eyes to see and value.

Each morning as a child, I walked to Saint Anthony Elementary School. I think that I was eleven or twelve years old when Father Vincent visited that parish. I know little about him to this day. What I know is the memory in my mind of him walking and praying on those early mornings. Prior to his visit, I had never seen a priest praying except in ceremony. The only reason I saw Vincent was that I often took a shortcut between an apartment complex that allowed me to walk through some paths into an open field that beached at the Saint Anthony playground. There, in the early unknown, Vincent prayed. Only the eyes of one fifth-grader saw what God saw every morning.

The problem of appearances reveals itself in a reader who thinks me less credible because I'm putting a Catholic man in a positive light, or because my calling was reached into me in that context. Others frown because I am no longer in that context. For either, these appearances are, sadly, enough to make a judgment about the quality of who I am.

So to understand a celebrity way of mentoring us, we have to come to terms with the deadliness of this approach to forego making right judgments on the basis of what quickly appears to us. It was this very thing that ruined Eve and Adam. "So, when the woman *saw* . . ." reveals the lynchpin of Eve's temptation to rival God (Gen. 3:6).

Those of us caught in this mind-set ourselves, or pained to serve others who are, take note that appearance making as a way of life roused the priestly poet to grow vehement. Jesus erupted into a sermon that had the phrase "Woe to you!" as its anchor clause (Matthew 23). With those words, Jesus takes up the prophetic mantle. The persons set upon by his rebuke are the Bible teachers, religious leaders, theologians, and their students of the day. "I see right through you!" he seems to shout, and there is now no turning back.

No one dared to speak to the divas of the religious world the way Jesus spoke. Any hope of power and position and advancement in the religious community had to go through this board. Any of us who knows what it means to have to save our careers can understand that only one truly freed from bowing to the appearances of men could have said what Jesus did. By his words, any of us who would follow him has a celebrity value system crushed before our eyes. An invitation to a different way beckons.

Coming to Terms with Glittering Images

What is it about a celebrity mind-set that Jesus opposes? To begin, the "glittering image" forms an apt metaphor for Jesus's sermon. In her novel by that name, Susan Howatch speaks to us about it through a clergyman who is no longer a whole person but split in his being. This clergyman, Dr. Ashworth, says of himself:

> They never meet the man I keep hidden. They just meet the man on public display. . . . I call him the glittering image because he looks so well in the mirror . . . but beyond him stands the angry stranger.[6]

Like Eve and Adam, we're all tempted to split between the appearance we make for others and the truth about who we actually are. For Adam and Eve, fig leaves became their appearance-keeping tool to veil their shame. Fittingly, the fictional character of Dr. Ashworth speaks of himself as a hidden man.

This is where ministry in a Jesus way begins. It is with this hidden man that Jesus wants to relate. Jesus's commitment to deal truly with the hidden man explains why Jesus sees hypocrisy in a negative light. By the term "hypocrite," Jesus draws the picture of a mask wearer who plays a part rather than lives it (Matt. 23:13, 15, 25, 27, 29). By his tone, expressed through repetition and exclamation, Jesus reveals how passionately he dislikes mask wearing among those who lead and claim to follow God. For Jesus, being authentic doesn't equate to cussing or finding edgy titles for our sermons. Authenticity means that our private and public selves merge.

Jesus begins by talking about our *public side of life.* He starts with our title and position. "They sit on Moses' seat," Jesus says (Matt. 23:1). (*You and I have to take note of the titles we have.*)

Then he talks about the public word making and actions that attend our titles. These leaders are publicly speaking sound words (". . . for they preach," Matt. 23:3) and publicly showing pious actions ("You build the tombs of the prophets and decorate the monuments of the righteous," v. 29). (*What are the job descriptions those titles require?*)

Then Jesus highlights the people who deal with our public side. Donors, members, and fans continue to find inspiration and express their gratitude by inviting these leaders to places "of honor at feasts" (Matt. 23:6). Like-minded organizations also yield to these leaders and congregants "the best seats in the synagogues" (v. 6). (*What kind of crowds are we meant to gather and preserve by the use of our title and the ordering of our public words and actions?*)

Because of this acclaim, the public side has become a trusted model of best practice for others to mimic. So people regularly seek them out for conferences and identify them as their teachers and parental mentors (Matt. 23:8–9). What criterion do we use to determine who should be mentors in our lives?

To look at this way of being from the outside would suggest that godly success is on display. A celebrity mind-set sees no reason to ask any further questions. We, with those who are considered the model of best practice, attend feasts and seats of honor. We are able to say that we know them or go to their church, and we have large crowds visibly enjoying it all. These signify God's blessing, because a celebrity assumption believes that appearances are reality.

But Jesus disagrees.

And this profoundly matters for us whom Jesus calls to follow him.

Those pastors who feel their jobs are on the line find comfort and sober challenge here as well. Jesus says that this public way of doing a day attracts lots of people. The famous are there, great information is given, everyone appears godly, and the place is full of buzz about it. Because of this, its leaders are praised and invited to lead others. But when maintaining a crowd has turned from the surprising grace that it was in the early days into a way of doing and preserving life, those we disciple begin to learn from our way of being that preserving and keeping people is the way of ministry God intends for us. The consequence? "You make them twice as much a child of hell as yourselves," Jesus said (Matt. 23:15).

The Jesus Way

Jesus rejects the glittering image as a way of being and as a line for measure. In contrast, what mind-set are you and I meant to cultivate in ourselves and in those we serve each day?

First, each of us is a human being, and so are those whom we esteem. Rather than relating to our neighbors through our title of "rabbi," "instructor," and "father," Jesus wants to teach us to relate to others humanly. In Christ, equally "you are all brothers" (Matt. 23:8). This means that titles do not lose their respect in our eyes, but they do lose their ability to make us be partial because of them.

After describing his excitement and fervor at the call of a particularly famous bishop for a meeting and assistance, Dr. Ashworth's wise friend asks him, "And if your own bishop were to telephone you today with the same request, how would you answer him?"

> In the silence that followed I felt my face grow hot as I shifted in my chair and stared down at my clasped hands. No reply was possible.[7]

As a seminary professor, I was considered humble because I would invite students to call me by my first name rather than by my title. Now that I'm a pastor in a church, or a neighbor in my neighborhood, to invite people to call me by my first name is nothing special. It reveals nothing. Calling one another by our first names is just what human beings do. Humility has had to take on a deeper human meaning for me. Whom do we overlook? Whom do we glad-hand? The One who cared for lepers, resisted audience with kings, and prized the desolate places intends to free you from partiality on the basis of these treasures that moth and rust devour (James 2:1–4). Others are meant to learn this from us in order to mature in Jesus.

Second, Christ alone is Jesus for us and for others. "You have one instructor, the Christ" (Matt. 23:10). After recovering our humanity and putting us in our places, Jesus distinguishes himself from us and sets himself as the true instructor, father, and rabbi for our lives. Others are meant to learn from us that he (and not we) are their hope and their sage.

Third, people are not meant for our consumption or our use or to prop up our crowd numbers. They are meant to experience a resemblance of Jesus's love from us in their ordinary troubles, limits, weaknesses, and sins. Jesus pounded those who were glad to have people attending their sermons but paid no further attention to what life was actually like for them (Matt. 23:4).

Imagine a pastor who declares that disobedience among children is the fault of the parents' inability to faithfully apply God's Word. In his congregation are the parents of a child with behavioral forms of autism. Such a pastor should have to babysit for at least one whole day the three-year-old whose sensory distortions throw her into tantrums. If with our voices we place burdens upon people, then with our hands we are meant in Jesus to help move these burdens.

Fourth, possession of doctrinal information does not equal spiritual growth. Jesus protests those of us who debate Scripture and lose sight of how our lives were meant to be reshaped by it in the first place (Matt. 23:16–22). Capability with information does not mean familiarity with maturity.

One brother left our church because he felt my expository sermon series through Luke, regarding the neighbors Jesus loves, was too basic. "I need meat," he said. "Talking about love and grace with people is important. But I need something more substantial in my life now." This same brother had great relational trials in his family that he did not know how to navigate. He was gifted and charismatic in personality. But his ability to love those closest to him was poor. He left to find more informational meat when the feast of maturity that he needed was before him. Sometimes we simply do not need another class on Romans. To think we do apart from ordinary resemblance to what we already know of Jesus emits an illusory view of growth.

Fifth, strong obedience in one area of life does not mean that we are obedient in every other area of our lives. Jesus declared that to tithe well does not mean that one is mature in terms of practical justice, relational mercy, or mundane faithfulness in the ordinary of a day (Matt. 23:23). Jesus wants us to graciously learn from him to live and minister in such a way that those who do life with us learn that, for all that they know and do rightly, they have merely scratched the surface. There are weightier matters to a life in community that still await their learning and practice in Jesus.

Sixth, care for our interior lives is a necessity. "First clean the inside of the cup and the plate," Jesus says (Matt. 23:26). Doing life and ministry without a way of life that places soul care front and center leaves us drinking froth. Jesus says of this, "You clean the outside of the cup and the plate, but inside they are full of greed and self-indulgence" (Matt. 23:25).

Littered about by the garbage dump his life had become, Dr. Ashworth receives these words from another who seeks to help him:

> In your pursuit of a success . . . you've probably tended to channel too much energy into your work as a scholar. . . . I feel you should now devote more time to cultivating your inner life so that you can achieve more than a mere outward semblance of your vocation.[8]

The achievement of a "mere outward semblance of [their] vocation" is not what those who follow us in Jesus are meant to find. Their souls and ours need a way of life that values and esteems a way of spending time that accounts for this.

I learned today of another friend leaving the ministry. We went to seminary together. He won awards. He was a standout leader in our class. He planted a new church that grew quickly and gave him accolades. He became one of those men whom others ask to speak at their conferences. There is no moral failure, no hidden and dark secret. He is simply dead inside, burned out by a way of life that gave him success in our eyes but dehydrated his humanity.

Finally, even religious people are prone to resist what would heal them. That they resist Jesus's way and choose to hold on to their own familiarity with celebrity makes them seem successful and makes Jesus seem a fool. But we know better than to believe this, don't we? Jesus ends his sermon here with the cry of lament:

Examining Our Mentoring

> I send you prophets and wise men and scribes, some of whom you will kill and crucify, and some you will flog in your synagogues and persecute from town to town. . . . How would I have gathered your children together as a hen gathers her brood under her wings, and you were not willing! (Matt. 23:34, 37)

The People Who Leave

Where does all of this lead us? Let's revisit the quandary of the pastor who feels that to follow Jesus's way will mean he will likely lose his job.

In short, he has two fears, and so do most of us: (1) people will leave; (2) we will be judged as failures. It is humbling to realize that the presence of these two fears reveals how deeply we ourselves are tempted to celebrity. These two fears reside in those we serve, as well. Without the gospel of Jesus, both of us will judge each other on these two mantras: keep people coming and keep up our approval rating—this after all is the celebrity way.

It is no small task to say, "Enough of this!" The courage required, the patience demanded, and the grace that is necessary humble us. Courage is required, because some will put our jobs on the line if we seek to make these kinds of changes to the celebrity mind-set (John 12:42). We will actually get passed over and reduced in influence should we persist. Patience is demanded, because Jesus's categories for success and being are so foreign to so many of us—this kind of change does not happen overnight. Grace is necessary, because who could risk such loss in our ecclesiastical and cultural worlds and who could love long and steady enough for change apart from him?

At this point, we need two reminders set before us.

First, people criticized, resisted, overlooked, and left Jesus. Remember, Jesus had a death threat on his life because he had healed someone. Jesus's family thought him insane and criticized him. Crowds of thousands were reduced to twelve because Jesus exposed them for following him for what they could get rather than out of true faith and love (John 6:1–15). Think about that for a while. Doing what will mend others in the gospel will rile and outrage some. Size of crowd has nothing to do with it.

If a crowd reduces because the leader has nothing of the manner of Jesus in his approach, then the leader rightly needs the grace to change. But if a crowd leaves because the actual manner and value system of Jesus is confronting and confounding the allure of the world/flesh/Devil mindset in their lives, then it is time to support that leader, get off his back, and admit that the crowds are immature and have a great deal to learn.

People were confounded, offended, and confused by Jesus's ministry way of prioritizing a life of daily disappearance for prayer; spending most of his time among the ordinary, messy and unknown; treating celebrities as if they weren't gods; teaching the gospel and exposing the hidden man; and valuing relational presence as time unwasted.

If people leave or overlook you or criticize you because you teach them to value this way of life, you are not exposed as hardened. They are. If with grace and patience you embody and teach that persons are not celebrities but human, that Jesus alone is the famous one and our preeminent instructor, that people are not meant for our consumption or use, that knowing doctrinal content does not equal spiritual growth, that obedience in one area does not mean that we are mature, that care for our interior life is a mandate, and that we are all prone to resist everything I just wrote, then you are in good company. You may be overlooked and ridiculed in this world, but not, dear friend, in the next. You know something of fellowship with your Master.

The Light We Shine

Earlier I shared a quote from Francis Bernardone: "You will see that one day, I shall be adored by the whole world." This rich young womanizer and poet was not wrong. Many of us do today, in Jesus, give thanks for him. Francis of Assisi is how most of us know him.

This Francis was my hero. In eighth grade, when I was confirmed in my faith in keeping with the Catholic practice in which I was raised, Zachary Wayne Francis Eswine became my spiritual name. I knew of Francis with the mind of a young boy and not as a theological debater or suspicious legend sifter.

What compelled me then is the famous moment in which Francis stood before the bishop and his worldly father and all of the townspeople who knew of his carousing and ruckus making. There, he handed everything he owned (including his clothes) to his abusive and money-hungry dad. He then walked off into the woods to spend his days rebuilding an old forgotten sanctuary, loving the poor, and living as one without the goods of this world. This choice humbles me still.

Examining Our Mentoring

Francis did become known in the world. His name was attached to greatness—but it was a greatness of a different kind. Surely this is something of what the Withdrawing One meant when he told us that "a city set on a hill cannot be hidden." When the Fame-Shy One said, "Let your light shine before others, so that they may see," it was our resemblance to him (not our names, our crowds, our money, our speed, or our largeness) that he believed would serve as a light in this dark world (Matt. 5:14–16). Jesus calls us to a greatness of a different kind:

> The greatest among you shall be your servant. Whoever exalts himself will be humbled, and whoever humbles himself will be exalted. (Matt. 23:11–12)

To desire to be an overseer is a marvelous thing. Aspire to greatness in it! Aspire to frequent the unknown, to bless the unnamed, to lose your fame and your reputation among the influential, in order to take a stand for an end to appearance making as a way of life and ministry. The woods await you. The chapel therein is broken down. It needs mending. You can leave the clothes of this world behind you now. He will meet you there. Jesus, the famous one.

Learning How to Return (to Obscurity)

The temptation to be like God for others by giving ourselves to the glittering image reveals to us our need for *returning*. Those of us who are prone to the spotlight or who are repeatedly placed beneath its lamps by others look to Jesus for this spiritual skill. What does it mean to learn how to return? Consider the Christmas shepherds with me for a moment.

It all seems so anticlimactic, doesn't it? Angels infiltrate the skies right before the shepherds' eyes. The glory of God thunders in chorus. Ancient promises are fulfilled and witnessed. Fear seizes these sheep men. Good tidings are spoken to them. "There is joy coming," the angels say. "The Savior is born, and this will be the sign that will confirm it for you." At this point, among the shepherds, I imagine this was a spectacular sign well fitted to confirm the Savior of the world. To see and hear angels was spectacular already. Imagine how spectacular the Messiah's sign could be. Perhaps God would reach down his hand and create a new planet. Then he will hold it between his thumb and index finger and place the planet in its new position in the universe right before their very eyes! Surely this would be a sign worthy of a savior from God!

But here the anticlimax begins. No planets were formed before the eyes. No tremendous demonstration came of frightening power and might. "You will find a baby," they said, "wrapped in swaddling cloths and lying in a manger." The sign of the celebrity of God lay in the aroma of cattle and hay—the placenta of new birth, the cries and warmth of an ordinary life.

> No stately form that we should know him
> There was no halo on his head
> No trumpets blowing
> No majestic fanfare
> He was born where animals are fed.[9]

The Savior is discovered, worshiped, and adored. To these ordinary sheepherders, God has revealed glorious and fantastic wonders! And now, the second anticlimactic moment confronts us. According to the Gospel of Luke, after beholding and participating in this too-grand-for-words event, "the shepherds returned" (Luke 2:20). They returned? That simply means this: after beholding the glory, the shepherds went home.

Same Old, Same Old

But what did they return home to? They returned to their responsibilities. They were shepherds, men who worked with their hands. The aroma of animal and outdoor living took up residence in their skin. These were blue-collar workers, salt-of-the-earth kinds of folks.

And these shepherds understood what it meant to work the late shift. "By night" Luke says, they watched their flocks (v. 8). *Watching*, make no mistake, is an adrenaline word. Responsibility meant keeping eyes open and skills poised when most in their community were closed and at rest with sleep. Years of this kind of labor creates a complaint in one's joints and bones. Add to this the scorn and jokes that were leveled against the shepherding way of life, and my question seems all the more valid. Why didn't the shepherds go on the road?

With all that they had seen, they could have started a conference series, planned a book tour, and instantly gained thousands of blog followers. These men were destined for greatness. They could have made a difference in their generation. Their job offered no room for advancement. "Same old, same old" was their routine. This routine stitched the fabric of their lives. Doing the same thing in the same place for the rest of their lives was their lot and their legacy. They could change all of that. The celebrity moment had found them. Greatness is too worthy a thing to demean by returning to the ordinary of life!

But right here, God in his grace disrupts us. By means of the shepherds returning, God seems to seriously imply that the glorious moment does not dismiss his people from their call into the ordinary of life. Yet, I think we have to admit that somehow the idea of being ordinary has lost its swagger among us.

Words such as *common*, *normal*, *mundane*, and *routine* are the descriptors that one uses when searching out antonyms for the word *exceptional*. To possess the opposite quality of someone exceptional is to have the honor of being average, usual, or humdrum. For many of us, the thought that we would live our lives as an average, usual, or humdrum person or pastor has scared us for years. The churches and ministries I have served have likewise bathed in this phobia.

That is why, if you take a moment to notice it, we seem to prefer living among the synonyms—these fortunate ideas that have the distinction of hobnobbing with the exceptional. These words invigorate our vision. They sound more appealing as the adjectives we would choose for our lives and ministries. *Olympian. Uncommon. Surpassing. Extraordinary. Special.*

The anxiety that troubles us is understandable. The difference an adjective makes says it all. Compare them and you will likely see what I mean.

> I aspire to serve as a common, ordinary, mundane, normal, routine, average, usual, and humdrum pastor for an unexceptional, commonplace, everyday, run-of-the-mill ministry. As a person I am unremarkable and middling.

Or:

> I aspire to serve as an Olympian, uncommon, surpassing, extraordinary, special pastor for a marvelous, remarkable, singular, exceedingly great ministry. As a person I am stellar and unforgettable.

The first descriptor feels like death. It punches the stomach of our motivations and kills the air. What potential spouse wants such a person? What parent is proud of such a person? What church wants to hire such a person?

In contrast, the second description inspires. It gives life. It breathes oxygen into the lungs of our imaginings and dreams. What potential spouse wouldn't want such a person? What parent wouldn't be proud? What church wouldn't want to call such a one?

We esteem little value to the first vision of humanity and life and terribly fear that we will go our whole lives or ministries without the second vision. It is little wonder then that it seems so wrong that, after seeing the glory, the shepherds would go back to the sheep stink.

Seeing God's glory, hearing his voice, receiving his good news, and beholding his love was never meant to deliver us from ordinary life and love in a place—it was meant to preserve us there. In Eden, God was the famous, unforgettable, surpassing, extraordinary one. Persons were not that. But because of him, they were noble and lovely in their relating to one another with love, in their cultivation of the ground, in their care for the animals. Meaning wasn't found in trying to become a celebrity like God. This was the mistake that ruined it all. The satisfied heart and the richness of ordinary joys were already given. Contentment was found with God in their world.

So if the shepherds don't return, what happens? To begin with, who will love their wives, their kids, and their aging relatives who have no pension—their friends? Celebrity opportunity does not remove the arrangements for neighbor love that still exist. Someone will need to care for the sheep, create clothes for others, provide milk and food for neighbors. And even if they did all get on a tour bus and travel around together, their need for and call to love each other and their neighbors, to eat, to bathe, to wash clothes, to seek and give forgiveness from each other in ordinary moments, to attend to sickness, to celebrate birthdays, and to seek God would not go away.

Every addict knows this. The glorious moment provided by the drug does not remove the ordinary call of life. That is the problem. The high doesn't last. We crash, and our loved ones are still there, longing to do ordinary life together and pained that it is being taken from them.

Every hero knows this. The man who hits the grand slam in the ninth inning knows that tomorrow night or next season he has to start again—another game is coming. He also still has to learn how to listen to his wife and cherish her, to resist exasperating his kids, to learn how to give his heart authentically to God and to receive God's love and wisdom for his life. The fireman who saves the life, the CEO who saves the day financially, the mother who saves the day for a child—the heaven-like moment thrills and celebrates. But it isn't heaven.

So for the shepherds "to return" is actually just an expression of wise and common sense. God's visitation empowers us to return and to live!

But also, that God gives a sign of his celebrity that is so vulnerable and ordinary tells us something about what God makes of the ordinary life the shepherds had to begin with. God seems to think that common and unknown things are great!

By his teaching concerning "the least of these," for example, Jesus establishes the run-of-the-mill as Olympian, the commonplace as surpassing, and the humdrum as extraordinary for our attention and value. Those with nothing notable in this world are those he sets before us for our time and esteem (Matt. 23:11–12).

Widows, orphans, children, the poor, the sick, the ordinary father or mother, ordinary shepherds, fishermen, and tax collectors are those whom Jesus prioritized his days around. Jesus was insistent to redirect his disciples' attention onto the poor widow and off of the wealthy tithers. Children were not to be despised, but welcomed; they were to be set as a model for what we are meant to become like in order to enter the kingdom. It was to the crowds made up of ordinary folks—those who were anxious about where their next meal, their clothes, or their drink would come from—that Jesus spoke of the Father's care for birds and flowers and said, "Are you not of more value than they?" (Matt. 6:26). To be truly great is to become the servant of all.

A Testimony amid the Humdrum

The heroic moment doesn't provide heaven for us. Yet it does give us a story to tell that inspires our hearts. Two years after that grand slam to win the game, one coworker at his midday break says to another, "Two outs, bottom of the ninth, and Pujols steps to the plate." The other coworker begins to smile. The two baseball fans recall the tale, laugh together, and shake their heads with wonder.

"Yah, that was something else," the one says to the other. "Shew! It sure was," the other responds. They stare off for a moment smiling. Then the one says, "Well, I guess it's time to get back to it!" "Yep," the other agrees. "Back to work."

This pictures something real about how God has made us. The shepherds returned with a testimony of God's provision, promise, redemption, and love. They returned glorifying and praising God. They learned what Jesus would later show the demon-possessed man whom he healed:

> The man from whom the demons had gone begged that he might be with him, but Jesus sent him away, saying, "Return to your home, and declare how much God has done for you." And he went away, proclaiming throughout the whole city how much Jesus had done for him. (Luke 8:38–39)

I am slowly beginning to picture those Christmas shepherds as if years later they sat around the fire in the cool of a late evening—children and grandchildren staring into the crackle and flicker with drowsy eyes and ready for bed.

Glory had not delivered them from the daily grind. It had not delivered them from Herod killing every two-year-old male, or from Roman occupation, or from a corrupt church that would in the end yell, "Crucify! Crucify!" Seeing the glory only called them further into the ordinary and the loss of what the ordinary was originally meant to provide.

One aged shepherd stokes the embers and says, "Did your old grandpa ever tell you about the time the angels—" Suddenly a chorus of grandchildren interrupts. Rolling their eyes, they moan, "Yes, Papa, we've heard that story before, many times!"

The old shepherd stokes the burning bark. He pauses and looks up and into their young eyes. His smile only broadens. "Let me tell you again," he'll say. And as the youth moan, tired from exulting in the same old thing, the aged man demonstrates his absence of fatigue. With awe and memory in his voice, and an ache in his back from the long day, he begins to retell the history. "It was an ordinary night and we were watching our flocks," he says.

And so an exaltation amid the monotony rises. Worship, hope, and testimony refuse to quit. As he speaks, the old man is looking at the daisies again, and the same old, same old is bringing life to his routine. For a moment, I feel his joy among the sheep. His kids will grow up and wonder. Something larger than this worn tent and long days had put a fire in Gramps' heart and life into his eyes. It is almost as if he had some news, as if God were with him, here among the sheep pens on this unforgiving hillside. Unknown by the world but known by God.

CHAPTER NINE

Immediacy

Managing a Jesus Way of Time

> I think the besetting sin of pastors, maybe especially evangelical pastors, is impatience.[1]

In some ways, the stress we faced as a church was beyond our control.

It was commonplace that people were leaving. People ordinarily leave a church with a new pastor for one of two reasons (and often within the first two years of the new pastor's arrival): (1) the new pastor is not enough like the previous pastor and things are changing too much; or (2) the new pastor is too much like the previous pastor and things are not changing enough. A pastor can learn to help a congregation through this, but he has little to no control over this kind of immigrating. The pastor must prayerfully and often painfully wait it out. If the church leaders understand this, it sure helps. Thankfully, I had this kind of help.

In addition, an atypical economic recession also pushed the source of some of the stress beyond our reach. Many not-for-profits and churches were suffering. The *Wall Street Journal* and *USA Today* published articles about pastors increasingly losing their jobs and about a national decline in charitable giving.

While our ministry of neighbor love was starting to powerfully take root, our giving was drying up significantly. We had increased our attention to prayer. Over the past eighteen months I had preached three messages about the nature of giving. We had hosted three congregational meetings to alert the congregation and to invite them to join us in prayer. And yet our giving was actually pretty fair, given the size of our church. The souring economy was simply crashing everyone's party.

The elders and I were initiating conversations with the pastoral staff about the possible implications for our jobs. We had already let one pastor go earlier in the year. The church provided him with several months' financial and community provision as best we could. He was our friend. The provision enabled care for him. But it hurt him and all of us.

So one night, our elders' meeting stretched late into the evening. Late-night meetings were becoming the norm. Chips and remnants of Chex Mix sat idly in cheap plastic bowls. A Mountain Dew can and a water bottle stood on the floor. We had looked at printed pages with numbered facts. We had examined taut budgets that would budge no further. In time, we might have to make harder decisions that would impact others of our team, and we were staring wordlessly at each other.

Questions about Power

I had led us in a devotional in this passage to begin our meeting: "Not by might, nor by power, but by my Spirit, says the LORD" (Zech. 4:6). This was the passage that was on our hearts. But what did resisting our kinds of power and might look like? What did leaning on his kind of power look like? We pondered these questions about his kind of power in a new way.

Meetings had increasingly featured tears, prayers, vigorous discussion, and long planning without answers. By his grace we had remained united. We had tried to love well, communicate clearly, and own the mistakes we saw in ourselves or that others showed us. But on that night his grace enabled us to feel even more certainly with our quiet stares what we had been learning and confessing for some time now: some of the stress we faced was of our own making.

It was the kind of stress a church planter feels in his first two years, or the stress a young pastor experiences in a rural church, or the stress a pastor with large potential and expectations senses. "I've served for two years, and we still have only twenty-five people," he says to himself. "Am I even called? Is God working at all? Should I move on to another place? Did I make a mistake in coming here?"

Our circumstances were different from that, but the underlying belief was the same. Because reality was smaller, slower, and seemingly ordinary, we were asking, "Why? What happened? Are we doing something wrong?"

We resisted sexy programs and splash. In my twenty years I had seen too much of this. Building programs and ministry initiatives hype everyone into excitement, giving, and volunteering. For a while the buzz generated is adrenalizing. Work gets done. Ministry happens. But subtly over time, people burn out. Gradually the programs and the hype become what has to be maintained. If a lull begins to creep in, we create a new hype with a new initiative to rally everyone again. It is like we are parents scared that our teen should ever feel bored. We confuse activity with achievement.

Over the years, such a church takes a long roller-coaster ride with an emotional up and down. Sometimes while the coaster is racing, everyone's hands are up, and mouths are wide with fun. It is dynamic both in feeling and accomplishment. But there is often little time on the ride to actually love people. One feels as if she is doing God's work, because we are all moving quickly with a lot of other people. The noise is real! But after the ride, sometimes our stomachs flip with queasiness. We look back and wonder if our ability to handle ordinary relationships and work has grown. Do we understand and practice prayer and solitude and love more Christianly than we did prior to the ride? Basic questions of what it means to handle our anger, our lusts, our spouses, or our drinking more Christianly do not seem resolved. We shouted and felt the wind. But what was the result?

So our elders wanted slow and steady, for the sake of a long and deep ride. We said so. We began to realize that our missional ideas had been ahead of our ability to carry them out. What I mean is, I had cast a vision of love for God and for neighbor in a local way for a global difference. *Missional* meant neighbor love. Yet we still had staffed ahead of the curve. And this is where we were inconsistent. By "the curve," we meant the numerical growth that was coming. Looking back now, we were asking ourselves, Why had we assumed the coming of a curve? Why did we feel we needed one? And why had we assumed that if it came, it would come quickly?

The answer we were realizing unsettled us. Unconsciously, it seems that we assumed that we would grow numerically larger in a short amount of time for the great gospel thing that God had for us in St. Louis. The concepts of larger, quickly, and for a great purpose slipped unnoticed into our ministry assumptions. We shook our heads and stared at the floor. The quote Eugene Peterson started, which was on my mind, finishes this way:

> I think the besetting sin of pastors, maybe especially evangelical pastors, is impatience. We have a goal. We have a mission. We're going to save the world. We're going to evangelize everybody, and we're going to do all this

> good stuff and fill our churches. This is wonderful. All the goals are right. But this is slow, slow work, this soul work, . . . and we get impatient and start taking shortcuts.[2]

The Attraction of Haste

Some shortcuts are gifts. Have you ever noticed that sometimes in grief or stress we laugh, and the laughter is good? It is almost like a cool breeze through a stifling room. It gives us a moment of respite between the tears or the demand. It doesn't start with a joke or some escape. It rises from an ordinary statement that somehow seems quite funny in the moment (even though it isn't). As a kid we called it "getting the giggles." Sometimes even elders need this grace of the giggles.

Amid our stares on that long evening, it was our feet that made us laugh. We laughed so hard, too hard, really, for something that wasn't that humorous. But it was grand! It all started when we considered making an appointment with the local school from which we rent space to inquire about lowering our monthly rent. I said something about it "probably being best that I wear shoes and not flip-flops to such a meeting," and something about how "of course the elder who would join me wouldn't have that decision to make because flip-flops are not part of his everyday fashion options." After a few moments with all of us laughing ourselves into lighter tears, all that I remember is Ty giving a rhetorical flourish in defense of flip-flops and persuasively concluding that "some people feel pain in their feet, and a good pair of flip-flops can ease the difficulty."

My point is that we said silly things that were only funny because we were there together sharing that aching moment with our feet on the road of a hard decision. Ironically, we were beginning to learn about our feet in a metaphorical and spiritual way.

Other kinds of shortcuts harm us. "Desire without knowledge is not good," the proverb tells us, "and whoever makes haste with his feet misses his way" (Prov. 19:2). Haste provides a kind of satisfaction for our soul desire. But the impetus it provides causes us, in the end, to miss the mark for which we originally put on our shoes. Haste works, but only in the short run. Haste in a direction provides short-term highs but a long-term crash. It messes with our feet.

A person who is late and in his haste drives past his exit on the highway has to slow down and turn around. "Walk," we say to my toddler son, who wants to run with his buddies beside the pool. I tell him to slow down not because I want him to miss his mark, but exactly because slowness is his best shot of actually hitting it. Speed promises destination. But often you slip on the wet concrete, and the resulting stitches slow you down anyway while also keeping you from where you hoped to be.

So, maybe we can describe *haste* as "feeling late" or "thinking we have to run." Wherever we are, it is like we are itching to leave. We have somewhere we are supposed to be, but where we are is never that place. So we constantly feel that we are missing out, losing our chance, or forfeiting what we could have had if we could just get there before the hourglass sand empties out.

In our case, we think we know now why we particularly felt late and thought we had to run.

1) To begin with, *haste is part of the air we breathe*. Most of us have been raised to resist boredom and to remain immediately entertained. We've been reared to seek to do the largest amount of work with the least amount of effort in the quickest amount of time. Slow equals waste. Boredom equals restlessness. Waiting is not considered a good use of an hour (much less a day or a week or a month). Our own hearts and our cultural assumptions steer us to impatience and to consider shortcuts.

2) *Our particular church's past*. Our church had been popular once, that is, prior to our split. The church had once had five hundred people and two services. We were up-and-coming in the community, and the talk was on the rise about what God was doing among us. And the church was not yet five years old. The prayers of the people who left the comfort of a home church to start this new gospel work were being answered. But then a devastating fracture between good people ransacked much of that. So, when I came, there was a palpable longing to gain back what had been lost. But in my first months, five marriages broke, two groups of folks slandered and ruined relationships, and a house group imploded in a thoroughly damaging way. We were now asking ourselves hard questions in the meeting that night. If our popularity was truly synonymous with health, how is it that our internal relationships careened so readily into division and fracture? A longing for revival and return can tempt us to impatience and to take shortcuts.

3) *We were not far from the "successful" church in town*. Down the road from us is a church that grew fast and large. Its resources are spread now

throughout the city. Some thought we were on our way to being like this church. Others were sad by how many of our folks had left to go there. Others were miffed or made insecure by how it feels to be like a small, locally owned store in the presence of a giant chain store and trying to compete as the chain store builds more and more stores around ours. Though most churches in America are not this size nor grow this fast, the rest of us are tempted to believe that their story, and not ours, is the gospel norm in the world. Measuring ourselves by the church down the road can tempt us to impatience and to seek shortcuts.

4) *I was considered the real deal.* Looking back, we are humbled by the hype about me, too. The previous pastor was my friend. Our heartbeat was the same. In our community, I was a medium-sized fish in a small pond. "Dr. Eswine" had come. We all expected that great things would follow. Maybe the celebrity mind-set that infects our larger culture was tripping us up. It is typical for a church to lose 20 to 30 percent of its congregation when a new pastor arrives. After my first year and a half, we had lost 50 percent of our attendance and $100,000 in giving. Even a Dr. Eswine in the world can be too much or too little like the previous pastor. Only God can give the increase, Paul had said (1 Cor. 3:6). The presence of a touted leader can tempt us to excuse impatience and shortcuts.

5) *Our heart for the gospel exceeded our skills with the gospel.* This church is remarkable. It did what few others would. It called a single dad with care of his three children to be its pastor. Trying to back out of the search process, I had said, "I do not know how to be a single dad and a pastor at the same time." They answered, "Neither do we, but we will learn together." I will talk more about this later. But for now, it is enough to say that we were like those who dream of serving as a missionary overseas who, one year in, wonder what they were ever thinking. What the commitment actually required of both of us to love each other was more real and tangible than the grace we had dreamed of giving. Trying to transition from a missional vision statement of neighbor love to actual neighbor love can tempt us to resort to impatience and shortcuts.

Patience as a Pastoral Virtue

The joke in Christian circles throughout my life has been, "Pray for anything except patience. You don't want to see what God will give you if you ask for that. Praying for patience is dangerous."

I've laughed and told this joke. Now I think the joke is on me. I never realized how the joke presumes that one can follow Jesus without patience. It also assumes that God will not bother with patience in our lives unless we ask for it. I have been wrong on both counts. One assumption in the joke is true: patience is often learned within the context of trial. The trials seem like interruptions to our otherwise good lives. But more often than not, the trials become the dogs that bark at the impatience and haste that sneak into the halls of our lives. We wouldn't see the intruder lurking to harm us without such barking. And impatience does harm to us. In God's eyes, it will do more harm to us than our trials (James 1:2–4).

Without patience, love is distorted; faith is not possible; hope fails. Impatience violates love, hurries us into walking by sight, and usurps God by putting the fulfillment of our hopes into our own hands. Perhaps this is why patience was a vital component in the pastoral theology that Paul passed on to his young ministry leaders.

For example, as Christians in community Paul apprenticed Timothy and Silvanus in the work. With them at his side, he wrote and taught the congregation in Thessalonica:

> We urge you brothers, admonish the idle, encourage the fainthearted, help the weak, *be patient with them all.* See that no one repays anyone evil for evil, but always seek to do good to one another and to everyone. (1 Thess. 5:14–15)

Paul shows them the pastoral care and discernment by which they will grow in community. "Make sure it is the idle and not the fainthearted that you admonish. Be clear that it is the fainthearted and not the idle that you are encouraging," Paul says. And then Paul reveals what their congregational work will require. "Whether a person is idle, fainthearted, or in need of help, whether you are admonishing someone or encouraging her, be certain of this," Paul said. "Be patient with them all."

Then, as if to illustrate the depth of patience Paul intends, he widens the ideals of commending patience. Along with exercising patience toward people's brokenness as a congregational way of life, Paul says they must also show patience in the presence of evil. Even when someone does them evil, he exhorts them to wait out their legitimate emotions. They are to bear a bit with their deep wound.

In our day, that would equate to waiting two or three days before responding to the e-mail and holding back the fury in an immediate voice mail. They (and we) are to find perspective and healing from a source other than the temporary gratification from rushing to repay the evil done to them. They are to wait until they can choose good for the enemy. Then this wrestling toward praise, prayer, and gratitude without ceasing for every circumstance they face, and seeking in it what is from God's Spirit (and letting go of what is not)—this reveals the pathway patience takes (1 Thess. 5:16–22).

As a pastor in the community, when Timothy is no longer apprenticing and is out as lead pastor on his own, Paul, from prison, will remind Timothy of this same necessity for pastoral work:

> The Lord's servant must not be quarrelsome but kind to everyone, able to teach, *patiently enduring evil,* correcting his opponents with gentleness. (2 Tim. 2:24–25)

Resisting the illusory desire for immediate defense, immediate remedy, and immediate relief is not easy pastorally. A patient gentleness requires courage and strength. For example, an e-mail is seductive bait for a quarrel. I noticed that I had not seen a dear family at church for a while. I contacted the family to inquire about how they were doing. I received an e-mail from the man in response. I hadn't seen the family because they had left our church. The e-mail reads like this.

> So. In short, despite the many good experiences we had at Riverside, and the people we really appreciated, we decided to try to find a church more suited to what we realized we need. Basically, we are looking for a church where the gospel is presented a lot; where doctrine is embraced and taught, where whole passages of the Bible are presented each Sunday. I don't fault Riverside for being the church that it is. It is a church going in the same direction that a LOT of American churches seem to be going. I trust that it is very effective for many people.
>
> Just so you know, we haven't found anywhere that fits us yet. It's getting very frustrating, and we have even considered (shudder!) trying to start a small home-church. I feel totally unequipped to do that. The thing is, though, I know several others (men in particular, and none from

> Riverside) who are equally frustrated with the modern American church and who have all talked about starting one ourselves. Not that we have the time, and of course none of us are preachers.

An e-mail like this—hearing that one does not present the gospel a lot, teach doctrine, or highlight the Bible, and that along with most churches we have more of sociology and therapy than we do the gospel—is tough. It can feel like a punch in the stomach that knocks the wind out, particularly when we know ourselves to pursue the gospel overtly and biblically in all we are attempting to do. Such criticism is made even more difficult when, in the context of friendship, the sender never mentions such things.

In addition, flaws or intentions to grow are given no room. When perfection to the desired standard isn't met, a person leaves rather than joining in. Finally, to slip away without conversation and isolate oneself is disconcerting to a pastor. But my rushing to defend, to (un)kindly instruct, or to try to immediately fix is likely unwise and will prove unhelpful. A waiting of some kind will be required. Waiting even applies to preaching and who we are as preachers:

> Preach the word; be ready in season and out of season; reprove, rebuke, and exhort, *with complete patience* and teaching. (2 Tim. 4:2)

We must resist the naive or manipulative assumption that just because we preached or said something to someone once, they should hereafter immediately, always, and forever get it right. That's impatient preaching. Impatient preaching enables the listener to avoid wrestling with a question; it expects the listener to always ask, feel, or think the right way immediately; it presumes that growing in Jesus does not require days, weeks, months, and years.

What Paul teaches pastors, he learned from his Savior. How is it that anyone can so overcome the trials of the world, the temptations of the flesh, and the assaults of the Devil? What methods does a pastor teach people and try himself? Jesus reveals that patience is the kind of power we will need. This is what Jesus said to us when he explained the parable of the sower:

> The seed is the word of God. The ones along the path are those who have heard; then the devil comes and takes away the word from their hearts,

> so that they may not believe and be saved. (Luke 8:11–12) [Assault of the Devil]
>
> And the ones on the rock are those who, when they hear the word, receive it with joy. But these have no root; they believe for a while, and in time of testing fall away. (Luke 8:13) [Trials of the world]
>
> And as for what fell among the thorns, they are those who hear, but as they go on their way they are choked by the cares and riches and pleasures of life, and their fruit does not mature. (Luke 8:14) [Desires of the flesh]
>
> As for that in the good soil, they are those who, hearing the word, hold it fast in an honest and good heart, and *bear fruit with patience.* (Luke 8:15)

Anything about resisting the Devil, overcoming trials, and handling temptations that we teach will need patience, this gracious fruit of our Lord's Spirit.

A Jesus Way of Time

The missionary was frustrated. Uganda, Africa, was his calling, but the work was hard—learning a new language, adjusting to a different cultural life—and results were slow and not immediate, glimpsed but not apparent. How does one gain a stamina for waiting it out and not leaving too soon? The advice from an older pastor came in this way:

> Give it your heart out of gratitude for a tender, seeking and patient savior. Make every common task shine with the radiance of Christ. Then every event becomes a shiny glory moment to be cherished—whether you drink tea or try to get the verb forms of the new language. . . . Always try to be daring but don't be in a hurry. . . . If you don't like what is going on in Uganda, wait a week. It'll be the opposite.[3]

Those of us in the long meeting that night were beginning as leaders to see our need for a greater stamina for waiting. But how do we grow in this? How do we learn to "wait a week"?

We knew something of this grace in our motto "No surprises." In practice this motto meant that we sought never to put anyone in the position of having to make decisions the first time he heard something. We often took at least two or more meetings over the course of a couple of months prior to deciding anything—the first month to introduce the situation, the in-between time to prayerfully consider, reflect, and discuss. We then strove to decide at a meeting one month later. Sometimes, we were not ready and we waited more. Weighty decisions can be delayed as a way to avoid deciding. We knew that. But weighty decisions are more often hastily made by tired leaders at the end of a long day who would think better of something in hindsight if given the chance.

We had also sought to lead our staff meetings differently. Each Monday-morning meeting lasted about an hour and a half. For one hour of that time, we began to read a book together out loud. During reading we reflected on it together and mulled over its implications for our team and for our ministries. Then we did our administrative bits for the last half hour of the time. We were now on our third book together.

At first, we were fidgety and nervous. Reading and reflecting made us feel that we were not getting our work done. Little by little, we've come to believe that this kind of contemplation and reflection is our work. Slowing  down, contemplating, and meditating on truth prayerfully and in community together is part of our agenda, not an interruption to it.

Yet, in the long meeting, we felt a deeper sense that we have much more to learn about learning to wait. Turning to Jesus, a little phrase comes to mind. I had preached on it some time ago: "Eight days later" (John 20:26). Thomas had said to the other disciples, his friends, that he would not believe in Jesus unless he saw Jesus. I know that Jesus heard those words of Thomas's. Thomas had once been courageous and willing to die for Jesus. But then the pain of betrayal and the loss of the one he loved became too much for him to try again or believe again. Cynical with loss, Thomas doubted. Jesus met Thomas and gave him the faith he needed. But he waited eight days to do it.

If Jesus's view of time was clock time, this willingness to wait and let Thomas stew in unbelief seems wasteful. Clock time manages minutes, subdues tasks, and accomplishes the most in the shortest amount of time to make much of being efficient and of making achievements. The calendar appoints us for tasks, and the days go by. Losing minutes is a waste of clock time. Through this outlook, Jesus should have immediately responded to Thomas when Thomas first exposed his struggle eight days earlier.

But Jesus seems to desire that our view of time be converted. Patience learns to grow here. For Jesus, time is something that has a fulfillment. This means that time belongs to something beyond it. There is an intended meaning to it (Mark 1:15). Because of this, time is a sign pointing us beyond itself to something we are meant to see and know (Matt. 16:3). Time is sacramental. It has been set apart as a means of revealing God to us.

Clock time has us believe that "the real thing is always still to come."[4] Grieving makes time slow down. Minutes feel like hours, making it a great accomplishment to get through a day. Clock time, in contrast, makes everything speed up. The minutes feel like seconds that are dropping like sand through our fingers. There is never enough time in the day to get to where we are trying to be. Clock time is a constant reminder that we are not where we want to be achieving what we were meant to achieve.

But Jesus time, or time as Jesus sees it, is not designed to drive us into what we want but cannot get to. For him, time is the means. It's the gift we are given by which we learn to locate the otherwise "unapparent presence of God."[5] Clock time teaches us to assert, get moving, make something happen. Jesus time calls us to listen, receive, pay attention, and learn of God. "What we are seeking is already here."[6]

Thomas is without faith for eight more days. But he is not without Jesus's presence alongside and purpose for him, waiting invisible alongside for just the right time. Clock time skews us into seeing prayer, listening, waiting, receiving, believing, meditating, temptations, and trials as setbacks or intrusions that waste our time. For patience to grow, Jesus must show us the meaning of himself in the time he has given us. With Jesus, even though eight days have gone by with no seeming result, all is not lost.

Impatience with the ticking clock's demands causes us to glance at a room that needs a new floor and then frantically rearrange the furniture. It would prefer that we move the furniture again and again and feel like a fix is taking place rather than do the tedious work of tearing up the floor for true stability. With the hype and the frenetic pace, everyone feels like they are doing something for Jesus. But few, however, may have actually entered the slow waiting of real spiritual relationship and growth.

By his grace, we were seeing that our assessments of what our church needed (and our solutions for meeting those needs) were right. Our ministries were growing stronger. But why did we think that we had to immediately implement those assessments and our solutions? Maybe we didn't know that the unfinished and uncomfortable time in between the assessment and the implementation would have revealed God to us. Maybe we had no category for handling time in any other way than by the clock. Could patience with how God would reveal himself in the meantime have settled us to believe that we could implement more slowly without losing out?

Learning the Words of Silence

Jesus's silence with Thomas for those eight days also reveals what a conversion of time will do to us. It will teach us that power and purpose are not tied to how busy we can make the day. Jesus needed no God words or any other kinds of words to fill up Thomas's days. While Jesus sat silent in Thomas's presence, maybe Thomas paced with agitation in the absence of Jesus's visible voice, filled minutes with conversations about what, if, and when he would do and not do. We don't know for sure. But what is certain is that Thomas slept and worked those days with no word, only presence, and this presence of Jesus was not felt or sensed. It unnerved him.

Maybe this is something of what Mary was learning and Martha needed. The good and noble clanking of pots and pans to get dinner ready is meant to cede to the presence of her Lord and not ignore it or fret about in order to make it worthwhile. Once he arrives, the meaning of his presence doesn't have to be achieved or conjured. It is already given (Luke 10:38–41). Every act of time is a revealing of his presence and our going to attend him, even if he sits with us but quietly.

If a curve never came and our church didn't grow much or fast, would our time have been lost and wasted? In the long meeting that night, we were beginning to learn that silence doesn't mean absence. Maybe it did when Adam stood by and said nothing to Eve or to the temptation they both met. But this is not the case with Jesus. He has been with us and will be still, even if he is as one who is silent or quieter for a while. We must learn this. More activity and increasing what we accomplish in clock time does not secure or signify his presence. His presence has little to do with clocks and schedules. He is already here.

The earlier quote about impatience being a besetting sin of pastors now reminds me of another who thought that our besetting sin as pastors is "too many words."[7] Impatience multiplies words. We forget that a day without relief is nothing more than that. Such days are not bereft of him. With him, unrelieved days of prayer become a year of active waiting for his lead. Such a year is no waste of time, even if the curve hasn't come. Patience quiets us. Words and activity fade in importance. Presence matters.

He Is Patient with Us

As I think about our meeting that night and all that we had seen in my first two years, I became most amazed by the strength of this church's core group. They had had three pastors in eight years. They left the stability of a larger, established church for the discomfort of believing that Jesus would empower a new gospel effort in this part of town for his glory. They were still here, waiting. How could that be? I thought to myself, "What if they were the truly honorable ones? What if their faith amid these days of small things revealed that they were the true spiritual success stories in our community?" Among these were the spiritual giants unknown to most. Somehow his grace had steadied them into waiting, when everything inside them could have felt that eight years of not getting where they had hoped must be waste.

Meanwhile, many had left who had invested much less for a quarter of the time. Down the highway there are churches where they could go and find what they wanted without waiting. I believe many of them had, unfortunately, delayed the issue that faced them. After they have been wherever they are for a while, life will happen, waiting will be required, and not all will be happy all of the time. They will then face the same questions there that they avoided here: Do you have a stamina for waiting on God when gratification isn't immediate, faith is sightless, and neighbor love is hard work? Is your Christianity merely a series of shortcuts designed to avoid the embrace of the mundane that real soul work requires? Patience waits for them.

I admired and learned from the patience of this core group, but I needed to learn patience with those who quickly drifted. And all of us required patience with me. I had tasted a kind of betrayal, including the sting of evangelicals who weren't at their best when they smell a scandal on you. I'd been scared of people, particularly church people, in a way that was uncomfortably new for me. The emotional abrasions from such a massive critique of my life and ministry had led me three times to try to quit in my first two years. Early on, the constant vulnerability as a single dad seemed too much. My eventual dating and marriage as a pastor in the public eye was sometimes cruel. But these elders, they kept saying that they believed God was at work. "Be patient," they'd say. "Hang on."

That night I shared my fears with my elders. I've worked in several churches with multiple groups of leaders. This was the first group with which I felt I could risk such a revelation of my heart. "Zack," they said, "if the worst ever happened, and this church we love folded, we will be standing there with you, the last to turn out the lights. We are with you and hope you will be with us even if it comes to that."

The patience in these men showed me the grace of Jesus. There is a strange sweetness that can be found amid the answerless ache of an impending threat. Going for days without what you know would be easier if you just had it in your hands. Patience says to your empty hands, God is here. Patience looks the worst in the face and says, "God will somehow be with us still."

The apostle Paul was called by God before he was born and while his name was still Saul of Tarsus (Gal. 1:15). Jesus waited to reveal that call on the violent road of Paul's bloodstained hands. Paul tells us about the patience of Jesus:

> But I received mercy for this reason, that in me, as the foremost, Jesus Christ might display *his perfect patience* as an example to those who were to believe in him for eternal life. To the King of the ages, immortal, invisible, the only God, be honor and glory forever and ever. Amen. (1 Tim. 1:16–17)

The patience with which Jesus ministers to us offers us a new way, a different perspective on time and words, a different kind of power for ministry. His is a long, forbearing power that endures days of small and even frightening things and says to such days, "You belong to me!"

Conclusion

Two men left home to plant a church in a city of need. One arrived prior to the other. He dreamed of a city reached for Jesus with the gospel. Through this prior pastor, people came to know Jesus, believers gathered, and a community of Jesus followers was born. It was a slow work, but it was happening. His prayers were being answered.

In time, he began to meet with the one who arrived later, in order to encourage the newcomer. The old-timer and the newcomer prayed for Jesus to reach the city for the gospel. Through the newcomer pastor, people came to know Jesus, believers gathered, and a community of Jesus followers was born.

Ten years later, the one who had come first pastors an ordinary church. Its two hundred–plus members demonstrate the love of Jesus in ways that did not exist there ten years earlier. The newcomer who came second pastors a famous church. Its thousands of members and multiple sites around the city demonstrate the love of Jesus in ways that did not exist there ten years earlier. The prayers of both men were answered. Why then is one of them sad?

CHAPTER TEN

Conversation with a Young Minister

Apprenticing with Jesus

> But you must understand, there are many ways of being in a place.[1]

"No matter what, I want to do all I can for the ministry."

My young friend said this earnestly. His passion inspired me, but its context worried me. He was revealing his hunger for ministry in relation to his struggle for him and his wife to love each other. They had been married two years and had two very young children. They were fighting often, and intimacy was strained. I took a breath and paused, staring down at the bowl of pad thai in front of me.

"If the ministry is what we will give everything for," I began, "then how we define 'the ministry' seems important." I took a bite and chewed.

"I just want to preach the Word," he declared. "I figure no matter what happens, as long as I keep saying what God said, he will bless it. As long as I keep preaching and teaching, he will be glorified. I know God has given me a purpose."

There was urgency in his voice and hurry in his eyes. Both were like a mirror to me. I twirled peanut and noodles around my fork (the chopsticks had long ago begun their humbling work with me). I was hunting for words.

"Yes, God will bless his Word," I ventured. "You do have purpose," I affirmed.

I lingered more with the bowl, trying to find what to leave unsaid there. "I spoke at a conference once," I said. "I preached five times. It was one of those moments when God's presence was tangibly felt. I had been experiencing this kind of impact regularly and was speaking at such places all over the country. In fact, after that particular conference, the rest of my year was planned full with preaching. So, I fully agree with you," I continued. "God does bless his Word. I've seen him do it firsthand.

"But," I said, and then stopped. I stood at a crossroads in my mind, wondering how to say what was next. I took the step. "On my way home after that last conference sermon amid the divine blessing of that night, my wife of fifteen years told me she was leaving me."

There was a quiet between my young friend and me. I sipped my Coke. I was afraid I'd said too much too soon. He knew the circumstances of my life. But was he ready to learn something of what such circumstances might have to teach us? Moreover, was I ready to try and give some kind of voice to it?

"I'm trying to suggest," I said, "that 'the ministry' involves more than the question of whether our sermons are useful or powerful for people. Going all out for God means more than going all out for our sermons."

We picked up with our noodles again. After lunch, we went back to my house. We sat on the couch and talked. He mentioned the secret sins behind the vault in our hearts. He spoke about how he still has sins that break him. He also revealed again that he could go weeks without really talking to his wife, about how the time flies by him and he doesn't realize how irregularly they truly find each other. He spoke about the books he had read over the years on longing and brokenness and carrying out the greatest commandment, to love.

"I've read all of this for years and I no longer trust a language of brokenness or relational love. I've tried to do all of that stuff and I just don't know how to love," he said with frustration. "I just want to minister to people. I want to glorify God!"

"It's strange, isn't it?" I muttered. "Frightening even, how we who are called to ministry can sometimes become cynical about things we've read for years and mastered with study yet not been able to practice in our ordinary lives."

We went on, shared music together, caught up on happenings. We ate again.

Later that night we stood beneath the stars.

Restless in Our Places

"When I get back home," he said, "I begin as a pastor. Maybe soon I can get to seminary and get equipped and then become a professor somewhere."

He looked up at the sky, and with longing in his voice he expressed, "I can't wait to get there. I just want to get out of where I am and get there. Two years as a pastor and then . . ."

I found myself staring at the gravel driveway like it was a bowl of pad thai. I searched again for what to leave unsaid. I heard my voice in his. I recognized my own ambition in him. He was restless to do something great for God, and yet he did not know how to include changing diapers in his definition of greatness.

"What if you are there already?" I tried. "I mean, what if you are already what God has in mind for you? What if the place of ministry where you are is the place where God meant for you to be with him?"

His face seemed pained.

"Please forgive me if I'm saying too much," I said. Then I paused.

Something he had told me earlier was nagging my thoughts. My friend was regularly sick, most recently with pneumonia. The hours he was keeping for ministry were wearing him out. I remembered my own ill health and fatigue.

"It's just that you are talking to a man," I mustered, "who got everything he dreamed of and lost most of what really mattered, and all of this in the name of going all out for the ministry and serving God. I'm just trying to say that it seems really important to know what we mean by 'the ministry' if we are going to go all out for it, you know? My desire is that what you are going all out for is the thing God intends with the definition God gives it."

"I don't know where to start with all that," he protested.

I nodded with agreement. "For what it's worth," I risked. "I'm coming to strongly believe that learning how to be human is the direction we need."

Hackled, he looked away into the sky again. "I can't answer all of this in one breath," he declared.

We lingered there a while longer. Frost clothed our breath and made it visible in the night. Beneath the star-strong sky we prayed. We thanked God for his humility, the holder of the stars, the one who shadows them into invisibility by his own light. He was hearing the voices of two pastors, two friends fragile in their ability to love him but full of longing. "What is man that you are mindful of him?" I thought (Ps. 8:4).

Homeless in Our Living Rooms

I thought a lot that night about what my friend wrestled with.

The following week, I sat for lunch with an up-and-coming pastor. The church he served was only four years old but had several hundred already in attendance. He was rising in our community as the next big thing.

Yet there was something troubling him. "The first two years of our explosive growth," he admitted, "I related poorly as a husband and father." He stared into his ice water and grimaced. "I hid in my success," he continued. "I think I used my success as a pastor to avoid my failing ways at home and in my heart."

This man was the epitome of what my younger friend was striving to be. But both men revealed the same struggle—the realization that one can receive accolades for preaching Jesus, yet at the same time know very little about how to follow Jesus in the living rooms of their ordinary lives. They could communicate love to a crowd from the pulpit or in an office or a classroom, but when called upon to give themselves (and not their gifts) they were fumble prone. I see this in me.

I wondered. What does it say about the way we're approaching the ministry if we who have been trained for it do not know how to follow Jesus when we have our pajamas on? Give us the role to play, and we know what to do. Take the role away on a day off or for good, and we stamp about restlessly. We know how to do things pastorally but struggle when asked to do them humanly.

As another pastor said, "I guard my day off well. I've built in a Sabbath rest weekly. But I don't know how to actually rest when the time comes. My kid is right in front of me with the Legos, but my mind drifts to pastoral stuff."

I think of my own life. Does our fidgeting in this way reveal that we are no different from any person working any vocation who is physically present but emotionally absent? The danger for pastors intensifies, however. We can justify our internal homelessness by spiritualizing it as all part of glorifying God. The truth is that we actually still might be immature in what it means to follow Jesus into personal rest among teddy bears and pacifiers or amid the quiet stillness of holding hands like lovers again with our spouse. Somehow we implicitly devalue these ordinary loves by our able willingness to constantly give our attention elsewhere.

A thought unsettles me. If I were Adam or Eve in the garden before the fall, would I be bored and think that my life was insignificant? Would I think that the garden was too small a place and the daily tasks too mundane to glorify God? Would I know how to stroll with Eve, clean the dirt off of my spade, and enjoy the food set before me? Or would I constantly say to Eve, the shovel, and the food, "Not now. I have things to do for God"?

A strange chuckle rises within me as I write this. I just remembered that I was once fired from a job. I was a window washer. I was terrible at it for two reasons. First, I'm scared of heights. I didn't climb a ladder; I clung to it for dear life. Second, I couldn't focus on the window at hand. My mind was never on the thing in front of me. I held the squeegee and stroked the window soap the way I was taught. But though my boss taught me the skill with the tools, I hadn't learned the skill of attention that he had learned to accompany the tool use. I mimicked the way he moved his hands and used a towel. But unlike him, I left streaks wherever I worked. I learned the hard way that the right use of tools in a job like this represents only half the learning required. My chuckle fades.

I'm beginning to think that we who train for the ministry would do well to think on that for a while. My young friend's frustration comes back to me. "I don't know where to start with all that," he had said.

Finding a Rule

Sometime later, my gifted young friend wrote to me during the first week in his new pastorate:

> I am full of anxiety, mostly about what I do with all this time. I am here each day. I am being paid and I keep asking myself, Have I done X-number of dollars of labor for the church today or not? I am unaccustomed to this free of a day, and it makes me anxious. I think things of myself like, I get things done better when my schedule is packed and I'm going a million miles an hour. I work better under pressure. I've known nothing but pressure for years and years, and now that God is providing space, I want to sabotage it somehow. How can I turn from this and find life?

Examining Our Mentoring

I heard my voice in his; his questions and assumptions in my own. He does not yet know how to do a day as a minister if speed, hurry, quantity, pressure, immediate results, and money-based evaluations are removed from him. The absence of these things harasses him into anxiety. He is not alone. I am pained with the knowledge that some of this he has learned from my way of being over the years.

I found myself inviting him to consider with me the things that you and I are exploring in this book:

> Most of us in ministry have a haphazard way of being. What I mean is that all of us have a way of doing each day, but few of us give much thought to it. Or we give thought to it for misguided purposes in light of how we have been mentored. The monks were onto something here when they recognized the need for a human being (especially those in ministry) to live by what they called a "rule." Whether we agree with all things monkish or not, there is no denying this insight. Each of us gives ourselves daily to habitual ways of doing life. For many reasons that will become apparent as we grow together, the rule that I commend to you is that you begin to look at each day as an apprenticeship with Jesus for his recovering of your humanity. Therefore, as you awake in the morning, set this prayer and commitment before the Lord: "By grace I will view this day as an apprenticeship with Jesus. He intends to recover my humanity so that by his Spirit I may support others as Jesus recovers their humanity too."

I then mentioned how we are well prepared to consider the "soul givens." By "soul givens," I mean what cannot be avoided and must be addressed regarding our interior lives by the ministry of the gospel. But we've been little prepared to account for how the gospel addresses the unavoidables of the body and how body-soul givens drape all over us and those we serve:

> Bodily unavoidables are things like time, weather, the senses, bodily functions, aging, eating, drinking, work, sex, gender, and skin color. We have likewise probably paid too little attention to the unavoidables of our place, because our theology of place (along with our theology of the body) remains immature.

I reminded both of us that wherever we are and no matter who we are, we and each person we hope to minister to will encounter certain things that are typical for any human geography and life. I tried to suggest what this implies for us:

> What recovering our humanity in Jesus means for us as pastors is that you and I have the opportunity to learn how to relate to time, how to relate to the weather, how to relate to what it means to work, to eat, and to feel in our bones the effect of our aging. To help you start, I commend reading the Wisdom Literature of the Old Testament and the Gospels with the following question: What does this show me about what it means to be human and, as a human being, to relate to God and my neighbors in the place that I inhabit? If you journey in this direction, you will soon discover, as just one example, what the way you handle your child's pacifier has to do with living the spiritual life as a follower of Jesus. In this discovery you will grow in mindfulness of the pacifiers held each week by some of those you pray for, preach to, and seek to point to Jesus. You will then begin to have psalm-like or Gospels-like speech, as if your two feet are standing in this world as you preach to us about the unseen world to come. In this, you will find that you are beginning more and more to teach in resemblance to Jesus, because you are more closely beginning to live in the manner he did with the bodily knowing of one's place that he had.

The "rule" Francis of Assisi set down for his monastic community was that they orient their days around "following the teachings and the footsteps of Jesus."[2] We don't have to fully agree with how Francis sought to imitate Jesus's footsteps to appreciate his larger aim. He connected our mentoring not just to Jesus's teachings but to how Jesus lived in the fullness of his humanity. This is important for us and for the rule by which we seek to orient our days.

This is why those we minister to are called to consider the outcome of our *way of life* (Heb. 13:7). They are meant to take notice of what comes from the way we relate to what attends each day. For this purpose, Timothy is encouraged by Paul not just to gain the right content to pass on from Paul's teaching but also to imitate and pass on Paul's way of life (2 Tim. 4:10–11).

So, like you, I need grace to ask myself not only what content of teaching I am passing on to those who hear me but also what way of doing a day I am apprenticing myself to and passing on to those who do life with me.

I hear the wise words of my friend come back to me from under the stars that night. "I can't answer all of this in one breath," he had said.

Now, the quandary is set before us. He does not yet know how to do a day without speed, haste, quantity of performance, and pressure. Yet what he needs Jesus to show him is something that must by its nature slow him down and take much of his time, for life in ministry is an apprenticeship with Jesus.

Apprenticeship

Throughout this book I have intended to make the point that each of us is already apprenticing ourselves to a rule, a way of life. My aim has been to give us tools for recognizing this fact and seeking Jesus about it. Jesus's grace saves us and trains us toward a different kind of apprenticeship. His design is to purchase and recover his apprenticing for our lives.

In order to solidify what an apprenticeship is, we can remind ourselves of Goethe's famous poem. In his *The Sorcerer's Apprentice,* the master has business to attend and leaves his young student to watch over things for a day.

An apprentice is one who attaches himself to the veteran of a craft so as to learn that craft, not only by rote but more so by inhabiting a way of life. The apostle Paul knew what this embodied learning meant, when he declared that he not just taught Bible studies like a Pharisee but also "*lived as* a Pharisee" (Acts 26:5). Elisha lived with Elijah. Timothy and Titus lived with Paul. Peter, James, and John lived with Jesus.

Apprenticeship assumes that knowing a trade not only comes by numbers and outlines but also by watching and inhabiting. Knowing is found in these forms, because teaching is. We teach not only by our words and assignments but also by the manner of our words and the ways we ourselves already embody the assignments we give.

This is why I cannot make the macaroni the way my mamaw did, even though I have her written recipe. Following the written recipe only approximates the taste Mamaw brought out of the pasta. My best hope of one-to-one correspondence is to sit with Mamaw and watch her ways of making it (a realization I made too late). Human beings who minister to others must enter this kind of embodied learning and teaching.

In his poem, Goethe reveals what happens to a student when he purposes to approximate by rote rather than embody by patience his master's ways. Ambitious, the young apprentice surmises that he is ready to fill his master's shoes because he has "memorized what to say and do."[3] Those familiar with the famed Disney version of this poem will likely remember the frenzy and damage that results. The apprentice has overestimated himself. Though he tried to imitate the tasks of his master, he neither embodied the ways of his master nor understood the depth of the powers that confronted him. Therefore, all of his efforts only worsened his plight until finally he humbled himself, begged the master's return, and received in surrender the master's gracious and powerful rescue.

Goethe's poem offers a morality tale by which one who has long embodied a way of being is contrasted with one who has merely memorized its words and mimicked its behaviors. The poet's point is obvious. Trying to access the power of a vocation by mere memory and incantation will shortly make a mess of things.

An example comes to mind. The veteran pastor of a very large and influential church brought his son, newly graduated from seminary, to become his successor. The damage wasn't far behind. Possessing a last name and a title does not mean that one knows how to rightly wield either. One has to be twenty-five before he can be fifty. Shortchanging this long embodiment is rarely wise.

And so the word *apprentice* has its biblical expression in the word *disciple*. Even apostles were disciples. But, like the apprentice in Goethe's poem (and like many, many of us), the disciples regularly made a mess of things. Because they could imitate words or mimic actions they had seen in Jesus, they presumed they were ready.

For example, while their Master is away, some of the disciples seize an opportunity to cast out a demon from a disheveled boy. They've watched Jesus do this many times. But though they are confident in themselves and accurately mimic his words and actions, they are unable to heal the boy. Why? "This kind," Jesus answered, "cannot be driven out by anything but prayer" (Mark 9:29).

Examining Our Mentoring

But did you notice what's absent from the play-by-play of this account? Jesus doesn't pray in the moment. We hear his words and see his actions in the moment, but we are not told that he is praying. That's because Jesus's prayer had preceded, prepared him for, attended, and continued on after this episode. The disciples didn't do this. They tried to recreate what their Master did without recognizing the way of their Master or the depth of the kind of evils that will confront them. The point is that there are kinds of evils that only this way of life will provide the capacity in him to handle.

The disciples had witnessed this rhythm of prayer as a way of life firsthand as they lived with him. But they did not connect the dots between how what he taught flowed from what he lived. Merging Jesus's teaching and footsteps would forge their only hope of overcoming certain "kinds" in the world. It did not occur to them that a way of being on a quiet day could prepare them for the moment of challenge amid the bone and soul of a neighbor screeching. As a matter of fact, right after their debacle they went on undaunted in their high esteem of themselves to debate who among them would be the greatest (Mark 9:34).

Similarly, several itinerant preachers had watched the apostle Paul cast out demons and perform miracles in Jesus. They determined that they could likewise do what Paul had done. So they happened upon such evil spirits and mimicked what they had observed in Paul.

"I adjure you by the Jesus whom Paul proclaims," one of them cried out. To which the demons retorted, "Jesus I know, and Paul I recognize, but who are you?"

Immediately, the preachers who tried to practice what they had not learned were overpowered and fled the scene naked and wounded (Acts 19:11–16).

The demons were astute. They recognized that no matter how much the preachers' words and actions resembled those of Jesus, the quality of Jesus's authority, life, and teaching was absent. Wreckage was the ministry result.

The Spell of Institutions

For many of us, apprenticeship has been made harder at times because we have sometimes been taught the ministry as if the gospel is a disembodied mastery. In other words, we no longer live with those we seek to learn from. My point here is not to advocate for one way of training over another. My point is to observe and take stock of what many of us know. We've learned the ministry differently than Timothy did.

To get at what I mean, consider what someone wrote to Henry David Thoreau who gave himself for a time to a hermitic life beside Walden Pond: "If I understand rightly the significance of your life, this is it," the man wrote. He continued:

> You would sunder yourself from society, from the spell of institutions, customs, conventionalities, that you may lead a fresh simple life with God. Instead of breathing a new life into the old forms you would have a new life without and within.[4]

This is an unspoken institutional mentoring that takes place for good and for ill in us as persons and ministry leaders. We already noted how this takes place in the providences of family life and ministry ambition. There is insight here regarding the kind of "spell" that our otherwise good institutional rhythms may have placed on us. This "spell of institutions, customs, and conventionalities" partly explains how my young friend is biblically competent but unfamiliar and anxious with how to do a human pastoral day and this with enjoyment. As we come to the close of our discussion, let's take a final and closer look at how our daily rhythms become apprenticed spells, rules, and ways of life.

Bible Training Spells

My seminary days not only taught me doctrinal content to make me sound; it also had a way of teaching that content that I surrendered to and oriented my life around for three years.

So, Dr. Calhoun's way of meeting with me in his home for tea each week modeled for me that hospitality is warm, personal, and more humanly offered in the home than in an office (even though he never taught me a class on hospitality).

In contrast, having to read three to five books for every class (twelve to twenty books in thirteen weeks) taught me a way of being that devalued slow meditation and prized instead speed, efficiency, and content management. It also required me to orient my family life around the heightened importance of "getting the reading done." Unwittingly, getting the reading done became a rule used to justify embodying an "other than Jesus" way of life during evenings at home.

We take such mentoring with us into the ministry. The former, for example, positively shaped the way I have sought to open my home, not just my office, as a pastor. However, the latter negatively shaped how I approached my family in light of my weekly sermon preparation. Likewise, I picked up the idea that a classroom and a syllabus of information offer the best paradigm for what it means to teach and to grow in maturity.

Most of us entered our first pastorates already exhausted because of the pace of life made necessary if we hoped to master divinity. Campus ministers and church planters often experience the same context of fatigue. That pace of life became a way of being for us. We could handle a theology assignment or an evangelism call, but we didn't know how to ask a girl out, love the one we'd married, or relate patiently or humbly to our place in life when things did not go our way.

I tried an experiment once as a professor. I assigned only one book for an entire semester class. It was the book that all others quoted on the subject. I proposed that we read this one masterful book slowly, that we meditate on it and discuss it thoroughly as our guide through the semester. My students complained, these future pastors, counselors, and ministry leaders who were in my class. They felt that I was not giving them their money's worth.

Yet these same friends who complained about my offering them more time to meditate often had one or two jobs and spent hours in the library to keep good grades. Already tired, some of them were married with children, and those familial relationships were strained. This weekly rhythm invisibly mentors us into acting as if fatiguing oneself to master a quantity of information amid the regular neglect of heart and family is necessary for pastoral life. After years of this way of doing a day, we no longer know what to do with ourselves (or with our spouse or children) if nothing more than ordinary life awaits us.

Our best administrators are beginning to see this. Our best deans are recognizing that theological education comes not just from the curriculum but from the way of life the stated curriculum requires of a student. Do our curriculum requirements promote a Jesus way of living humanly?

Local Church Spells

The local church also apprentices us in wonderful but also sometimes misguided ways. In my first pastorate, our small church of sixty people (down in size because of a split) offered thirty programs from their mortgaged eighteen acres of land within their new million-dollar facility. We paid eighty thousand dollars a year in interest alone. The day we cut our programs from thirty to five, an outrage erupted from some. "We are going backwards," I was told. "The gospel compels us to do more for our community, not less. You don't care about the gospel, and you are ruining this church."

The problem was that our people were exhausted. Our concern about "going backwards" and "missing the gospel" did not seem to include or take seriously what our activities for Jesus were doing to the bodies and souls of our members.

Some of them put up their own property as collateral for the church building. The twelve church members doing 80 percent of the work had little time for a presence at home, in their neighborhood, or to hear their own heart before the Lord. The presence they did have was a fatigued and hurried one. Somehow the gospel going forward had been measured in ways that excluded rest, limits, patience, and timing. We were a church competing rather than apprenticing. Because of that, we were teaching a way of life in Jesus's name that was "doing great things" but damaging people in the process. Our view of greatness somehow did not include nurture of the soul. It was from this vantage point that I was mentoring my young friend.

Missional Organization Spells

Similarly, each quarter a large number of area pastors and church planters gather together. To attend this gathering is to find blessing and encouragement. But to attend is also to find the question that seems to be on everyone's mind when conversations are started: "So, how big is your church?"

This question not only challenges me as one whose church is smaller than most of the ones they serve, but I think often of the church planters that I've worked with in various settings. Those who have only thirty or fifty or eighty congregants after three to five years actually struggle to know that they are called; they often receive pressure that something has gone wrong. "What do you tell donors in your regular newsletter if big things aren't happening?" one church planter asked. This mentoring comes from somewhere. It can suggest that Jesus values large movements in short amounts of time. It tragically suggests that one's calling correlates to how quickly the crowds gather.

Or consider another venue. I heard a good ministry leader give a report of successful ministry in another country. The report demonstrated how the number of programs along with the number of those attending had grown from the previous year. The report glowingly spoke of the new initiatives to be implemented in the new year. Everyone, including me, gave thanks to God for his blessing.

Not long after, I had the opportunity to visit that country. I met some of those indigenous leaders numbered in that previous ministry report. They spoke of the challenge they were having with the American missionaries who were relationally hurting people and disrespecting the initiatives of their own local leaders. Culturally, these indigenous leaders found it difficult to state these concerns plainly to their American brothers.

I was sobered. I had given thanks to God because we were measuring success and faithfulness by numeric tallying of persons and initiatives. Yet those who were the actual recipients of that ministry were beseeching God to give them wisdom and grace to heal from the hurt of those numeric steamrollers. This ministry had to reevaluate how Jesus would measure success for them. We all did.

Cultural Spells

At least in America, we get this competing mind-set of greatness, honestly. Competition and free market form the air we breathe. Consider what I mean.

I listened to another State of the Union address by the United States president last night. I've heard more than forty years' worth of these kinds of speeches from both sides of the American political aisle. As always, our ideals are captured with such terms as *moral vision, technological innovation, becoming number one in the world* at such and so, and *rebuilding a better America* so that we can compete and win more on a global scale. I am grateful for my home.

Don't get me wrong—it's not that I'm opposed to trying, for example, to have the most college graduates of any country in the world. I just wonder why we don't say that our goal is to have the *best* college graduates of any country in the world. *Best*, you see, has nothing to do with *more*. I wonder why our value for praise is located for us in the word *more* rather than in the word *better*. I'm also no longer sure why we need to devalue the quality of graduates we have if we aren't number one in comparison to someone else's number of graduates. At the end of the day, what good is it to us that we can jubilantly say to some other country, "We have more than you do!" Who decided that we are meant to measure ourselves on the basis of what another country does, anyway?

What concerns me is that my experience with churches and ministries and my own heart say that if we are not careful, the church can mirror this similar value system. We become competing institutions, striving to offer goods and services that best or rival other churches or like ministries in our communities. Some congregants even approve of this approach. If they do not like the children's ministry, they go to church elsewhere. Few Christians have been mentored with a "family" rather than a "consumer" paradigm. It rarely occurs to them that they could stay through the unsettledness, enter a dialogue with others, pray together, and become part of finding a solution toward strengthening the children's ministry. How is it that Jesus followers often have little stamina for working through with others what unsettles them? We can often take Bible classes and quote from the Bible, but we still know very little about patience.

So a pastor's time becomes concerned with demonstrating quantifiable innovation and progress (as if progress in Jesus is tied more to physical movement or advancement than to our portion being found in him).

Ironically, any pastor who works with small groups knows that genuine growth often occurs among smaller amounts of people over a longer period of time. But purposefully pursuing this approach to leadership within a culture that esteems celebrity and equates influence with size is not easy. It probably means letting go of opportunities to be quoted and referenced. It will admittedly require a Jesus way of value that is both painful and challenging to move toward (remember the rich young ruler of Mark 10). Leaders would have to learn again how to live outside of the limelight amid the faithfulness of small and daily relational life. They, as Paul did, would have to learn contentment in doing all things through Jesus, who strengthens them whether they have little or much (Phil. 4:11–13).

Examining Our Mentoring

These and other kinds of unspoken environmental ways sit behind the anxiety my friend wrote about in his note above. He has learned biblical content and worldview wonderfully, and in that light he is well prepared. But the institutions he has known, along with his own heart and his family mentoring (including my own mentoring in his life), have made meditation, waiting, patience, self-control, and time given to unquantifiable purposes, such as prayer and relationships, unfamiliar as a way of Christian living and ministry. Such things feel like waste.

So, like many of us, he does not yet know how to do a day as a husband, father, or pastor without the categories of becoming more known, growing larger, and praising the quick achievement of quantifiable tasks, even though Jesus highlights none of these traits for his disciples. We offer an anxious presence to unanswered or seemingly overlooked moments when attention seems focused everywhere other than on us. This is problematic for us. Our humanity in Christ is being sabotaged. Which means that Jesus's proper place is as well. I finished writing to my friend:

> The three rival rules—celebrity, consuming, and immediate gratification—teach us to use our days in order to make a name for ourselves by using people and things to make something bigger happen as fast as we can. I hope that as you look at these rival rules, you will see how obviously at odds these values are to what Jesus taught us and modeled for us and purchased for us. These rivals form our nemesis. We need help. Only God is everywhere, knows everything, and can fix everything. Our foolhardy attempts at his glory teach us to orient our days misguidedly. This way of ordering a pastoral ministry will slowly ruin us and those we try to serve. We and they may be and feel "successful," but we will little resemble the way of Jesus. Jesus has a different way of being in mind for us. His grace has a mentoring to it. He intends to recover his place and, therefore, to put us back into ours. He died and rose to do this.

Conclusion

Saying all of this to my friend, I remember myself as an adult in my first pastorate. There I was sitting on that porch eating Mamaw's spice cake. The words of a children's book come to mind:

> Nothing is sweeter in this sad world than the sound of someone you love calling your name.[5]

A memory of myself as a boy comes back to me, for pastors were children and grandchildren once. I remember Mamaw calling out at suppertime. Sometimes she chose two quick thumps with the heel of her hand. She'd slip her feet into her plain canvas shoes of faded red and stand on the gravel drive just outside of the carport. She'd hold the door open with her left hand. With that right hand she'd lean down and knock the wind out of the steering wheel. In response to Mamaw's strength, the worn car horn would burst into gasping and thrust two goose-like wonks into the air.

At other times, she would speedily whack an old can with a wooden spoon. The spoon became a drumming instrument for making rhythm and causing loud clatter to rise into the neighborhood air at sunset.

My uncles and the neighborhood kids used the same can for the game I loved. "Kick the Can" was the game's name. I was young, and Mamaw forced her two sons to let me play. They were too young to be uncles but could do nothing about that. They had to let their nephew tag along.

I loved it. I felt older, like I belonged. It is remarkable the happiness an old plain can is able to offer a neighborhood of kids. This aspect of the can sometimes reminds me of people too. Equally remarkable is how useful the same can was in Mamaw's hands.

But the honking goose horn and the clanging soup can both fade in comparison to those times in my memory when Mamaw simply chose to use her own voice to call us home. Maybe we were down by the Guthries', hiding like soldiers in the bushes, or climbing trees. She would call my uncles' names first and then mine. She would call out first for my Uncle Bud. "Bbbbbuuddd." Then Adam. "Aaaaddddaaaammmm." Then me. "Zzzaaacckkkk."

Sometimes hearing Mamaw's voice calling on the wind annoyed me. Supper was ready. It was time for me to come home, but I didn't want to. I wanted to play, not eat. I wanted to ramble through the neighborhood, not sit in my spot at that same old table. It was time to come home. And I refused. A foreshadowing of an obstinance in my heart that would harm both me and others in time.

But other times it stirred me to hear my name in Mamaw's voice calling at dusk. The older boys weren't always fair. They could make a game of me rather than inviting me to play at one with them. I knew what it meant to hear her voice carrying our names at that time of night. Food was waiting. Rescue was certain. My heart could leap, my tears subside. It was time to come home. And I did.

I see in this scene a reminder of how Jesus calls any of us into this life and to this ministry. He called us on some street in a local place as those who belonged to somebody somewhere and whose family name had become our own. I was an Eswine and a Guernsey. I played games like "Kick the Can." I played Tonka trucks with my uncle Adam. I drank pickle juice (thanks to my uncle Bud). I heard my papaw finally speak of Jesus at the American Legion Hall in Henryville, Indiana. It was Thanksgiving (yes, it was).

I preached about Jesus at my mamaw's funeral. She died on Christmas Day. Songs I had written were played on the CD player as family and friends gathered. I was ordained to preach by the Great Lakes Presbytery. But I spoke of Jesus that day as Pauline's grandson, the broken son of Vern and Jan. I was that boy that Mamaw called "Charlie Brown" and a "dandy" (as she did others of her grandchildren). Afterward, we ate fried chicken and macaroni with tomatoes right there in the basement fellowship hall of the Henryville United Methodist Church.

Papaw died a little over three years later. In spite of the doctrinal convictions about women as pastors on the part of his grandson, Pastor Wilma had nurtured my old Papaw's young faith. She had tended to him faithfully and spoke wholeheartedly to him of Jesus. As we all sat in that funeral, she invited us to the same Savior that had pursued, found, and forgiven Bud, the same Savior that had answered Mamaw's prayers. More fried chicken followed, and then home.

What I'm trying to say is that life and ministry are an apprenticeship in Jesus in which, by his grace, he recovers our humanity, and for his glory he enables others to do the same. Bernanos had it right. "Grace is everywhere."[6]

Notes

Chapter 1: Preaching Barefoot

1. Carl Dennis, "Smaller," in *Unknown Friends* (New York: Penguin Poets, 2007), 16.

2. Archibald Alexander, *Practical Sermons; to Be Read in Families and Social Meetings* (Philadelphia: Presbyterian Board of Publications, 1850), 6.

3. John Calvin, *Institutes of the Christian Religion*, ed. John T. McNeill, trans. Ford Lewis Battles (Philadelphia: Westminster Press, 1960), 1.1.2.

4. Teresa of Avila, *Interior Castle*, trans. E. Allison Peers (New York: Image Books, 2004), 15.

5. Thomas Merton, "Whether There Is Enjoyment in Bitterness," in *In the Dark Before Dawn*, ed. Lynn R. Szabo (New York: New Directions, 2005), 183.

6. C. S. Lewis, *Reflections on the Psalms* (New York: Harcourt, 1986), 5.

7. For a guide meant to aid us in this way, see my *Preaching to a Post-Everything World: Crafting Biblical Sermons That Connect with Our Culture* (Grand Rapids, MI: Baker, 2008).

8. Zack Eswine, *Kindled Fire* (Ross-shire, UK: Mentor, 2006).

Chapter 2: Recovering Eden

1. Leif Enger, *Peace Like a River* (New York: Grove Press, 2001), 28.

2. Ranald Macaulay and Jerram Barrs, *On Being Human: The Nature of Spiritual Experience* (Downers Grove, IL: InterVarsity, 1998).

3. William Stafford, *Even in the Quiet Places* (Lewiston, ID: Confluence Press, 2010), 25.

4. Ranier Maria Rilke, *Letters to a Young Poet*, trans. M. D. Herter Norton (London: Norton, 2004), 27.

5. Richard Lischer, *Open Secrets: A Memoir of Faith and Discovery* (New York: Broadway, 2002), 45–46.

6. Francis A. Schaeffer, *Speaking the Historic Christian Position into the 20th Century* (privately published, 1965), 125–26.

7. Herman Bavinck, *Reformed Dogmatics*, vol. 1 (Grand Rapids, MI: Baker Academic, 2000), 362.

8. Herman Bavinck, *Reformed Dogmatics*, vol. 4 (Grand Rapids, MI: Baker Academic, 2000), 435.

9. Richard Baxter, *The Practical Works of Richard Baxter*, vol. 18 (London: James Duncan, 1830), 409.

10. Martyn Lloyd-Jones, *Preaching and Preachers* (Grand Rapids, MI: Zondervan, 1972), 97.

11. Eifion Evans, *Daniel Rowland and the Great Evangelical Awakening in Wales* (Edinburgh: Banner of Truth, 1985), 48.

Chapter 3: Everywhere-for-All

1. Wendell Berry, *A Timbered Choir: The Sabbath Poems 1979–1997* (New York: Counterpoint, 1998), 216.

2. John Calvin, *Institutes of the Christian Religion*, ed. John T. McNeill, trans. Ford Lewis Battles (Philadelphia: Westminster Press, 1960), 3.20.6.

3. Walt Whitman, *Leaves of Grass: 1855 Version* (Ann Arbor, MI: Borders Classics, 2003), 32.

4. Matt. 13:54; Luke 2:4, 39, 51.

5. Brooks Williams, "Mystery," in *The Dead Sea Café* (Raleigh, NC: Silent Planet Records, 2000).

6. George Mallory in 1922, http://www.mnteverest.net/quote.html (February 2, 2006).

7. David Breashears and Audrey Salkeld, *Last Climb: The Legendary Everest Expeditions of George Mallory* (Washington, DC: National Geographic, 1999).

8. "After his disappearance on Everest close friends would say that Mallory had taken the decision to return with foreboding, telling them that what he would have to face this time would be "more like war than adventure" and that he doubted he would return. He knew that no one would criticize him if he refused to go, but he felt it a compulsion. It is impossible to say now whether these were more than fleeting moments of guilt at having to leave his wife Ruth yet again with all responsibility for their young children. Be that as it may, once on the road to Tibet again, Mallory was his usual energetic self. "I feel strong for the battle," he wrote to Ruth from Base Camp, "but I know every ounce of strength will be wanted." "I have to look at it from the point of view of loyalty to the expedition," he wrote to his father as he vacillated, "and of carrying through a task begun." Audrey Salkeld, "Mallory," http://www.pbs.orgwgbh/nova/Everest/lost/mystery/Mallory.htm.

9. Charles Cummings, *The Mystery of the Ordinary* (New York: Harper & Row, 1982), *ix*, 10.

10. G. K. Chesterton, *Orthodoxy: The Romance of Faith* (New York: Image Books, 1990), 39–40.

11. James Waddel Alexander, *Thoughts on Preaching* (Edinburgh: Banner of Truth, 1975), 118–19.

12. Chesterton, *Orthodoxy*, 60.

13. Czeslaw Milosz, *To Begin Where I Am: Selected Essays* (New York: Farrar, Straus & Giroux, 2000), 11.

14. Czeslaw Milosz, "Nobel Prize Lecture," December 8, 1980, http://www.nobelprize.org/nobel_prizes/literature/laureates/1980/Milosz-lecture.html.

15. Milosz, *To Begin Where I Am*, 12.

16. Berry, *A Timbered Choir*, 216.

17. Dennis Okholm, *Monk Habits for Everyday People: Benedictine Spirituality for Protestants* (Grand Rapids, MI: Brazos Press, 2007), 89.

18. Francis Schaeffer, *True Spirituality*, in *The Complete Works of Francis A. Schaeffer: A Christian Worldview*, vol. 3 (Wheaton, IL: Crossway, 1991), 280.

19. Aleksandr Solzhenitsyn, *One Day in the Life of Ivan Denisovich*, trans. H. T. Willetts (New York: Farrar, Straus & Giroux, 1991), 3, 182.

20. For more on this see *Dictionary of Biblical Imagery*, ed. Leland Ryken, James C. Wilhoit, and Tremper Longman III (Downers Grove, IL: InterVarsity, 1998).

21. Kathleen Norris, *The Cloister Walk* (New York: Riverhead Books, 1997), 1.

22. Kathleen Norris, *Acedia and Me: A Marriage, Monks, and a Writer's Life* (New York: Riverhead Books, 2008), *xiv*.

23. For a helpful reflection on dreams see Archibald Alexander, *Thoughts on Religious Experience* (1844; repr. Edinburgh: Banner of Truth, 1989), 80.

24. I am basing this idea loosely on the "prayer of examen" indicated by St. Ignatius of Loyola, *Personal Writings* (New York: Penguin Books, 2004), 293.

25. G. K. Chesterton, *The Everlasting Man* (San Francisco: Ignatius Press, 1993), 9.

Chapter 4: Fix-It-All

1. Benedict Ward, *The Sayings of the Desert Fathers* (Kalamazoo, MI: Cistercian, 1975), 7.

2. Richard M. Cohen, *Strong at the Broken Places: Voices of Illness, a Chorus of Hope* (New York: Harper, 2008), *xvi.*

3. Westminster Larger Catechism, Q. 23 and 28.

4. Mary Felstiner, *Out of Joint: A Private and Public Story of Arthritis* (Lincoln: University of Nebraska Press, 2007), 89.

5. Ibid.

6. Henri Nouwen, *The Wounded Healer: Ministry in Contemporary Society* (New York: Doubleday, 1979).

7. C. S. Lewis, "The Inner Ring," in *The Weight of Glory* (New York: HarperCollins, 2001), 154.

8. Ibid., 150.

9. Ibid., 145.

10. Ibid., 149.

11. Eugene H. Peterson, *Under the Unpredictable Plant: An Exploration in Vocational Holiness* (Grand Rapids, MI: Eerdmans, 1994), 104.

12. See, e.g., Psalms 3, 7, 18, 30, 34, 52, 54, 56, 57, 59, 63.

13. John Updike, "Stolen," in *Endpoint and Other Poems* (New York: Knopf, 2009), 33–34.

Chapter 5: Know-It-All

1. Wendell Berry, *The Memory of Old Jack* (Washington, DC: Counterpoint, 1999), 142.

2. First published in my *Listening for the Sound of Reality*, http://www.covenantseminary.edu.

3. G. K. Chesterton, *Orthodoxy: The Romance of Faith* (New York: Image Books, 1990), 33.

4. D. Martyn Lloyd-Jones, "Knowledge False and True," in *The Puritans: Their Origins and Successors* (Edinburgh: Banner of Truth, 1991), 28.

5. Not this dear man's real name.

6. Fyodor Dostoevsky, *The Idiot*, Novels of Fyodor Dostoevsky, vol. 2 (New York: MacMillan, 1916), 55.

7. Ibid., 599.

8. Jonathan Edwards, "Some Thoughts Concerning the Present Revival of Religion in New England," in *The Works of Jonathan Edwards, vol. 4: The Great Awakening* (New Haven, CT: Yale University Press, 2009).

9. Augustine, *On Christian Teaching*, Oxford World's Classics, trans. R. P. H. Green (New York: Oxford University Press, 1997), 27.

10. Steve Garber, "The Epistemology of Love," Washington Institute (http://www.washingtonist.org/163/the-epistemology-of-love/), 2.

11. J. Gresham Machen, *The Christian Faith in the Modern World* (Grand Rapids, MI: Eerdmans, 1965), 13.

12. Zack Eswine, "Land of the Living" (unpublished song).

13. Billy Joel, "And So It Goes," *Storm Front*, 1989.

14. Wendell Berry, *The Art of the Commonplace: The Agrarian Essays of Wendell Berry* (Berkeley, CA: Counterpoint Press, 2002), 12.

15. Ibid., 11.

Chapter 6: Physicality

1. Marilynne Robinson, *Gilead* (New York: Picador, 2004), 4.

2. Czeslaw Milosz, *To Begin Where I Am: Selected Essays*, ed. Bogdana Carpenter and Madeline G. Levine (New York: Farrar, Strauss & Giroux, 2001), 1.

3. Eugene H. Peterson, *The Contemplative Pastor: Returning to the Art of Spiritual Direction* (Grand Rapids, MI: Eerdmans, 1989), 62.

4. Gerard Manley Hopkins, "The Caged Skylark," in *Hopkins: Poems and Prose* (New York: Knopf, 1995), 17.

5. Belden Lane, *The Solace of Fierce Landscapes: Exploring Desert and Mountain Spirituality* (New York: Oxford University Press, 1998), 31.

6. Ibid., 25.

7. Peterson, *The Contemplative Pastor*, 62.

8. See Rom. 16:16; 1 Cor. 16:20; 2 Cor. 13:12; 1 Thess. 5:26.

9. Augustine, *The Rule of St. Augustine in Selected Works*, The Classics of Western Spirituality (Mahwah, NJ: Paulist Press, 1984), 488.

10. Dennis Okholm, *Monk Habits for Everyday People: Benedictine Spirituality for Protestants* (Grand Rapids, MI: Brazos Press, 2007), 49.

11. Carman Fowler Laberge, "In the face of death, church is bearing witness to life in Joplin, Missouri," *The Layman Online* (Thursday, May 25, 2011), http://www.layman.org/news.aspx?article=28568.

12. For more on handling criticism, see my *Preaching to a Post-Everything World* (Grand Rapids, MI: Baker, 2008).

13. William Stafford, "Malheur Before Dawn," in *Even in Quiet Places* (Lewiston, ID: Confluence Press, 1996), 49.

Chapter 7: Seeing

1. Frank Bidart, "Golden State," http://www.poetryfoundation.org.poem/177901.

2. Jean-Pierre de Caussade, *The Sacrament of the Present Moment* (New York: HarperCollins, 1989), 67.

3. Switchfoot, "Amateur Lovers," *Oh! Gravity*, 2006.

4. T. S. Eliot, "The Hollow Man," in *Collected Poems: 1909–1962* (New York: Harcourt Brace, 1991), 81.

5. Louise Gluck, "Under Taurus," in *The First Four Books of Poems* (New York: HarperCollins, 1995), 95.

6. Wendell Berry, *Life Is a Miracle: An Essay against Modern Superstition* (New York: Crosspoint, 2001), 10.

7. Ibid., 11.

8. J. R. R. Tolkien, *The Fellowship of the Ring* (New York: Houghton Mifflin, 1994), 58.

9. U2, "When I Look at the World," in *All That You Can't Leave Behind* (Interscope Records, 2000), emphasis mine.

Chapter 8: Celebrity

1. John Updike, *A Month of Sundays* (New York: Ballantine, 1996), 7.

2. Nathan Foster, *Wisdom Chasers: Finding My Father at 14,000 Feet* (Downers Grove, IL: InterVarsity, 2010), 41.

3. Paul Sabatier, *The Road to Assisi: The Essential Biography of St. Francis* (Brewster, MA: Paraclete Press, 2005), 7.

4. See, e.g., Matt. 8:4; 9:30; Mark 1:44; 3:12; 5:43; 7:36; Luke 8:56.

5. Eugene H. Peterson, *Under the Unpredictable Plant: An Exploration in Vocational Holiness* (Grand Rapids, MI: Eerdmans, 1994).

6. Susan Howatch, *Glittering Images* (New York: Fawcett Columbine, 1987), 209.

7. Ibid., 173.

8. Ibid., 276.

9. Excerpt from Zack Eswine, "The Least of These," unpublished poem.

Chapter 9: Immediacy

1. Eugene Peterson, "Spirituality for All the Wrong Reasons," *Christianity Today*, 49 (March 2005), http://www.christianitytoday.com/CT/2005/march/26.42.html?start=y.

2. Ibid.

3. C. John Miller, *The Heart of a Servant Leader: Letters from Jack Miller* (Phillipsburg, NJ: P&R, 2004), 22–23.

4. Henri Nouwen, *Turn My Mourning into Dancing: Finding Hope in Hard Times* (Nashville: Word, 2001), 55.

5. M. Craig Barnes, *The Pastor as Minor Poet: Texts and Subtexts in the Ministerial Life* (Grand Rapids, MI: Eerdmans, 2009), 22.

6. Nouwen, *Mourning into Dancing*, 55.

7. Henri J. M. Nouwen, *The Way of the Heart: Connecting with God Through Prayer, Wisdom and Silence* (New York: Ballantine, 1981), 48.

Chapter 10: Conversation with a Young Minister

1. Teresa of Avila, *Interior Castle*, trans. and ed. E. Allison Peers (New York: Image Books, 2004), 6.

2. Francis of Assisi, *Francis and Clare: The Complete Works*, trans. Regis Armstrong and Ignatius Brady (New York: Paulist Press, 1982), 109.

3. Johann Wolfgang von Goethe, "The Sorcerer's Apprentice," http://www/has/vcu.edu/for/Goethe/zauber.html.

4. Henry David Thoreau, *Letters to a Spiritual Seeker*, ed. Bradley P. Dean (New York: Norton, 2004), 34.

5. Kate Dicamillo, *Tale of Despereaux* (New York: Random House, 2006), 258.

6. Georges Bernanos, *The Diary of a Country Priest* (New York: Knoll & Graff, 2004), 298.

General Index

Scripture Index